KEEPING CLIENTS SATISFIED

MAKE YOUR SERVICE BUSINESS MORE SUCCESSFUL AND PROFITABLE

Robert W. Bly

PRENTICE HALL
Englewood Cliffs, New Jersey 07632

Prentice-Hall International, Inc., *London*
Prentice-Hall of Australia, Pty. Ltd., *Sydney*
Prentice-Hall of Canada, Inc., *Toronto*
Prentice-Hall Hispanoamericana, S.A., *Mexico*
Prentice-Hall of India Private Ltd., *New Delhi*
Prentice-Hall of Japan, Inc. *Tokyo*
Prentice-Hall of Southeast Asia Pte., Ltd., *Singapore*
Editora Prentice-Hall do Brasil Ltda., *Rio de Janeiro*

© 1993 by
Robert W. Bly

10 9 8 7 6 5 4 3 2 1

Libray of Congress Catalonging-in-Publication Data

Bly, Robert W.
  Keeping clients satisfied : make your service business more
successful and profitable / Robert W. Bly
    p. cm.
  Includes index.
  ISBN 0-13-514183-4
  1. Customer service—United States. 2. Service industries—United States. I.
Title.
  HF5415.5.B58 1993
  658.8'12—dc20   92-35379
CIP

ISBN   0-13-514183-4

PRENTICE HALL
Professional Publishing
Englewood Cliffs, NJ 07632
Simon & Schuster, A Paramount Communications Company

PRINTED IN THE UNITED STATES OF AMERICA

Acknowledgments

I'm indebted to Donald Libey, JoAnna Brandi, Dr. Jeffrey Lant, Dr. Andrew Linick, Ed McLean, Joan Harris, Mitch Hisiger, Bob Jurick, Herman Holtz, Jeff Davidson, Dottie Walters, Pete Silver, and the other authorities on client satisfaction mentioned throughout the book. You can learn by doing and by watching, and I've certainly benefited from watching them in action.

Appreciation goes also to the late Howard Shenson, who discussed many of the ideas in this book with me during our phone conversations

And thanks to my clients. By showing me what you want, you have helped me to teach others how to satisfy and keep their clients, too.

There are many other people I've met with over the years who have helped me develop and refine the techniques presented in this book. I won't name them all here. But to all, thanks, folks!

I also wish to recognize Ruth Mills for her patience and understanding, and Zsuzsa Neff for her help in preparing this manuscript.

And, finally, I thank my wife, who took care of the baby while I wrote this book.

About the Author

Bob Bly is the director of CTC, a consulting firm that specializes in helping clients improve business communication and customer relations skills. CTC presents workshops and seminars in sales, marketing, business communication, and customer service to corporations and associations nationwide.

Bly is the author of 25 books including *How to Promote Your Own Business* (New American Library); *Create the Perfect Sales Piece: How to Produce Brochures, Catalogs, Fliers, and Pamphlets* (John Wiley & Sons); *The Copywriter's Handbook: A Step-by-Step Guide to Writing Copy That Sells* (Henry Holt); and *Selling Your Services: Proven Strategies for Getting Clients to Hire You or Your Firm* (Henry Holt).

Other titles include *Out on Your Own: From Corporate to Self-employment* (John Wiley & Sons), *Secrets of a Freelance Writer* (Henry Holt), *Direct Mail Profits* (Asher Gallant Press), *The Elements of Business Writing* (Macmillan), and *The Advertising Manager's Handbook* (Prentice Hall).

Bly's articles have appeared in such magazines as *Direct, Business Marketing, Executive Business, Amtrak Express, Writer's Digest, New Jersey Monthly*, and *Cosmopolitan*. His clients include Value Rent-A-Car, Sony Corporation, Associated Air Freight, Philadelphia National Bank, Executive Enterprises, Timeplex, Myron Manufacturing, and EBI Medical Systems.

Questions and comments on KEEPING CLIENTS SATISFIED may be sent to:

Bob Bly
CTC
22 E. Quackenbush Ave.
Dumont, NJ 07628
(201) 385-1220

Contents

Preface

Keeping *Clients Satisfied* has been written to give you complete, step-by-step instructions on how to accomplish the one task that is essential to your continued long-term business success, namely:

Keeping your clients happier longer.

We are now entering an era of unprecedented opportunity in business—but also unprecedented competition. In the 1970s, the "Age of Plenty," you simply had to offer a superior service, and people would beat a path to your door.

In the 1980s, the "Age of Marketing," merely having a good product or service was no longer enough. Competition was crowding the marketplace, and so to succeed, you had to promote your product and service—aggressively—through advertising and marketing. Still, you could basically run your business the way you wanted to—and find plenty of buyers for what you were selling.

In the 1990s and into the year 2000, all that has changed. Now, it's not enough simply to offer a great product or service and advertise it aggressively. To succeed, you have to be in the business of *making clients happy and satisfied*, not just providing products and services.

We are living in the "Age of the Customer," a time when the client is sovereign. The successful entrepreneur or executive is dedicated mind and body to one simple but vital task: doing everything possible to service the client. According to a recent survey of The Professional & Technical Consultants Association

(San Jose, California), the number one concern among its members is "finding and keeping clients" (selling is the number two concern).

Competition for clients is fiercer than ever. People are spending more cautiously, and in fields where there was only one or two vendors five years ago, the clients can now choose from among dozens of firms offering the same (or similar) services.

Getting clients is tough, requiring aggressive sales and marketing. With clients so difficult to get, each client on your client roster becomes a precious asset—one to be nurtured, guarded, and protected at almost all cost.

"Any time you have a slowdown in the economy, you are forced to do things differently," says Stan Gault, CEO of Goodyear. "You have to expand your efforts, you have to be more thorough, and you have to be more professional."[1]

Every day, your competitors are trying to sell similar services to your customers in an attempt to win them away from you. Only by keeping clients happy and satisfied can you prevent this. Only by providing great service to your customers can you generate maximum business revenue from your valuable client base, year after year. And only by working continuously to prevent, anticipate, and correct problems can you stop clients from becoming unhappy or dissatisfied.

That's what this book will help you do.

The book is in three parts. Part I puts forth the idea that the best way to ensure client satisfaction is to choose clients with whom you can get along in the first place. I'll tell you how to establish a "Desirable Client Profile" so you can select and work with the best clients and get rid of those whom you could never please.

Part II presents specific techniques for keeping clients happier longer. In this section, you'll see why great customer service by itself is *not sufficient* for keeping clients happy—and what else you must do to ensure a satisfied client. You'll also learn how to easily and inexpensively make clients happy by giving them more than their money's worth . . . effective communication techniques that let clients know you care . . . little but important details that can make or break the vendor/client relationship . . . and how to make the breakthrough to providing extraordinary client satisfaction.

---

[1] Source: *Personal Selling Power*, September, 1992, p. 26.

Part III gives you specific guidelines for handling a wide variety of problem situations. Problems and dissatisfaction will ruin your relationship with your client—unless you catch them early enough and handle them in the proper fashion. This section presents comprehensive advice for dealing with a wide range of client problems including price complaints, dissatisfaction with the quality of your service, coping with difficult clients, how to prevent an unhappy client from leaving you, and how to cope when, occasionally, you *do* lose that important client or major account.

A direct mail piece I received a month ago had a line that caught my attention: "We are living in hard times." Many businesses are suffering as a result of the recession of the early 1990s, and are having a hard time coping with the changes taking place in the pace and method of doing business today.

But not you. When you master the techniques of keeping clients satisfied, you will be assured of a bright and prosperous future. A full roster of satisfied clients is the most precious asset any business can have. *Keeping Clients Satisfied* describes how to hold onto yours.

Part I
DEVELOPING STRONG CLIENT RELATIONSHIPS FROM THE START

CHAPTER 1

Doing Business in the "Age of the Customer"

You bought this book because it's tougher than ever to succeed in business and you want to gain a competitive edge. And you figured learning new client satisfaction techniques would be valuable to you in your business.

How right you are! In today's marketplace, it *is* tougher than ever to get and keep new clients. Several factors have contributed to this: a recessed economy, increased competition, more sophisticated technology, less time (and therefore more time pressures), and less money to spend.

SURVIVING IN A RECESSION

First, the economy. In the early 1990s this country experienced one of its most severe recessions of all time. What effect did that have on business? What was once a *seller's* market suddenly became a *buyer's* market. People spent less. Sales were down. Companies put spending programs on indefinite hold. As a result, business became scarce. Instead of having more business than they could handle, many previously busy and successful firms *did not have enough business*. And it's supply and demand that puts you in a weak or strong position.

For example, when you have more business than you can handle, you can be more selective about the jobs you take. You can require clients to conform to *your* schedule. And, if you're really in demand, you can charge pretty much top dollar—and get it—because you're negotiating with the client from a position of *strength*. When you know you'll continue eating well even if you lose the job, you can more easily stick by your guns and get what you want. After all, *you really don't need the work.*

This was the situation during the 1970s and 1980s. Clients had money to spend and were lining up at your door to spend it. Sure, maybe you did some advertising, marketing, and selling, but it was *easy*: you pretty much knew that running your little ad or sending out your mailing piece or making some sales calls would quickly bring you as much business as you desired.

There is a temptation in such a circumstance to be lax about client service and courtesy. After all, when you are turning down three clients for every one you take, it really doesn't matter if a few of them walk. Perhaps you became difficult, stubborn, a prima donna, hard to deal with. Or maybe you were generally good to your customers, but didn't worry about or notice any lapses or infractions committed by your employees.

Clients were thick-skinned and fairly loyal: they tended to stick with their vendors unless the vendor was totally inept. And even then, it might take several bad experiences before the client began looking elsewhere.

On the other hand, when you don't have *enough* business, the picture changes drastically—again, a function of supply and de-mand. When the demand for your product or service diminishes, you're not sitting so pretty. You realize just how difficult it is to make new sales and get new clients—and you also realize what a precious commodity a good client is.

Advertising and promotion are more expensive than ever and don't work half as well as they used to. The phones aren't ringing. Salespeople and telemarketers become demotivated, hit harder by constant rejection and prospects who are shopping around more or are simply not buying.

In the early 1990s, clients began to realize that they *could* go elsewhere—and rather easily. They saw that they, not you, were now in the driver's seat, so to speak. You need the business; they have money to spend. So they expect to be courted—and treated like royalty.

And in essence, that's the business attitude that will domi-nate for the entire 1990s and into the twenty-first century: *ulti-mate customer service*: the client is king. They know it. You know it. If you want their business, you must treat them accordingly.

This does not mean that subservience or sycophantic behav-ior is necessary. Far from it. In business, the central transaction is an exchange of value for value: their money for your product or service. For the relationship to work, you have to be peers with the client, equals, partners. However, in the 1990s and beyond, your clients are going to be a little more equal than you!

STAYING AHEAD OF THE COMPETITION

A second factor contributing to this new era of business in which keeping the client (and keeping them satisfied) is the central focus is the growing competition. Simply put, there are more products and more services out there competing for the consumer's or businessperson's dollar than ever before.

Perhaps you started off with a "minimonopoly," because your business was unique or you specialized in such a rare area that you were basically the only person prospects could turn to for your particular expertise or service. Such people are becoming rarer and rarer.

Now, everywhere you look, competition abounds. If your business is a commodity product, you see new competition springing up every day.

Example: Three years ago, in my small town of New Milford, New Jersey, there was one video store. Now there are three. Not only that, but you can also rent videos at the stationery store and the A&P.

Now, a video you rent from one store is exactly the same as the video you rent from another store. So what makes the difference? *Service to the customer.* Each new video store began offering more and more services that the first store didn't offer, including

- A broader selection
- More copies of popular movies available
- Late-night drop-off of tapes
- VCR repair service
- Selling of sodas, popcorn, and candy to eat while you watch your movie
- Cleaner, nicer store
- Better location
- No initial membership fee

The original video store, sadly, went out of business. It was unable—or unwilling—to change its operation and suffered accordingly.

Although commodity product sellers are facing stiffer competition than ever, with superior customer service being the only competitive weapon available, even specialists are feeling the heat of increased competition. People in small niche markets and highly specialized businesses no longer have their comfortable "minimonopoly." Why? Because other entrepreneurs looking to get into business see the niche market or specialty service and copy it.

Why is there so much more competition today than in the 1980s? A major contributing factor goes back to the weak economy. With the massive business failures and downsizing of corporate America, more and more people at all levels suddenly found themselves out of a job, with dim prospects for being employed elsewhere any time in the near future. According to Drake Beam Morin, the world's largest career transition consulting firm, in 1992 it took the average professional who was fired 7.2 months to find a new job.

Many of these terminated corporate workers, seeing a lousy job market, decided to go into businesses of their own, either as consultants or running some other small enterprise. This meant a tremendous increase in competition in almost all fields of business.

What's more, these beginners tended to charge low fees. That didn't mean they would beat you out for a job. But it did mean your prospective clients had another option. Now they could tell you your price was too high and quote much lower prices from these low-bid sources. And so they gained leverage in negotiation of prices.

Prices for a wide range of services dropped dramatically in the early 1990s. At the same time, customers became more demanding than ever. As a result, many businesspeople complained they were working harder but are earning less. And that change may be permanent. You can still make nice money in business today, but you *will* have to work harder. Instead of fighting it, face it, make peace with it, and push forward. The gravy train of the 1980s is gone.

KEEPING UP WITH NEW TECHNOLOGY

A third factor that has contributed to this new era and made the 1990s the "Age of the Customer" is technology. Modern technology may have its benefits, but it has speeded up the pace at which our society moves *enormously*. Voice mail, modems, on-line databases, facsimile machines, electronic bulletin boards, and the accessibility of overnight delivery services have created a consumer who wants it *now*, if not yesterday.

The customer has come to expect instant gratification. The service provider who does not provide it is at a competitive disadvantage. In many aspects, small businesses are at a competitive disadvantage with larger ones, because they cannot afford the staff or equipment to render such a high level of service.

But what a smaller company lacks in resources it can make up in customer treatment and customer contact. A big organization, for example, may have inflexible policies that the customer service person is not authorized to break, and this inflexibility can infuriate the customer if the policies prevent customers from getting what they want immediately.

At the smaller company, the person serving the customer usually has the authority to break, change, or make new policy *on the spot*. Not being locked into a rigid way of doing things controlled by a long chain of authority gives you the freedom to do whatever it takes to keep and please the customer.

ACCOMMODATING CLIENTS' TIME PRESSURES

In addition to the weakened economy, increased competition, and technology, a fourth factor adding to the creation of "Age of the Customer" is *time* or, specifically, the customer's lack of it.

Everybody seems to be busy today, to have more than he or she can handle. The workweek has not decreased, nor do people have more leisure time today, as was once thought would be the case by now. If anything, corporate employees are working harder than ever before.

The reason is the economy again. With corporations downsizing and terminating employees daily, managers realize they are no longer indispensable, and they cannot count on the corporation to provide them with a lifelong job and financial security. That era has passed and will probably never return.

With high unemployment and fewer jobs, corporations, as employers, have the advantage over their employees. It's supply and demand again: when positions are scarce, employees want to hold on to their jobs, so they complain less, ask for less, and work harder.

The happy 1950s scene of the husband on the commuter train coming home to a martini, pipe, slippers, and a barbecued steak in the back yard is also long gone. Now both spouses are working demanding full-time jobs and are exhausted from doing that and raising a family at the same time.

The upshot is a society of time-pressured consumers demanding a higher level of service than ever before. Clients want you to *save them time*, and they get impatient very quickly if you don't.

The customer is similarly pressured at work. Downsizing means there are fewer staffers to handle the work, and increasing competition means there is more work to do. As a result, everyone's too busy and pressed for time.

In business-to-business selling, vendors are finding that clients want the vendor to do—preferably at no cost—what should really be the *client's* job. The client is time pressured and wants to hire not necessarily the vendor who can do the best quality job but the vendor who will be a "partner" and help shoulder the load.

To some degree, clients have always wanted their vendors to give them some extras and not see a bill for it. The difference today is, the vendors—at least the ones who want the business—are doing it. This helps strengthen the client/vendor relationship but again requires the vendor to do *more* work for *less* pay. This cuts the profit of all firms and is personally wearing on the small business owner who must work harder to accommodate this new type of customer.

COPING WITH CLIENTS WHO HAVE LESS MONEY TO SPEND

The last factor that has resulted in the 1990s being "Age of the Customer" is what I call *downward mobility*. Simply put, although we make more money than our parents, we are actually less well off, because the cost of living has outstripped the increase in salaries.

For instance, about 25 years ago, a three-bedroom house in my county might have sold for $20,000, and the person buying it was earning maybe $15,000 to $25,000 a year. Today, that same house goes for $200,000—ten times as much—but the buyer is earning $60,000 to $75,000—only three times as much. What this means is that while we make more than our parents, our expenses are proportionally greater, so we're not living as well.

How does this affect you? Disposable income is less. Consumers are still buying, but they are spending more carefully. Interestingly, they are buying some small luxury and expensive items (air-pump sneakers, gourmet ice cream, take-out sushi) to compensate for the fact that they can't afford the big-ticket items. They're also buying services that save them time, such as house cleaning and baby sitting, but are cutting back in many other areas.

Downward mobility reduces buying power and makes your customer extremely deliberate about purchase decisions.

THE SEVEN MAJOR CHANGES IN THE WAY CUSTOMERS AND CLIENTS BUY IN THE 1990s

As a result of all the factors just discussed, there has been a fundamental shift in the way consumers and businesses acquire products and services, and in their relationships with retailers, service providers, manufacturers, dealers, and others who supply these goods and services.

Understanding these differences, and accepting that this is the way it is in the 1990s, will make your life easier in two respects. First, instead of being frustrated by the changes taking place, you'll recognize them and accept them. You'll still have to meet these challenges, but you'll at least learn to accept reality and stop longing for better days that will never return.

Second, the first step in solving a problem is *understanding* the problem—not the apparent problem, but the true nature of the challenge you are facing. By recognizing that these seven fundamental shifts in the customer/vendor relationship have taken place, you'll be better able to adjust not only your customer service and product quality to meet these new demands, but also your sales and marketing efforts to sell this new consumer.

Here are the seven key changes I see in today's consumers and business buyers—along with some ideas on how to adapt.

Fundamental Change 1: The Market Has Become More Price Sensitive

As a direct result of the recession of the early 1990's, your customers have become more price sensitive. This does not necessarily mean that price is the only concern, or that the low price or low bid will be the one that makes the sale.

But it does mean that business and consumer buyers *are more concerned than ever about what things cost*. Price is always a factor, to some degree. But its importance has escalated dramatically, and the way you price your service is a major factor determining whether the client is happy with you or whether they will begin to look elsewhere.

Consumers evaluate many purchases more carefully. In the corporate world, the manager is increasingly rewarded for *being a good buyer*, which translates into getting vendors to do the job for as low a price as he or she can negotiate them down to.

In the 1980s, firms would choose their area of superiority and offer that as the reason to hire them. Basically there were three options: price, quality, and service.

Some vendors got jobs on *price*—they always bid low and won contracts from prospects who look to get it as cheap as possible. Other vendors stressed *quality*. They said, "We take our time, and you'll have to wait, and we charge a lot. But if you want the best, you have to pay for it." And customers looking for quality responded to the pitch. A third group of vendors stressed *service*: they weren't the cheapest, and they weren't the best, but they would do anything the client asked them to. If the client said "jump," they asked, "How high?" If the client said call me to go over the report at 10 o'clock at night, they said, "Yes, sir." Customers who valued service above all else gravitated toward this type of vendor, even if the price wasn't low and the quality wasn't absolutely the best.

Now, however, all that is changed. You can no longer "specialize" in price, quality, or service. *Your customers want all three*. They want a top-of-the-line product, but they also want a "good price." They want you at their beck and call, and *they want it yesterday*. This is a difficult bill to fill, and it's why many service providers long for the golden years of the 1980s. But it's what you'll learn to live with in the 1990s and beyond.

The market is more price sensitive, but as I've said, this does *not* mean being the cheapest price is an automatic winning strategy. With some customers, yes; with others, no.

There has always been a segment of your market that buys primarily on price. What has happened is that *the size of this segment has increased*. Not everyone is a price-buyer, but more people are. Pressured by lack of disposable income or a corporate mandate to control spending, they want you to give them a break on price, price, price.

Coping with "Price-Buyers." To the price-buyer, the winning bid is selected by the bottom-line dollar amount: the job goes to the firm who can do it for the least amount of money. They figure it will be "good enough," and so do not consider higher bids.

You must be able to spot the price-buyer and decide if you are willing to play this game. As a rule of thumb, when a customer calls you and the *first* thing they ask is what so-and-so will cost—with no apparent interest in your qualifications, track record, product features, or experience—you are probably dealing with a price-buyer.

Some industries have been harder hit by an increased emphasis on price-buying than others. In contracting, for example, independent contractors who do home remodeling and building face stiff competition from bigger firms that advertise standard-design family rooms, dormers, or other add-ons at a low-package price.

"These firms generally don't do good work and can rip you off," one independent contractor told me recently, "but that low, low price does sell for them. Prospects ask me, 'Why do you charge so much when so-and-so firm advertising in *TV Shopper* can do it for $10,329?' And it's a problem: many don't understand, don't believe, or don't care when I point out the difference between our work and the bargain-basement contractor's. And we do lose business to them."

So part of this price-consciousness trend is that a portion of the market that were not previously price-buyers have been converted to price-buyers.

Coping with value-conscious buyers. As for those customers for whom price is *not* the major issue, most of them have changed as well; they have become more *value conscious*. That is, they aren't necessarily going to buy the low price, but they do want to be sure they are getting the most *value* for their money.

Be aware that the value-conscious buyer is going to be a demanding customer. But there are very few *non*demanding customers left. So you've got to adjust. Be prepared to provide more service, to do more, and to act faster, for the same or lower price than you were getting five years ago.

Value-conscious buyers will often meet your price but in return wants to make sure they are getting the most they can out of you, and everything you do will be scrutinized carefully. These buyers are less shy than the 1980s consumer about complaining when they're not happy, and they'll often complain about small things—every detail must be to their liking. Get used to it and prepare to accommodate them. This is business in the 1990s.

An important note: If you are going to give extra service to a customer, do it immediately, pleasantly, openly, and willingly without griping about it. If you give the customer a hard time, and there is some argument, and you give in and do it, customers will not be grateful that you did what they asked; after all, they think that's just part of what they're entitled to.

They *will*, however, remember that you gave them a hard time. And that's the quickest way to get your valued client flipping through the Yellow Pages and calling your competitors for a bid on the next job.

The best way to respond to the value-buyer who wants more and more from you is to agree immediately and pleasantly and act as if it's a pleasure for you. As Lou Weiss of Specialty Steel & Forge says, having a can-do attitude is what works in today's marketplace.

If a customer's request catches you off guard when you're in the middle of something else, you need time to think. Say you have another phone call or are in a meeting but will get back to them in five minutes. Then you can think about how you wil respond and do so in a calm, polite manner, without showing anger or annoyance.

Fundamental Change 2: The Average Purchase Is Smaller in Size

People and businesses will always have to spend money. They need products and services and can never totally do without them. However, today they are spending less, and the average dollar value of their purchase, investment, or contract is likely to be far smaller than it was in the 1980s.

There are two reasons why the average purchase has shrunk in size. The first is purely economic: people and businesses are on tighter budgets and want to save money and spend less; they might like to buy more, but feel they can't afford to.

The second reason is that consumers are fussier and prefer to "test" a vendor, product, or service before making a larger commitment. The small initial purchase is one way of testing you without a large risk or investment. If they like what they get, they'll probably come back for more. If they don't, they figure they haven't lost much.

This buying habit is hard on vendors for one simple reason: in many cases, it takes just as much effort to close a sale worth $10,000 as it does to close a sale for $1,000. So you spend just as much time courting the client, only to be rewarded minimally for your efforts. It's frustrating and tiring. Again, you're working harder and making less.

Part of coping is simply to acknowledge and accept this fundamental change in buying habits as the way things are now. However, there are a few specific things you can do both to increase your ability to get business from clients as well as to boost your revenue.

Repackage you product or service. First, because the customer wants to spend less initially, you should repackage your product or service to accommodate this desire. What you're doing is lowering initial entry cost for the client to do business with you. This gets your "foot in the door" and paves the way for repeat business, which is the lifeblood of most companies.

For example, I know one software vendor whose product costs $1,999. Because that's a lot of money and people are hesitant to spend that, he offers what he calls a "Small Project" version of the program for only $50. The Small Project does everything the $1,999 "Commercial" version does, except it restricts the user from entering more than a few pieces of data, so that it cannot handle any real-world application. For $50, many more people buy and try the software, and those who like it then move to the next step and upgrade to the $1,999 commercial version.

In another situation, a company was selling a kit of tools and raw materials for building certain products at home. The kit cost $599. The company owner realized that the price was a barrier to many prospects who would prefer to make a smaller initial purchase. So to those who did not take the $599 offer, he offered a "starter kit" for only $99. This proved enormously profitable; when the entry point was lowered, customers bought.

Services can also be repackaged to accommodate this trend of buying in smaller increments. A $1,600 a day consultant, for example, might offer an initial half-day consultation at a reduced rate, say, $600 instead of the usual $800. Many clients who find $1,600 a day hard to swallow see a $600 "starter package" as more affordable.

Offer a wider range of options.   You should also think about organizing your product line or service menu so that there are a wide range of options from which the buyer can choose, from a low-priced item to an expensive purchase.

One company selling information on how to be a better public speaker sent me their literature. I was interested in their material, but not sure it was what I wanted or that it would be good, and because of that, I didn't want to subscribe to their newsletter for $100, take their seminar for $250, or buy their audio-cassette album for $180. So I did not buy.

Later, when they mailed me a catalog, I saw they had produced a $10 book that contained some of the basic material in the other items. I ordered immediately and became a customer. I have since bought many other things from them, moving up the price scale with each new purchase as I become more comfortable with them.

Lower or waive your minimum order requirement.   If you have a "minimum order," you should think about lowering or eliminating it. What happens when a valued customer picks up the phone to place a small order and is told she can't, because it doesn't meet your minimum order amount? She'll probably remind the order taker that she is a regular customer and request that the order be taken anyway. When the order taker says he can't, she will *immediately* call your competitors—because she's in a hurry and has no time to waste.

The competitor fills the order, and your customer realizes, "Hey, it's the same product, and it's just as easy to order, and they helped me out." And suddenly she has moved all her business to your competitor—a loss you could have prevented by being more flexible and accommodating.

A key strategy to keeping clients satisfied is to remove all barriers to doing business the way they want to do it and to be totally accommodating and flexible. Waiving the minimum order requirement for existing accounts is one example of doing that.

In the 1990s, the average project will be smaller in scope, the average purchase smaller in size. Accommodate that with a lower-priced starting point so the client can "sample" your wares before making a bigger commitment.

This applies to existing accounts as well as new business. The size of the average order you receive from your customers will probably be substantially less than it has been in the past. Yet they will expect the same level of service, care, and concern they received when they were a bigger account.

Do not let clients know you are annoyed or unhappy at their reduced spending. They care about themselves, not your profits, and remember: *they can always go elsewhere.* No matter how good you are, you're not indispensable. Keep that in mind.

Fundamental Change 3: Purchase Decisions Are Made by Committees Instead of Individuals—and They Take Longer to Finalize.

You are going to face enormous frustration serving your clients and customers on an ongoing basis if you do not recognize and accept the fact that they're going to take longer to make up their mind and may require more hand-holding and prodding to get them to act.

With so many households needing two incomes, buying is more and more a shared, joint decision. With money scarcer, major purchases become frightening, and so people use their friends, relatives, and associates as an ad hoc buying committee— asking twenty different people their opinion and getting twenty different answers.

In business-to-business selling, the buying authority of many managers has been reduced or is lower than it used to be. When I was twenty-four years old and in my second job out of college, I had a junior-level position with an engineering firm, yet I could spend $5,000 or even $10,000 without someone higher up having to sign off or making a presentation to management.

Now as a seller I deal with corporate clients in their thirties, forties, and fifties who have to consult with many different people and get approval from a management committee before they can authorize a $2,000 or $3,000 expenditure for consulting or training services! The atmosphere is cautious and the buying mode is by committee.

This becomes agonizingly frustrating, not to mention time consuming, for the vendor who has to deal with corporate clients. You might have to prod and push and call fifteen times to get a client to give you the final go-ahead on a project or authorize the next step of an ongoing assignment.

Often this results in total disruption of your schedule. The client, of course, originally wanted everything the day before yesterday, and you moved heaven and earth to accommodate him.

You submit the first phase of the project—and they sit on it for weeks before getting back to you.

The temptation is to read the client the "riot act" and say you'll have no more of it. But don't. Remember, the client is looking to you for support and has hired you to make her job *easier*, not harder. The best strategy for keeping your client satisfied in this situation is to be flexible, accommodating, cheerful, and helpful.

Don't complain about the delays they have caused, and don't say you can't do your end because they're not doing theirs. Instead, just say you are checking into the status of the project and is there anything you can do to help move the process along?

If you *must* have the client respond to you with a check, contract, or other action before you can proceed, remind the client, but do so nicely—as a friend, partner, and teammate, and not, as so many do, as an adversary.

Another sticky issue when dealing with clients who are slow moving and do things by committee is: When is a contract really a contract? In the old days, when you had a good relationship with a client, the verbal go-ahead from your contact person at the client company—to be followed leisurely by a purchase order or letter of agreement—was taken as a "go."

Now, that's not the case. Remember, your corporate client *is no longer the decision maker in authority*: they have to run everything by the committee. So be aware that when he approves your estimate or tells you to schedule the first meeting for the twenty-third, it's *not* firm yet.

More and more clients, both business and consumer, are having second thoughts and great anxiety over purchase decisions. So what's firm in your mind may not be firm in theirs. Make sure your paperwork is signed, sealed, and delivered before you count the job as yours. Even then, cancellation is possible. (We'll deal with what to do when the client cancels after the contract is signed in Chapter 8 on coping with problems.)

Today's client moves slowly, but expects lightning-fast response from you when they're finally ready to roll. They can operate at a snail's pace, but they won't allow *you* the same luxury. It doesn't matter that you're busy and have scheduled other work because they delayed the contract—they want you *now* and the meeting is tomorrow morning. Expect to jump through more hoops to keep clients satisfied in the decades to come. The client expects you to be there instantly when he needs you, and if you aren't, your competitors will be.

Fundamental Change 4: Customers Are Buying Products and Services in Small Increments Rather than All At Once

Even if the client has a big need, today's customer is more likely to buy incrementally rather than all at once. Even your "regulars" aren't going to give you the big orders you once got; instead of buying everything on the menu, they just want item 3 from column B.

The trend will be for clients to give you authorization for smaller pieces and parts of what they need rather than the full package. Even if they eventually purchase the full package, it is not going to be bought all at once.

As a result, you are less likely to walk away with that big eight-part project; rather, the client will assign the work to you one piece a time and then wait and see what their needs and finances are in the weeks or months ahead before going forward with the next phase or step.

Don't fight the client on this or push too hard for a bigger order; this piecemeal buying is pervasive among customers today, and they are looking for you to accommodate it rather than fight it. In fact, you will score points with your customers by showing them how to do things less expensively and spend less rather than more.

In this era of reducing spending, clients often get the feeling that their suppliers and vendors are always pushing for them to buy more product or use more services, not in the best interests of the client, but because it means a bigger sale—and more profit—for the vendor.

To a degree, they're right. If you're a contractor specializing in adding family rooms to houses, and you get paid by the square foot, aren't you going to push the prospect to get a bigger family room rather than a smaller one? Your rationale on the surface is that they'll enjoy the bigger room, and even though it's tough for them to swing it now, they'll thank you later.

This may be true. But at the same time, you know there's a little voice in the back of your head saying, "And also, I'll make more money on the bigger project." So the client's mistrust of vendors and belief that they are out to "get" the client is partially valid.

While the bigger job brings you bigger bucks, losing the client because they think you're only looking after your own interests means no bucks at all. So let me suggest an alternate strategy:

Every once in a while, recommend to the client that they *not* buy your product or use your service, or at least that they buy less of it.

This instantly raises the client's trust and opinion of you by an order of magnitude. It comes as a shock because it's directly the opposite of what they expect from you. They *expect* you to try to sell them; when you show you are trying to *help* them instead—especially if that help involves spending less money rather than more—it gets their attention. And it strengthens the client/vendor relationship substantially: *You* are the one who's recommendations they can trust; why bother to go elsewhere?

An effective strategy for dealing with the customer trend of buying in small increments is to offer the customer a *menu* of products, services, or options from which they can select what they want, rather than bundle everything together and force them to take the "whole package." Make the identity and cost of individual elements clear rather than try to hide them.

If you offer customers a high-priced "take-it-or-leave-it" all-encompassing package, they're more likely to leave it than take it. Which means they will soon be dealing with another vendor instead of you.

On the other hand, if you let your customers buy a little now, and then go back for more later, they'll be more likely to do business with you on a basis that accommodates their limited budget and more "timid" 1990's buying habits. Obviously your profit on the sale is smaller. But the idea is to maintain a good relationship so that you make it up on many future sales.

Fundamental Change 5: Less Important Jobs and Projects Are Now Being Done by the Clients Themselves

Consumers have always been into "do-it-yourself" to some degree. And business clients have *always* done some of the type of work you do for them in-house. But now the trend is, because of economic necessity, to save money by doing more in-house—especially "low-end" projects that do not warrant the expense of costly outside help.

You may immediately be thinking that I am in error. "The trend is downsizing," you say, "so actually, businesses are cutting staff, which means more work for outside vendors." This is true, but only to a degree, and here's what's really happening: Although businesses are cutting back on staff, they are *investing* in in-house systems and technology that make them less dependent on costly outside services.

As an example, consider graphic arts. Corporations have scaled back communications departments, so companies that once had five or six graphic artists on staff now have none. You would think that would mean lots more business for independent graphic design studios. And it did, for a while.

But what are these companies doing now? They are acquiring desktop publishing systems and training support staff to use them to produce newsletters, bulletins, reports, fliers, and other materials that were once farmed out to the graphic design studios. Secretaries are now producing materials that professional typesetters and designers once charged clients a pretty penny for.

Yes, the clients still use the freelance graphic artists for the "important stuff": annual reports, color product brochures, posters. *But the trend is for clients to do more of the easier, less important, or nonessential tasks in-house themselves.*

Consumers, despite lack of time, are the same way. People who would once have called a professional to paint a room or put up wallpaper are buying do-it-yourself Time-Life books and videos and are watching Bob Vila, the home improvement spokesperson for Sears Roebuck. People who once spent freely in the 1980s are suddenly *concerned* about what things cost and how they can save their money.

What does this mean for you as a vendor or supplier? Much of the low-end of the market for your service or product will shrink or vanish altogether. As a result, you will be competing with more firms for a smaller number of projects or sales. Again, this makes the environment more competitive and puts the customer, not you, in the driver's seat.

How to cope? One strategy is to redesign your business so that you can handle the smaller jobs and nonessential projects so efficiently and cost-effectively that clients give them back to you instead of doing it themselves.

For instance, in the 1980s, when desktop publishing began to get noticed, ad agencies and graphic design studios laughed it off as fad: after all, the client was not a graphic artist, so just having a computer instead of a ruler or paintbrush wouldn't allow them to replace the agency or studio, they reasoned.

The graphic arts industry, therefore, was slow to implement the new desktop technology. But their corporate clients embraced it and were suddenly turning out reams of material and telling the agency, "We don't need you for this."

Many agencies and studios responded by acquiring their own desktop capability and offering it as a faster, less costly graphic service, making it once again attractive for clients to go to the agency or studio instead of doing it all themselves. In this way, the agencies and studios regained some of the work they had previously lost.

Or you may decide the low-end stuff isn't worth having and allow the businessperson or consumer to do it themselves, concentrating your own efforts on services the customer is *not* going to perform in-house. The choice is yours, but you must be aware of the do-it-yourself trend and have some strategy for responding to it.

The do-it-yourself trend has also created a new source of competition for you: lower-priced service alternatives designed specifically to handle these low-end tasks at low cost. To continue with our graphics example, the rise of desktop publishing resulted in numerous people starting "desktop publishing services": people bought Macintosh computers with page layout software and told corporations, "We'll do your newsletters and bulletins for you—and we'll charge one-third of what your ad agency is charging."

Ad agencies looked down on such services or laughed them off initially, but they aren't now. The desktop publishing service has created a permanent low-priced alternative source to the more sophisticated ad agency or graphic design studio solutions. Ad agencies and design studios must respond to the challenge by offering similar service when needed or more effectively bonding themselves to the client as the number one vendor for design services through some other means. But the options of "do-it-yourself" or do it through a low-priced alternative are here to stay.

Fundamental Change 6: Customer Loyalty Is a Thing of the Past

When you have been dealing with a customer for a while, you develop a zone of comfort with that customer that causes you to relax in your dealings with them. This follows from the principle of "familiarity breeds contempt." I'm not saying you have contempt for your customers. Far from it. You probably like them, and maybe even consider some friends.

But the way you treat your old, steady clients is not the way you treat your new customers or the hot prospects you are pursuing. It's not even close to the way you treated the old, steady client when they were a new account.

When you're pursuing a prospect, you put your best foot forward. You tell the prospect all the good things about your firm, none of the potential negatives or weaknesses.

When you first get the customer, you do everything in your power to ensure that the first order is fulfilled quickly, efficiently, and without difficulties or delays. You realize that the new client is not yet really "yours"—and that if you don't deliver the superior service you promised in your sales pitch, you won't have them as a client for long.

As time goes on, and the customer continues to buy from you, your attitude becomes, "Well, they've become a regular for us. The pressure is off." You assume that the customer is happy with you and always thinks of you when they need the types of products or services you sell.

This may have been true—at one time. But it is no longer. In the competitive 1990s, your competitors are pursuing your best accounts and doing everything in their power to take them away from you—almost on a daily basis. Worse, your key accounts do not have the loyalty to you that they did in the 1980s—even though you may think they do. This means that, *unless you're at your competitive best at all times, in every dealing with the client, you're at risk of losing that client at almost any time.*

Therefore, the habit of relaxing and taking it easy when the account becomes "yours" is a pattern that must be eliminated from your behavior and the behavior of your employees. Every day, every interaction with the customer, every product shipped, every service rendered, every problem handled, all must be done with the same excellence you would show *as if this were your first order from the client and he was testing you on a "trial" basis to see if you'll work out as a vendor.*

Loyalty to a specific service, product, vendor, or supplier has not vanished completely, but it has significantly diminished. Your customers want it their way. They want it cheap. They want it great. They want it fast. If they can't get that from you today, tomorrow, or the next day, they're not going to stick with you because you "have a relationship." Instead, they are going to search for alternative sources—and be extremely receptive to your competitors' sales pitches.

You cannot relax today when servicing an account or nurturing a relationship with a customer. Customers are quick to "see red" and become annoyed when things are not done exactly their way.

You are, in essence, never really through "selling" the client. The "sale" is not something that happens once and ends when you get the contract, check, or purchase order. "Selling" is something that takes place before, during, and after the service is rendered or the product is delivered: it's an ongoing process that lasts for as long as that person or company is your customer.

This also affects how you price your product or service to existing accounts. Again, in the past, you might have developed a comfort zone that said to you, "Well, they're in love with our product, they love our service, and we're fulfilling all their orders within 48 hours. Where else can they get such great service? They can't, and they know it. So they're not looking around—and I can charge them a little extra because they won't mind paying us a bit more than we've been charging. They probably won't notice and, after all, we're worth it."

In the 1990s, the "Age of the Customer," that thinking doesn't hold. The account you think you have a "lock" on is much less attached to you as a vendor than you would like to believe. In fact, you'd be surprised to learn how many of your clients are now closely scrutinizing price quotes and cost estimates on orders they once would have approved automatically.

Customers are reviewing your pricing much more carefully than ever before, and they are seeking other bids on many jobs you thought were "yours"—and doing it without your knowledge. So don't get too comfortable in the way you charge your best customers because you think you can "get away with it." You can't. Half the time, it's a competitive bid situation, and you, as the "incumbent" vendor, don't even know about it until it's too late and you've lost the job.

The key strategy here is to treat every client as if they were your most important client and every job as if it's a highly competitive bid situation. Avoid complacency in customer service; it can cost you business.

Fundamental Change 7: Customers Want More Services Without Paying More

Today's customers want as much as they can get for as little as they can pay for it; they want "extras" and "freebies" and discounts.

The higher-priced supplier or vendor used to be able to combat this type of buyer with the argument, "I know we cost more, but if you want a Rolls Royce you have to pay for it." Now the customer expects a Rolls Royce for the price of a Mercedes or even a Cadillac—and, in many instances, there is competition out there offering it to win the customer away from you. In fact, many of them are offering quality comparable to yours.

Negotiation in all aspects of business is becoming the norm rather than the exception. Many vendors will tell you their pricing is firm, but when you don't buy, and they call back, suddenly there's a reason why they can offer it lower if you act now.

Many authorities on selling will tell you always to stick by your price and never back down. I gave such advice myself in the books I wrote and published in the 1980s.

But today you need all the competitive weapons you can get to win the business war, and you need me to be completely honest with you. So let me tell you: almost *everyone* today negotiates or bargains at least part of the time. Anyone who says he doesn't is a megastar in his field, has a virtual monopoly, or is a liar.

Does this mean you have to "give away the store" to make the sale? Fortunately, not. Customers are reasonable and understand, to some degree, that you have to make a profit; they don't expect a $25,000 home improvement job for $10,000. However, the 1990s buyer *is* likely to get you to throw in some extras with the job—extras you'd normally charge for—and then get the whole package for $24,000 or $23,000.

What do you do? Chapter 4 goes into great detail about how to accommodate the buyer who wants a little extra, a little something for nothing. You'll see that meeting this request halfway is easy, inexpensive, and can make you a hero with your customer. Being totally inflexible and rigid about your pricing or policies is likely to cost you a lot of business this year and next.

WHY CUSTOMER SERVICE IS THE NUMBER ONE PRIORITY IN RUNNING A SUCCESSFUL BUSINESS TODAY

If you look at these seven fundamental shifts in customer behavior, you'll see one common theme to them: *the customer wants and demands more service from you.*

Increasingly, customers see the services and products they buy as looking more and more alike. What differentiates one source from another in the customer's mind is *how you treated them.* Did you deliver on time? Was your advice good? Did you answer all questions promptly? Did you bill the amount you said it would cost? Did you save them money or improve their operations in a a way they didn't expect? Excellent customer service—not product design or service methodology—is increasingly the differentiating factor that determines whether you keep or lose clients.

HOW TO KEEP YOUR CLIENTS HAPPIER LONGER

This book will show you how to render excellent customer service, resolve problems so they do not harm the vendor/customer relationship, and keep your clients happier longer.

An important, but often overlooked, element in ensuring a long list of satisfied customers is to start the relationship on the right foot in the first place. This means accurately determining what the customer really wants and matching your product or service to satisfy those wants.

More important, it means choosing the right customers— *customers you know you can satisfy and will enjoy dealing with—* and not taking on customers who don't fit that bill.

Let's talk about how to do that in Chapter 2.

CHAPTER 2

Selectivity: The Key to Longer, Happier Client Relationships

If you don't enjoy dealing with your customers any more, and if your client relationships are fraught with problems, difficulties, and stress, maybe you aren't the cause of these problems. Instead, *maybe you need new customers.* That's a need that can be met—but how much better off you'd be if only you would *choose the right customers in the first place!* This chapter is written to help you find, get, and keep the right customers for your business.

SELECTIVITY IS THE KEY TO BETTER CLIENT RELATIONSHIPS

There are many factors affecting your relationships with your customers. Your service, product quality, courtesy, prices—all these can cause customers either to be happy with you or dissatisfied with you. We all know this: it's obvious.

But another "obvious" fact that most businesspeople ignore is that one of the most powerful strategies for assuring good customer relationships—that is, customer relationships that last a long time and are profitable—is to *choose the right customers in the first place.*

Choosing the right customers can eliminate 80 percent of problems *before* they occur and make your life a lot more pleasant and stress-free. Choosing the wrong customers can give you headaches, ulcers, stress, worry, and a sour disposition from continually fixing problems, mending fences, and being at odds with people you depend on for business but with whom you can't seem to get along.

Many of the problems you have keeping clients satisfied will not happen if you stop taking on clients whose requirements you know in advance will be difficult if not impossible for your particular product or service to satisfy. And many of the collection problems you have chasing deadbeats would not exist if you enforced your credit policies and avoided doing business with people who are obvious credit risks in the first place. In short, many of the problems you experience coping with difficult customers will be alleviated if you choose to do business with people who are easy to get along with.

Clients Choose You, but You Also Choose Clients

For many businesspeople, especially during an economic downturn, the concept of "choosing" clients is alien. "What do you mean 'choosing clients'?" you object. "In today's economy, we take all the business we can get."

That may seem a sensible strategy when things are slow, but it will get you into trouble almost every time. There are better ways to cope with a business downturn, as we will see.

Clients choose vendors, no doubt about it. Every order you get, every sale you make, every contract you sign is the result of some sort of review process on the part of the prospect. They are the client, the customer, the buyer; they are the ones spending money, and they have the power to hire you or not hire you.

But to ensure maximum client satisfaction down the road, this selection process should not be a one-way street: just as clients choose you, you choose clients. You should look at each potential customer carefully; analyze their needs, wants, personality, and buying power; and make a yes/no decision about whether to accept them as a customer.

This screening process is done silently by you and should not be made obvious. Although the customer is making clear that you are one of several vendors under consideration, you shouldn't let *them* know they are one of many clients you are considering working with or not. You just smile and say you're glad they're interested in your services, but unseen by them, you are holding a magnifying glass as close to them as they are to you.

THE FIRST STEP TO SCREENING A CLIENT: USE YOUR "MENTAL RADAR"

Whether you know it or not, you're screening potential customers every time you see, talk with, or meet a first-time prospect.

Let's say someone calls you on the phone in response to your Yellow Pages ad and begins inquiring about your service. If they are well-mannered, articulate, pleasant, and seem intelligent, you probably form an instant positive impression. Within a few seconds, the prospect has passed your first-stage screen: you've made the decision that, if all other factors work out, this is someone you'd like to have as a customer.

Now a second prospect calls. This person is loutish and ill-mannered. He immediately begins questioning your credentials in a challenging tone, frequently telling you how he hired this competitor of yours and that competitor and no one could please him. Within seconds, this prospect begins to grate on your nerves; you take an instant dislike to him. You run this data through a subconscious screening process, and your mind gives you the result: this is a customer you don't want. You quickly make some excuse about being busy or not having any product in stock and get off the phone.

Actually, what is happening is that you are running the input you receive from each prospect—appearance, demeanor, personality, budget, requirements—through a checklist of what you do and do not like in a customer. Only you are doing this *subconsciously*: you have never deliberately created such a checklist or set of guidelines, but your subconscious has: based on years of dealing with good and bad customers, your mind has compiled a list of likes and dislikes, do's and don'ts it goes through when evaluating a new prospect.

Is this a bad thing? On the contrary, it's a good thing: you're already doing, to some degree, what I've been advocating—being selective about the kinds of customers you do and do not work with.

However, the problem with relying solely on your "mental checklist" is that it's easy to skip one or more items in your hurry to make a decision about a particular prospect. That's why I recommend creating a Desirable Client Profile as a tool to help you select those customers with whom you are most likely to build a good long-term relationship with and screen out those who are likely to become "problem" accounts.

BUILDING THE DESIRABLE CLIENT PROFILE: MONITORING CLIENT CHARACTERISTICS

The Desirable Client Profile is a checklist you use to evaluate prospects and decide whether they're a good "fit" for your product or service. There is no particular form I use or special format I can give you as an example, because the profile isn't that formal. All it is, is a list of points or questions against which you measure each potential customer.

Ideally the list should be typed or written neatly on one side of a single sheet of 8½ × 11-inch paper and posted or kept in a place where you have easy access to it when potential customers contact you. If you have a notebook you use to track sales leads, tape or clip the profile to the inside front cover. If you do a lot of telephone selling, keep the list posted on the wall in front of your desk.

Okay. Let's say you want to build a Desirable Client Profile. What are the key points that should be covered?

THE SEVEN CHARACTERISTICS OF THE DESIRABLE CLIENT

There are probably dozens of criteria by which you can measure whether a prospect is a good potential customer for your business. But the most important qualifying characteristics fall into the following seven categories:

1. Level of client need
2. Type of client need
3. Type of client
4. Buying power
5. Buying authority
6. Personal chemistry
7. Match between your product or service and the client's requirement

Let's build your Desirable Client Profile by looking at each of the screening factors in more detail.

Compatibility Criterion 1: Level of Client Need

Level of need means how seriously or urgently your prospective client needs what you are selling. A prospect's initial inquiry may be extremely casual—perhaps nothing more than requesting a brochure out of idle curiosity—or it may be highly specific: the firm needs a certain type of service and wants to evaluate whether you can fill that need.

Which type of prospect you feel is the best fit for you depends on the nature of your business. Most businesspeople would probably say they are primarily interested in dealing with customers who have a real and immediate requirement for their product or service. This leads to a faster sale and an opportunity to please the customer and establish a relationship.

Some businesspeople, on the other hand, are in fields where a longer "courtship" between seller and buyer is typical, and anyone "needing it tomorrow" is looked upon with suspicion and not taken as a serious prospect. An example would be the world of professional speaking. Most associations plan their annual conferences six to twelve months in advance or more. So if a speaker got a call from someone claiming to be an association executive, who said he was looking for a speaker to be on a program to be held in four weeks, the speaker might suspect something not quite right was going on.

Maybe the caller was someone who did not have the authority to hire speakers but was just curious to see what types of brochures professional speakers use. Or perhaps it wasn't really an association executive, but a competitor trying to get his hands on the speaker's media kit.

Most businesses, however, consider the best prospect to be a "serious player"—someone who seems to have a genuine requirement for the seller's product or service and will need it now or in the near future.

Compatibility Criterion 2: Type of Client Need

What the prospective client needs quickly identifies her either as a hot prospect or a not-so-hot prospect. For instance, the other day I received a call from a corporate training director who said he was looking for a consultant to do an in-house training program. Great! I was excited—that's what I do, and here was an immediate requirement.

I asked what the topic would be, expecting it to be in my specialty areas of sales, marketing, and client satisfaction—after all, why else would they call me? But my happiness vanished when the training director said he needed a training session on presentation skills. Unfortunately, I don't have a seminar on that topic.

When I explained that, the training director said, "Oh, well don't worry. Send me literature on what you *do* offer. I'm sure we'll have a need in the future." But this lead had gone from a 10 to a 1 on a scale of 1 to 10—from a hot prospect with an immediate need for my specific product to someone who had called the wrong vendor and now just wanted to collect a brochure so as not to make me feel disappointed.

The type of need the prospect has, therefore, is a major factor determining whether they will be a good or bad client for you. If they need a product or service you normally provide, then they would score highly on this portion of your Desirable Client Profile.

On the other hand, if they need a product or service you *could* provide but don't normally, they may not rank so high. You could make the decision to pursue the customer, take on their job, and then create a customized product or service to satisfy them—but do you really want to? Taking on such a customer will probably be a pain in the neck and may not be worth your while. So a customer who needs something other than your "standard" offering is not so desirable as the customer who is buying exactly what you're selling.

Compatibility Criterion 3: Type of Client

Some clients are good prospects for you. Others are not. So the type of person or company is a major factor in determining whether you want to work on or pass up the contract being offered.

Many companies that sell to consumers, for example, have established certain demographic and psychographic criteria against which they screen prospective customers and select which are likely candidates. For example, Club Med used to advertise primarily to singles, while Perillo Tours seemed to target the over-50 crowd.

For whatever reason, you may know that a person of a certain age, economic status, social background, political beliefs, or whatever wouldn't enjoy and benefit from what you are selling. So they are listed low on your Desirable Client Profile in this category. On the other hand, people who are of the age, income bracket, habits, social background, or whatever that would make them likely to enjoy and benefit from your product or service would rank high as desirable clients here.

It is the same with business prospects. In my consulting business, for example, I know that I do best when working with clients in industries where I have a lot of experience—banking, computers, electronics, software, and so on. So when I get an inquiry from such a prospect, they rate high on my Desirable Client Profile: I'm really going to pull out all the stops to get them to hire me.

On the other hand, I know that prospects from industries that demand specialists and in which I am *not* a specialist—fashion, cosmetics, packaged goods—would not make good clients. First, it's unlikely they'll hire me in the first place, so the lead is not worth pursuing. Second, even if they hire me, I won't have the track record and experience they're looking for, and this will only cause problems later on. So when I get an inquiry from someone selling perfume or fashions, for example, I rank them low on my Desirable Client Profile and tend to shy away from them.

Compatibility Criterion 4: Buying Power

Buying power is a major factor determining whether a prospect would make a good client for you. The rule of thumb is simple: if they have the resources and budget to afford you comfortably, they'll probably become a happy and satisfied customer, all else being equal. That's because they're accustomed to paying the kind of money you charge for the level of service you provide, and your invoices will not represent serious financial hardship or strain for them.

On the other hand, the prospect who can barely afford your asking price, or for whom paying your fee is a hardship or a stretch, is more likely to be difficult and become dissatisfied. There are a couple of reasons for this. First, because paying your fee is a strain, he's going to become unhappy when he sees your bill. Yes, you told him the price in advance, but the client who wants you but really can't afford you has a way of "forgetting" money discussions until the invoice comes due. Then he asks why you have to charge so much, complains that he can't afford it or that you overcharged him, or begins to nitpik over your invoices item by item. This gets you frustrated; soon you're angry with the client and the client is angry with you—a good sign that the relationship will not last much longer.

Another reason why prospects who can barely afford your product or service are not desirable customers is that they are more demanding than are those for whom the purchase is not a hardship. If you've been in business for any length of time, you've discovered this amazing but true fact: the client who readily agrees to your fee and pays your price is usually the most pleasant and least demanding. Conversely, the client who nickels and dimes you, pays your bills grudgingly, and feels the pinch of every penny is the one who's most demanding.

In a way, that's understandable: the "poor" client can less afford not to get the most out of every dollar than the cash-rich client. Be that as it may, however, this doesn't make the poor client a good client to work with. So another major factor that makes a client "desirable" is having the money to afford what you are selling.

Compatibility Criterion 5: Buying Authority

Just because someone appears to have the money to afford you doesn't mean they have the authority to spend it. For this reason, a key measure of the desirability of a customer is *buying authority*: Do they have the authority to go ahead and authorize the purchase of your product or service themselves? Or must they consult with a cosigner, partner, or corporate buying committee, or even a spouse or parent before they can sign on the dotted line? Here is an informal hierarchy of customer desirability:

- The ideal, or most desirable, customer is the one who has ultimate buying authority and can sign your contract or cut you a check today if he or she decides to buy what you are selling.
- The second most desirable prospect is the one who essentially makes the decision but may have to check with one or two people before you can get the purchase order or signed paperwork.
- Less desirable as a customer is the person who has responsibility for buying your type of product or service but no real buying authority or clout, and must go through a long chain of approvals even for rather minor expenditures.
- The least desirable customer is the assistant or go-between whose job is to act as liaison with vendors, collecting infor-

mation, communicating instructions, and passing messages back and forth but who has no authority to buy, specify, or even recommend products or services.

The lower down your potential customer is in this hierarchy, the less desirable they are. Dealing with go-betweens can be frustrating and wasteful, because you can spend hours selling the person only to discover that your "real" customer has no interest in your product and never had.

This criterion of client desirability can also be applied to dealing with consumers. If you're a contractor, for example, and you are selling to a single person, you know that if you convince that person, you've got the job.

On the other hand, if you're dealing with a customer where the partner is the real decision maker, but your primary contact is with the other partner, you may never get to overcome the decision maker's objections or present the benefits of your offering to that partner, and your efforts may be wasted.

The higher up on the decision-making hierarchy the prospect is, the higher they should rate on your Desirable Client Profile.

Compatibility Criterion 6: Personal Chemistry

Personal chemistry is difficult to define, explain, or measure quantitatively. Yet you can judge it fairly accurately within the first three minutes of meeting the prospect in person or during your initial telephone call.

What it boils down to is this: Some people you take an instant liking to and know you can get along with: these people rate high on your Desirable Client Profile. Other people you take an instant dislike to: either they rub you the wrong way, or you just decide, based largely on instinct, that you're better off staying away from them. These prospects rate low on your Desirable Client Profile.

Other people you are neutral about: no strong feeling one way or the other. These prospects get a medium rating on your profile.

Personal chemistry is probably more important for someone rendering services to clients than for someone selling a product. But if there is to be an ongoing relationship necessitating frequent contact between you and the customer, then personal chemistry is definitely a factor, and you should not ignore it when selecting which clients to work with and which not to.

Compatibility Criterion 7: Match or Fit with Product or Service

This has to do with the prospect's particular application or situation. It is probably the least important of the seven criteria, but it still should be considered when evaluating any new potential client.

"Fit" refers to how well your product or service can satisfy the specific requirement or application of a given customer. Sometimes you find your product or service is a "natural" fit to the client's requirement. Great! That client rates high on the Desirable Client Profile scale.

For instance, one of my colleagues, a successful consultant, has a gruff, almost abrasive manner when dealing with clients. This is because, unlike many of his peers who try to be diplomatic or avoid offending clients, my colleague feels the only way to be effective is to be totally honest and blunt: no pussyfooting around. Some clients appreciate his candor and value him for it. Others are turned off by it and won't put up with it.

His service, then, is a good fit for clients like owners and entrepreneurs who want the truth and are concerned only with making money from his excellent advice. His service is *not* a good fit for middle-level corporate managers who risk being embarrassed by his abrasive manner and having him insult their colleagues and superiors when he must present his recommendations in a workplace meeting.

Rather than fight this, the consultant recognizes this, and has written his marketing brochure to make the fact clear up front. He is open and candid about his to-the-point way of dealing with people and suggests that those who don't like it or have to be concerned with "pleasing a boss" *not* hire him.

That may sound arrogant, but in fact, it's sound business practice. He is ensuring a much higher client satisfaction rate than he would otherwise get. He accomplishes this by selecting, in advance, only those prospects who are an excellent fit for the way he renders his service and conducts his business.

Were he to take on nonideal clients, he would end up in a lot of fights, offending a lot of people and having to chase after them to get his invoice paid. Instead, he deals only with like-minded individuals and, as a result, has excellent relationships with clients who are willing and happy to put up with his idiosyncrasies in exchange for his superior level of advice.

SCREENING POTENTIAL CLIENTS USING THE DESIRABLE CLIENT PROFILE

In its most basic form, the Desirable Client Profile consists of these seven questions:

1. Does the prospect have a genuine need and, if so, how urgent is that need?
2. Does the prospect have a requirement for the specific types of products and services we sell?
3. Is this the type of person or firm we like to do business with?
4. Can they afford us?
5. Does this person have the authority to make the purchase?
6. Is there good personal chemistry between our people and the prospect?
7. Is our service or product a natural "fit" with the prospect's unique requirements, or would they be better off getting it elsewhere?

With each prospect you are considering taking on as a customer, ask yourself these seven questions. If most of the answers are positive, the prospect is desirable as a customer and should be taken on, if you can get the contract. The positive answers point to a good, long, happy working relationship.

On the other hand, if most of the answers are negative, think long and hard before taking a down payment from this buyer. You may want the money now, but it may not be worth the aggravation and heartache later on.

For a slightly more precise rating method using the Desirable Client Profile, follow the instructions in Exhibit 2-1.

WHAT IF YOU CAN'T BE AS SELECTIVE IN CHOOSING CLIENTS AS YOU WOULD LIKE?

As previously stated, you may be thinking, "This idea of being selective and choosy about your customers is fine and good for those who have more business than they can handle. But our industry is in a downturn right now, and we need all the business we can get. So does the Desirable Client Profile really apply?"

Exhibit 2-1. Desirable Client Profile

INSTRUCTIONS: Rate the prospect according to these seven criteria using the following scale:

5 = Agree strongly
4 = Agree somewhat
3 = No strong opinion either way
2 = Disagree somewhat
1 = Disagree strongly

1. The prospect has a definite and urgent requirement.

[ ] 5 [ ] 4 [ ] 3 [ ] 2 [ ] 1

2. The prospect is a candidate for using one or more of the specific products or services we sell.

[ ] 5 [ ] 4 [ ] 3 [ ] 2 [ ] 1

3. The prospect fits the profile of the type of individual or company we like to deal with in terms of demographics, psychographics, job title, job function, industry, geographic location, and so on.

[ ] 5 [ ] 4 [ ] 3 [ ] 2 [ ] 1

4. The prospect can readily afford the fees we charge for our product or service.

[ ] 5 [ ] 4 [ ] 3 [ ] 2 [ ] 1

5. The person to whom I am speaking has the authority (or can easily get the authorization) to purchase our product or service.

[ ] 5 [ ] 4 [ ] 3 [ ] 2 [ ] 1

6. I have a good feeling about this prospect—I like him or her and feel we would work well together.

[ ] 5 [ ] 4 [ ] 3 [ ] 2 [ ] 1

7. Our product or service is a good match with the prospect's requirement and can serve them much better than other products or services on the market can.

[ ] 5 [ ] 4 [ ] 3 [ ] 2 [ ] 1

Write your total score
here:_____

SCORING:

28–35

The prospect is highly desirable and would make a good customer. The relationship would probably work out well, be mutually beneficial, and be relatively free of problems and conflict.

21–27

The prospect would make a decent client, and the sale should be pursued. But, keep on the look-out for signs that would indicate more potential future difficulties than the initial profile indicates. If no such signs show up, the relationship will probably work out.

14–20

You have doubts; many signs indicate that this prospect is not a great match for your business. Proceed with caution. If you can work out or ignore the differences, pursue the sale. If things go from bad to worse, get out.

7–13

This prospect would not make a good client, and you should consider passing on the business, possibly referring it to a colleague who is more suited to handling this type of prospect.

Yes, but with a slight modification. You should still establish a Desirable Client Profile checklist so you have rational guidelines for selecting customers and clients whom you are likely to be able to satisfy both over the short and long term. After all, client satisfaction is the name of the game.

At the same time, during an industry slump, recession, slow economy, or personal business downturn, you obviously can't be as choosy as you like. Rather than throw out or ignore your Desirable Client Profile, use this strategy: You *slightly* downgrade your Desirable Client Profile until business improves, then reactivate your original Desirable Client Profile when things get busy again.

This means you don't throw out your standards in a soft economy, but you do relax them to a degree. How much you relax them depends on how slow things are and how much business you need.

For instance, if you downgrade your Desirable Client Profile slightly, and the slight lowering of standards allows you to reach enough prospects you wouldn't ordinarily deal with to get you busy and profitable again, then that slight downgrade is all that's needed.

If you downgrade your Client Profile slightly and the new business it opens up to you is still not enough to make up for lost sales, then you downgrade it even further—gradually—until it's at a level that works for you.

For instance, if you have a house cleaning service and you normally charge a minimum fee of $60 and clean no house smaller than three bedrooms, and the recession has caused many of your customers to cut back on using your service from weekly to monthly, you need more business. So you might lower your minimum to $50 and agree to do smaller houses. But you probably wouldn't lower your minimum to $20 and agree to do studio apartments: it's just not worth making the trip out to the customer's home. So you lower your standards slightly, but don't throw them out all together.

During a soft economy, you want to be flexible and accommodating, not rigid and unyielding. Treat the Desirable Client Profile as a set of helpful guidelines for choosing clients, to be modified as circumstances dictate, not as a set of commandments etched in stone.

USING SALES AND MARKETING TO UPGRADE CLIENTS ALONG THE DESIRABLE CLIENT PROFILE

When you use the Desirable Client Profile (Exhibit 2-1) to rate clients, you will find a portion of your clients falling into the top category—let's call them A clients. These are your top clients, the best you have, the ones you want more of.

Another segment of your client list will fall in the second category; label them the B clients. As the grade implies, B clients are good clients but not great clients. Still, they are worth having.

A third segment, the less desirable clients, are the C clients. This is the third category on the rating scale in Exhibit 2-1.

And, finally, a small portion of your clients will fall into the fourth category of least desirable—let's call them D clients. These are the ones you tolerate because you've had them a long time, or they're good references, or you need the money, but often you dream about getting rid of them, if only you had more A and B clients.

Ideally, your goal would be to get rid of D clients, convert C to B clients, convert B to A clients, and get more new A clients. The result of this would be a roster of mostly A and B clients. And with better clients, you'd have fewer problems and a much higher overall rate of client satisfaction.

How do you do this? By marketing and selling your product or service aggressively on a daily basis. Many people mistakenly think marketing and selling are something you do only when you don't have business and need more of it. But while marketing can give you more business, it can also give you something just as important: freedom of choice.

Remember the supply and demand equation. When you need business, the clients are in the driver's seat. But when you have more business than you can handle, you can be more selective and choosy in who you take on as a client—and who you do not.

An ongoing sales and marketing campaign, applied rigorously and on a daily basis, can fuel demand for your product or service, giving you more sales leads than you can handle. With more leads than you can handle, you can afford to be choosier about which leads you pursue—and which you don't.

As you convert more of those leads to sales, you gain new customers—so many that you can't handle them all. At that point, you begin to say to yourself, "Hey, with all this business, I'm not sure I want to continue working for Joe Shmoe Company any more. They've always been difficult, lousy, bossy, and demanding, and they want everything as cheap as possible. I needed them when things were slow, but now, business is booming, so *perhaps I should resign the Joe Shmoe Company account.*"

Whether you do or not is not the issue. The point is that when you have more business than you can handle, you can begin to improve your mix of clients as represented on the Desirable Client Profile. When you can literally afford to turn away one, two, or more prospects or even current clients, you can get rid of some of the C and D clients in favor of new A and B clients.

People in business often ask me, "When is it okay to confront a lousy client and tell them you can't put up with them any more?"

My answer is: When you are willing to risk not having their business anymore and feel you can do so comfortably, both financially and psychologically. An aggressive *sales and marketing* campaign[1] can make the demand for your services exceed the supply, giving you the freedom to *pick and choose the clients you want to do business with.* It's a wonderful feeling—and one of the primary benefits of active, ongoing self-promotion.

Your goal concerning client satisfaction should be always to upgrade your client mix so you have more A and B clients and fewer C and D clients. Remember, the key to having more satisfied clients is choosing the right clients in the first place.

HOW TO SAY "NO" TO CUSTOMERS YOU ARE TURNING AWAY

Being selective about the customers you choose to do business with naturally means there will be some customers you will be turning away. It's important that you do this as politely as possible, without making the person feel inferior or rejected in any way. The reason is that some day this person or company may be in a position to hire you, may become an A or B prospect, and they will remember how you treated them. It never pays to treat people shabbily. It never pays to burn bridges.

So how do you say no to a customer without letting them know outright that you consider them not worth doing business with? Don't tell them about your client profiles and whether they rated a B, C, D, or whatever. Instead, make an excuse based on your not being available or able to help them.

For instance, if a client wants to hire you and you don't want the business, say, "I'm sorry, but we just took on a big project for IBM, and so we would not be able to handle your assignment. But do think of us again in the future." Or if they are ordering a product, say, "I'm sorry, but we are short of stock on that item and have

---

[1] Since this is a book about customer satisfaction and not selling or marketing, a discussion of *how* to sell and market your product or service effectively is beyond the scope of this chapter. I've written a number of books on sales, marketing, and promotion you may want to consult. These include *The Copywriter's Handbook* (New York: Henry Holt, 1990), *How to Promote Your Own Business* (New York: New American Library, 1983), *Selling Your Services: How to Get More Clients to Hire You or Your Firm* (New York: Henry Holt, 1991), *Direct Mail Profits* (Westbury, NY: Asher Gallant, 1987), and *Ads That Sell* (Westbury, NY: Asher Gallant, 1988), and *Business to Business Direct Marketing* (Linwood, IL: NTC, 1992).

reserved it for a big shipment to AT&T. After that, we may not be carrying it. So you may want to check another supplier."

An alternative is to take the business but at a price or on terms that make it worth dealing with a less than ideally desirable customer. For example, you could quote a higher than normal fee, and if they accept, then the extra money compensates you for the trouble of dealing with them. Or if you think they are likely to give you a hard time over paying your invoice, you can simply say your policy is payment up front. This eliminates billing complaints and collection problems later on.

Some C and D customers, even after being turned down, will still try to keep you on the phone, pump you for information, and pick your brains for free. If you render services and get paid by the hour, it's perfectly all right to say, "I normally charge X dollars an hour to give such advice; however, I'll give you five minutes free starting now." Answer their questions for the five minutes and then explain you're busy and must go on to other projects.

Similarly, if a client who is not a desirable prospect and with whom you do not want to do business keeps asking for quotes that are time consuming to produce, you can tell him you charge a certain sum for putting together proposals and that it is payable in advance. Since he is not a serious prospect, this will end the requests for quotations.

CHAPTER 3

How to Satisfy Your Clients by Understanding Their Needs

As we discussed earlier, there are two steps you can take to assure that you will have good relationships with your clients and minimize future problems even *before* you begin selling products or rendering services to those clients.

The first step, covered in Chapter 2, is to select the right clients in the first place, that is, choose clients with whom you are likely to have a good working relationship and avoid doing business with customers who are likely to be difficult, troublesome, or hard to please.

The second step is to make sure you understand exactly what your customer wants from you—and how your product or service addresses this requirement—before you start doing business with them. "Understanding client needs" is a key factor in ensuring client satisfaction and is the subject of this chapter.

WHY IT'S ESSENTIAL TO UNDERSTAND WHAT YOUR CUSTOMER REALLY WANTS

The idea that the purpose of business is to deliver goods or services in exchange for money is outmoded and archaic. You are not in the business of providing goods or services. You are in the business of *satisfying customers and clients*. That means you must deliver not only the good or service the customer ordered, but you must deliver an entire *transaction* that satisfies the customer at every step. This starts from the second the customer steps into your store and ends when the customer no longer owns your product or terminates their relationship with you.

Let's take the purchase of a television set as an example. My wife and I wanted to replace our old, tiny Philco with a 27-inch color TV set. After shopping around, we settled on one brand, which we could have purchased at any one of a number of local stores. We chose a particular store because of the recommendation of a friend. The friend had told us that by mentioning his name, we would get a "good price," but the price was no better than anywhere else. Still, we went ahead.

The company delivered the TV and it worked, so you would assume that the transaction had been fulfilled and we were satisfied. Not so. Remember, your business must deliver a satisfactory transaction from beginning to end, at every step of the way.

Here's the problem. In our case, the remote control stopped working. The set had come with a free one-year in-home service contract covering all components, and the owner's manual provided a toll-free 800 number we could use to locate a certified repair shop. We called the number and got a name. So far, so good.

The trouble started when we called the repair shop. "Why don't you bring it in?" the owner asked, amiably enough. I replied, equally as amiably, that while that was a reasonable request, we were extremely busy and didn't want to spend our time making the trip—that was why we had purchased a model with an *in-home* warranty—and would he please send someone either to pick it up or repair it on site.

At this point, the owner began arguing with us, explaining that he too was busy and didn't have people to spare to come out to our house. This didn't make sense to me, because if the problem had been in the set itself, they would naturally send someone out.

Then the owner told me the warranty covered only defects in the product itself, not damage caused by the owner, and that the remote control wasn't working because I probably dropped it or banged it too hard. I didn't, I replied. It just stopped working. "How do I know that?" asked the owner.

Wait a minute, I thought, *now I have to PROVE my case to the company before they'll honor the warranty*? You see the point: delivery of a product or service is not enough in today's market— not nearly enough; you have to deliver *continuous customer satisfaction* to assure a long, profitable relationship. I doubt I would buy from this store, use this repair shop, or even purchase from the same manufacturer again.

How does this relate to achieving client satisfaction by understanding client needs? In this way:

> To assure customer satisfaction, you must find out what the customer *really* wants, not just what they *say* they want, and fulfill that need.

This point is so important, so obvious and simple-sounding, yet so fundamentally ignored, that it bears repeating: to assure customer satisfaction, you must find out what the customer *really* wants, not just what they *say* they want, and fulfill that need.

Focusing on What Your Client Wants—Rather than on What You Can Offer

Let's take a look at how this principle works and how you can apply it in your business.

In my case, what I really wanted was a trouble-free, easy-to-work TV set that would operate reliably and not give me any headaches. Did the seller uncover and identify this need of mine? No. In the store, the salesperson made a big deal about the set's superior stereo sound, which he insisted was better than any similar TV set.

That's great. Problem is, I'm not tone deaf, but close to it. Many audiophiles would probably appreciate the great stereo sound in my TV set, but I'm not one of them. I don't know the difference between a woofer and a tweeter and can barely distinguish the sound quality differences between a child's record player and a $2,000 stereo.

Therefore the fact that the transaction delivered to me a TV set of superior sound quality did not ensure customer satisfaction, because the customer was unconcerned with sound and even unable to determine the quality or lack of it in the sound system.

If the salesperson had bothered to ask, "What are you looking for in a TV set?" I would have told him: "We want something that's easy to use, doesn't have a lot of complicated programming or other controls to learn, and is reliable. Our young child loves to watch baby videos, and we want a TV that is reliable and doesn't have downtime."

At this point, the salesperson could have steered me toward a less elaborate, more reliable model if one was available. Or he could have warned me that remote controls sometimes break, or needed special care in handling, so at least I would have known in advance and not become angry when it broke so quickly.

Or he could have given me in advance the business card of the most reliable repair shop he knew of, or sold me a better type of warranty, or anything that would have fulfilled *my* real wants rather than what *he* considered important in such a purchase.

To serve clients successfully, you must provide a product or service that meets their needs. The best way of ensuring this is to understand fully—and possibly even help the customer formulate or define—what those needs are.

The best, simplest, and most direct way to find out what your customer or potential customer wants is to *ask* them. Ask and they will tell you, if they know. Just be aware that what people *say* is not always what they *mean*. So sometimes you need to ask more questions to find out what the customer *really* wants.

The needs may be assessed either through visual inspection, conversation, or through a written needs assessment or other diagnostic tool. These methods are described in the rest of this chapter.

ASSESSING CLIENT NEEDS BY VISUAL INSPECTION

One way businesspeople assess the means and needs of potential clients is through visual inspection and other "clues" that indicate whether the client would be compatible with the way the seller does business.

For instance, real estate agents at open houses make quick (though silent) judgments about potential home buyers based on looks—both on the way the visitor is dressed, as well as the car they drive. A prospect dressed neatly in business or leisure clothes driving a BMW gets treated differently at the showing of a $650,000 model home than the man who comes in wearing dirty work clothes, with his name embroidered over the pocket, driving an '84 Chevette.

It's true that visual inspections are not always accurate. I know many people of limited means, for example, who wear $900 suits they can ill afford or drive leased luxury cars that drain their entire disposable income. At the same time, I have seen many millionaires who pad around their neighborhoods in torn jeans or wrinkled sweat suits.

However, visual indications should be taken into consideration. It's not *always* true that you can't judge a book by its cover; sometimes you can.

For example, in my consulting practice, I know that my service is better suited to some clients than others. Also, the service is priced to be affordable to ongoing businesses already generating revenue, not kitchen table operators or garage start-ups.

Therefore, when a prospect contacts me, I want to make a judgment whether I am a good "fit" for their business. If I am not, I will pass on the assignment and refer them to another service that can help them. Why? Not because I don't want the business, but because I know that in the long run, you build a successful business by *satisfying clients,* and therefore, you should try to deal only with clients or customers whose requirements you can satisfy in the first place.

Very small businesses—by small, I mean start-ups and one- or two-person operations, and most home-based businesses—have needs for services I don't provide and requirements I cannot handle. Therefore, I can assess the "fit" of my service to the client by determining the nature of the client.

When a potential client doesn't have a separate phone line for their fax; when the name of the company is the same as the name of the owner ("Chuck Jones of Chuck Jones Enterprises"); when I call and get an answering machine during business hours, when the client sends me a letter not on company letterhead, but on plain paper, and there is no phone number on it; or when the client doesn't understand the basics of the marketing tools I help my clients develop, I know I am dealing with a person whose need would not be ideally filled by my service—and I do not take them on as a client.

Visual inspection is an especially useful tool for service providers who must work within an existing setup. For example, I know one company that makes molds manufacturers can use to make complex components, parts, and products. Most of his potential clients do not themselves know whether the shape they want to manufacture is of the type this moldmaker can handle. Therefore, it helps the moldmaker to inspect a model, blueprint, or drawing of the part or product to be manufactured and then make a decision whether to accept the assignment.

If the product to be manufactured is too simple, the moldmaker can do the job, but knows the client doesn't really need his level of sophistication and can probably get it done faster and cheaper elsewhere. If the product has a complex shape other moldmakers cannot make but this moldmaker can, then he pursues the contract, realizing his service could satisfy the client in a way others could not—resulting in successful completion of the assignment as well as a great referral and future business.

In some cases it may pay you to visit customers at their homes or offices before making a decision about taking on their job. Based on visual inspection of a job site, for example, an architect may see whether it's worth the client's money to retain him to do a drawing or whether the site simply is unsuitable for the type of projects that particular architect creates.

One way to assess the client's need, then, is simply to look.

ASSESSING CLIENT NEEDS IN CONVERSATION

A second, and more powerful, way of assessing the client's requirement is through conversation. This involves asking a series of probing questions so that you uncover their real need and also explore with them whether your product or service, as you provide it, would be likely to satisfy them or not.

This method can be used with any business seeking good customer or client relationships, but is especially valuable for those where the customer evaluates the product or service based on subjective criteria.

Two examples that come immediately to mind are interior decorators and caterers. Take the caterer. He can provide a sumptuous feast of delicious lo-cal, fat-free dishes, but if the client is a meat and potatoes lover, they'll hate it. The interior decorator can create a stunning antique-filled house in a grand Victorian style, but if the homeowner prefers the light, airy feel of Early American, they will proclaim that you did a terrible job.

As a novice in business you may tend to be a prima donna; feeling that you are the one with knowledge and taste and that the client should follow your lead. More and more, however, clients are taking the lead rather than being led around. Ironically, in a society that is becoming more and more specialized, where generalists are vanishing and everyone is a specialist, people are listening to their own instincts more, and are trusting experts less.

Therefore, to succeed, you're going to have to ask prospects to tell you what they want and then tailor your product or service to fulfill that need. And if your product or service cannot be so adjusted, you should think long and hard about taking that client on—because they will only be disappointed in the end. You may get paid (or maybe not), but that doesn't matter: you will have left an unhappy customer behind. That means no referrals, no testimonials, no repeat business. It builds nothing for the future and is ultimately a waste.

What questions should you ask? I can't give you a script or checklist, because every business is different. Based on experience, you already know most of the questions you need to ask to evaluate properly the needs of a customer. The problem is: *you don't ask them,* or if you do ask them, *you don't really listen to the answers.*

Why don't you listen? Because when you really probe into the customer's requirement, you allow for the very real possibility that the customer will have a requirement for which you are *not* the ideal vendor, or a need that other suppliers are better equipped to handle.

And in a slow economy, *you don't want to hear that.* In tough times, we naturally want to make all the sales we can—and so we are less selective about the customers we serve, the clients we pick, the projects we choose.

Is that a mistake? Yes and no. No, in the sense that when things are slow, you need revenue and cannot afford to be as selective as you would like about the assignments you take on. Yes, in the sense that the less selective you are about choosing the right customers—those who can be satisfied by what you are selling— the more likely you are to have problems, bad relationships, and headaches later on.

Twelve Characteristics of Your Service that Can Help You Evaluate a Client's Needs

While I cannot, as I've said, give you a script for your particular business, I can provide some general guidelines for assessing customer wants, needs, and preferences. There are twelve basic characteristics customers look for when evaluating any product or service; these are listed in the following sections. By questioning, you can see which are important to your customer and which are not.

If you can adjust your product or service to deliver those characteristics important to the buyer, you will be well on your way to ensuring a satisfied client and a long, profitable relationship.

If your product or service *cannot* be adapted to suit the buyer's preferences, watch out—the chances of delivering the product or service and ending up with a happy customer are slim at best.

Here are the twelve characteristics or categories in which customers rate products and services.

1. Quality.   Quality has become a buzzword in American business today. Seminars and lectures are given on the topic. Books have been written about it. Ford Motor Company once claimed that "Quality is job #1." And an ad from Siemens observed, "If the word 'quality' seems used too frequently, it's because quality is seen too rarely."

We won't haggle over technical definitions here. Instead, let's take the everyday definition: to the customer, a quality product is a product that's good, excellent, or one of the best. A quality product uses the finest ingredients, the most expensive materials, the most reliable components. A quality product is made with superior craftsmanship—and is backed by excellent service. Quality, to many people, simply means buying the best—whether they are buying a product or your service.

You must assess what quality level the customer needs, expects, and is willing to pay for. "But that's a silly question," you might object. "Doesn't everyone want top quality?"

Surprisingly, the answer is no. In today's highly competitive, time-pressured, fast-paced world, quality in many things is not as appreciated or desired as it once was. The image of the old-world craftsman carefully making his product by hand, one step at a time, is outdated and archaic—the customer doesn't want to wait 12 weeks for it to be finished or pay what handcrafting costs. Instead, the customer is perfectly happy with a decent but lesser quality product that rolls off an assembly line, because it's half the price and is available now.

Let me give you a concrete, real-world example. Years ago, a friend of my family started a business making compact discs for record companies. His job was to transfer older recordings from record or tape to a CD master that the record company could duplicate and sell. To accomplish this is not an easy task—the old records have lots of hisses, pops, scratches, and other noises, and the overall quality of the original recording may be poor, which makes creating a "clean," high-quality master difficult.

This man is a music lover and a craftsman. When he started his business, he won several industry awards and favorable reviews for the excellent quality of his work. As a result, he was soon in heavy demand, with more contracts than he could handle. With a hefty backlog, he planned to raise his fees and schedule work far out into the future.

Alas, the plan did not come to fruition. What happened? In the 1990s, his customers changed. Pressed by hard economic times and increasing competition, the music companies needed to get new recordings out faster, but also had reduced budgets, so wanted to pay less. Also, many people saw that they could make money doing what our friend was doing and went into business for themselves—so now there was more competition.

Were the music companies willing to pay more and wait longer for the higher level of quality our friend provided? *No.* He was told point blank: "It doesn't have to be that good, but we need it in a week and we can only pay this much. Can you do it?" In his industry, the clients began to value *speed* and *price* over quality: they want it good, but not *that* good; the incrementally better sound his recordings achieved—perhaps discernible only to experts and audiophiles—was not needed and not worth the extra time and expense.

The lesson: *Don't assume every prospect is a quality buyer.* Some want top quality and will wait in line or pay a premium for it; others want it fast and cheap.

Your product or service is at a certain level of quality. Be sure to assess whether the customer's needs will be satisfied by the quality you offer. It's possible, for example, that your product is well suited to the everyday customer but not of high enough caliber for the *aficionado.* Therefore, you must either take on a higher-quality line to please these fussier customers or decide not to service that segment of the market.

On the other hand, your product may be *too* good, as our friend's was, for the needs of your market. If that's the case, you need to find customers who appreciate and are willing to pay for that level of excellence or else not be as particular and offer a lesser product at a proportionally lesser price.

2. Service.   Many, many customers today value *service* far more than they value quality. Their attitude is basically, "It doesn't have to be great, perfect, or even excellent; good or even okay will do. But I'm busy and I'm pressured. So please do *what* I want, *when* I want it, exactly the *way* I want it."

For this customer, you need to have the "can-do" attitude: whatever the customer asks you to do, you do it—gladly, and with a smile. This customer is quick to forget all the good work you've done for her if a problem arises, is impatient if she doesn't get what she wants right away, and cannot tolerate being told "no" to any of her requests.

Earlier I said that some businesses incorrectly strive to achieve a level of excellence in quality that their customers really don't care about and are not willing to pay for. With service, the opposite is true: the majority of customers today want and demand as high a level of service as you can give them, and most businesses fail to meet this expectation—they deliver a level of service that, to the customer, is subpar.

When a customer switches suppliers today, the cause is usually not that the product is bad but that they were dissatisfied with the service. In the 1990s, the "Age of the Customer," the customer has become *enormously* difficult to please. Service must be at the highest levels, the effort to render excellent service must be continual and unrelenting, and the service must be *consistently* good: one small lapse can undo, in a moment, customer relationship building that took weeks or even months to achieve.

The need to render consistently superior service is the area of greatest vulnerability but also of greatest opportunity for most businesses today. It's the area of greatest *vulnerability* because no matter how hard you try, you will slip up, sooner or later. Why? Because it's virtually impossible for an individual or an organization to be at their best 100 percent of the time. Other pressures, both business and personal, can cause any owner or employee to "slip up" at any time and treat the customer in a manner that is below satisfactory. To put it in plainer language, we all have bad days where we get tired or ticked off, say or do the wrong thing, and get the customer angry.

When this happens, the customer becomes dissatisfied at that instant. The dissatisfaction may not last long, and there are things you can do to minimize both its level and duration (these are discussed in Part III of the book). But during that period of dissatisfaction, you become vulnerable: your customer is receptive to competitors who are continuously pitching to try to get the business away from you, and if they happen to hit the customer with a phone call, sales letter, or TV commercial during the period of dissatisfaction, the customer is much more likely to respond—

and possibly to defect—than when they are generally satisfied with you and your service.

Consider this example: A woman attending a seminar I gave on how to become a freelance writer told the following story: "When I was a corporate communications manager, I received many sales calls and letters from freelancers who wanted to work for us—and, being busy, I routinely ignored them.

"But one day, one of our regular freelancers turned in some copy I was not 100 percent happy with. When I sat down with her to discuss changes, she became belligerent, angry, defensive, and uncooperative. She *argued* with me, telling me our requested revisions were wrong and that the piece was accurate and perfect as is, which it was not.

"After she left, I went to my desk and found yet another letter from a freelancer seeking work from us. However, this time I picked up the phone and *called that freelancer right away*. He came for a meeting, showed his work. I liked it, and him. The next job went to him, not the regular writer. Soon we were giving him steady work. As for the woman who gave me such a hard time—I never used her again."

In today's competitive marketplace, few of us can afford to be prima donnas. The customer wants, and demands, the highest levels of service on a continuous basis.

Take the time to ask the customer what they expect in terms of service. Without doing so, you are likely to do something that violates an unspoken expectation of the customer. And even though the customer never openly expressed that expectation, not meeting it will immediately put the whole relationship on shaky ground.

It's far better to find out what level of service the customer wants, and how they want it delivered, at the start. This eliminates major potential problems and goes a long way toward ensuring your ability to please the customer on a continuous basis.

3. Speed.   Closely related to, but not the same as, service, is the speed of delivery. A major concern of today's customer is: How fast can I get it? And increasingly, they want it faster and faster, and are unwilling to wait.

As discussed in Chapter 1, modern technology is responsible for "spoiling" today's customer and creating the expectation that every desire can be instantly gratified. A recent TV commercial shows a business executive flying on an airplane. He suddenly realizes he has forgotten to send his daughter, a college student, her monthly allowance. Instead of having to wait until he gets to the airport to call his wife and ask her to mail a check, he pulls out the on-board telephone from the seat in front of him and uses his bank card to instruct his bank to write a check for him *that minute.* With such technical marvels, is it any wonder the customer who comes in Wednesday doesn't understand why his job can't be ready Thursday morning?

Another factor fueling the demand for faster service is the busier pace of life in the 1990s: people are more time-pressured and have their hands full just trying to keep up. In the rush to get today's work done today, there is less and less time for advance planning. As a result, your customer has not made provision to allow for "normal" turnaround on his order. But he still needs it when he needs it. So you, as the vendor, are expected to make up for his lack of planning by "jumping through hoops" and getting it done faster.

As businesspeople, we have two ways to attack this problem, and rather than being mutually exclusive, they are complementary. One is to work faster, and the other is to ask your clients to expect more realistic deadlines.

Work Faster. The first solution is to do everything in your power to give the customer quicker delivery, process their work faster, and respond more rapidly. To do this, you may need to take one or more of the following actions:

- Add more telephone lines
- Keep longer hours
- Hire more employees
- Upgrade to a faster computer system
- Put in a modem
- Make three trips a day to the post office instead of one
- Implement an electronic data interchange (EDI) system
- Be open on weekends and holidays
- Offer additional service options with more rapid delivery
- Take on less work so you can do existing projects faster
- Schedule your time more efficiently

Or you may need to do whatever else it takes to enable your company to provide faster delivery.

A good indicator of the fact that more and more customers desire fast service can be found in mail order catalogs. Notice that more and more catalogs now offer, for an extra fee, delivery of merchandise via Federal Express (instead of United Parcel Service) as an option. Not only that, but mail order buyers are taking advantage of the availability of such service, despite the added $5 to $7 or more service charge per order.

What's more, what was the accepted standard for rush service yesterday is no longer an adequate solution today. Overnight delivery, for example, was once the ultimate expression of fast customer service. Now at least one industry leader, Associated Air Freight, has added a nationwide same-day service promising delivery within two to eight hours from any pick up location in North America *to* any zip code in the United States. Customers with emergencies have a need for faster-than-overnight delivery, and the company responded accordingly.

Ask Your Clients to Expect More Realistic Deadlines. The second strategy for coping with the customer's demand for fast service is to attempt to educate them so that their expectations become more realistic.

For instance, an uneducated customer may not understand why it takes two weeks to get a color catalog sheet printed when local printers offset resumes in a day. Take him on a tour of your plant and show that, while modern scanning and pre-press equipment has cut printing time on four-color jobs from four to six weeks down to two or three weeks, there is still much custom work involved, and those steps cannot be skipped or compressed.

If your customers have a genuine understanding of what it takes to produce your product or render your service, they will be more willing to accept a longer delivery period.

Does this mean their "rush, rush, rush" attitude will vanish? Not by a long shot. The customer is still pressed for time, pressured by their own boss or customer and too busy to plan as far in advance as you would like them to. As a result, the demand for fast service will continue.

The best solution is a combination of the two methods just described. Improving your operations, while not allowing the "instant" turnaround your customer would ideally like, can help shorten the time frame considerably, while the education process can help the customer become a little more patient and understanding. The combination may buy you the time you need.

Because missing a deadline or delivery date is the quickest road to creating major customer dissatisfaction, you should carefully assess each customer's deadline requirements, and then evaluate whether you are able to live with those time frames.

For example, if you're a printer competing for a job printing labels, and you know it takes you a minimum of five days to print such labels, it is wrong and harmful to promise faster service when you know full well you can't deliver it: the client will leave you after the first late delivery and may not even want to pay your bill.

Repeated failure to meet customer deadlines also risks harm to your reputation in the business community. So ask customers about turnaround times—what they expect normally, how important fast turnaround is to them, what they expect in an emergency or rush situation, and how frequently they anticipate having rush orders. Also discuss whether they expect speedy service as part of the norm or are willing to pay a premium for it.

4. Price. As discussed in Chapter 1, a fundamental change that has taken place in business today is that the consumer is more price-conscious than ever before. That means a greater percentage of clients have become "price-buyers"—customers for whom price is a major factor (if not *the* major factor) in their buying decision. And even those who are not price-buyers have become much more value conscious—they may spend a lot of money and pay your asking price, but if they do, they're going to make certain they get their money's worth, and more.

A necessary function in keeping clients satisfied is to deliver to them on a steady basis the products and services they want *at prices they find reasonable and are willing to pay.* This means that you must understand what your customers will and will not pay for the various products and services they buy from you and, in most instances, price what you sell accordingly.

The customer will tolerate occasionally not being able to afford a particular product or service because you charge a bit more than he or she is used to paying for that specific item. But if every price quotation or cost estimate results in shock, dismay, anger, upset, and an ensuing argument or protracted discussion, the relationship will quickly sour. No customer likes to feel continually abused and ripped off by a vendor he perceives as being too greedy or charging too much. And no vendor likes haggling with a customer over the price on every order or continually defending his fees and pricing structure.

How do you assess compatibility between your fees and the customer's budget requirement? There are two techniques: you can tell the client flat out what your fees are, or you can ask the client what his budget is.

Disclose your fees as early as possible. This can be done by sending customers price lists, fee schedules, or rate sheets that outline what you charge for the different products and services you provide.

The prices can be exact, or the schedule can show a range of typical fees for a given item. The point is to communicate, in a nonconfrontational way, what you intend to charge the customer as she orders various things from you.

Some customers might scream that every price is out of line and twice what others charge. If you are not willing to sell for less, fine—you now know that this client's budget requirements are not compatible with your business policies.

On the other hand, if the client with fee schedule in hand asks for a firm quote or cost estimate, it's fairly certain that he will find your price acceptable or close to it, if it does not vary greatly from the ranges quoted in the sheet.

Ask your client point blank what his budget requirement is. If you do consulting work for corporations, for example, you could say to the client, "Assuming you find my service appropriate for your needs, my fee is $3,000 for a two-day consultation. Is this within your budget?"

A yes or no answer quickly tells you where you stand. Don't be afraid to be direct—after all, if they won't pay your asking price, and you are not willing to come down, what's the point of prolonging the inevitable? Find out what you need to know, then move on.

Although more and more customers are price-conscious these days, there is still a certain segment of the market that will pay your asking price *or much, much more* for the special treatment they are looking for. In some cases, these special considerations are so important to them that price is not even an issue!

In general, customers shift out of the price-buying mode and become willing to pay a premium price in exchange for one or more of the following benefits: quality, service, fast delivery, convenience, security, or support. All these factors are discussed in this chapter.

5. Reliability. Reliability as applied to a *product* means that it performs as promised, efficiently and effectively, without interruptions, breakdowns, or need for frequent repair.

In contrast, reliability as applied to a *service* means that you keep your promises to your client and what you say you will do, when you say you will do it, for the price you quoted.

Here is another major area of opportunity for you. Most firms doing business today are not as reliable as they could be: Their product may be of good quality and their service decent, but they have a habit of breaking promises and not fulfilling commitments.

The customer will tolerate this to a degree, and especially if the infractions are minor, lack of reliability will likely be accepted with a sigh and a groan rather than drive the customer to seek new vendors: it's not nearly as grave an offense as poor service or rip-off prices.

However, lack of reliability creates a vulnerability in that the vendor loses the customer's confidence: the customer no longer believes the promises you make to them, and the track record does not enable you to contradict this negative impression.

Therefore, you are vulnerable to competitors who come in and *do* make promises. Even if those promises are not realistic, the customer believes your competitor more than they believe you *because the competitor has not yet given the customer any cause to doubt them*. Therefore, if they promise price, quality, or service superior to yours, the customer is inclined to try it and not listen to you when you say the competitor can't make good on those promises.

How much the customer values reliability is one requirement that is difficult if not impossible to assess in advance. The reason is that, if asked, virtually everybody would say they value a reliable vendor; who would say they like dealing with unreliable people?

Also, while it seems okay to ask a potential customer if your prices are within their budget, it's trickier to ask them in advance how they'll react if you screw up—because that implies you mess up frequently with other customers and will with them too (otherwise, why would you bring it up?).

Yet the truth is, some customers are more tolerant of lapses in reliability than others. One may not care if the paperwork on a project is a day or two late; another may scream if a vendor shows up even five minutes late for a meeting due to traffic or car trouble.

Your experience with your customers will reveal what each customer's requirement is in terms of your reliability. A good rule of thumb is to strive to be as reliable as possible with every customer: you shouldn't make promises unless you plan to keep them.

However, by grading the reliability tolerance of each customer, you know that in case there is an emergency and some slippage or other problems cannot be helped, you can allocate your resources accordingly.

For example, let's say you have two printing presses churning out two jobs for two clients simultaneously; both are due at 5 p.m. Client A, an executive with major responsibilities at a large firm, is a stickler for reliability and intolerant of anything less than 100 percent on-time performance. Client B owns his own small business, is a relaxed person, and won't throw a fit if something's a day or two late.

Now one printing press breaks and only one job can be completed by 5 p.m. Having accurately assessed each client's needs in terms of tolerance for error in advance, you can take appropriate action. You call Client B to let him know the press broke and see if he can have the job tomorrow instead of today. He says yes, fine, and thanks for calling and letting me know—no problem.

You then take Client B's job off press and run Client A's job, which is delivered by 5 p.m. You don't even tell Client A about the broken press, because it would raise the concern of your shop being underequipped. In any event, both jobs are performed to the satisfaction of both clients, with both relationships firmly intact.

Had you not taken the different levels of tolerance for error into consideration, you might have tried to run both jobs and delivered them later that evening. Client B would be okay with this, probably, but Client A would have fired you. Again, this is the importance of evaluating the client's needs to assure continued client satisfaction.

6. Convenience.   Convenience has become much more of a factor in the customer's choice of vendors than ever before.

Consider this example. Convenience stores are prospering. This means that even in a tight economy, consumers will gladly pay $3.50 for a fire log that costs $1.99 in a supermarket, or $1.29 for a bottle of soda that costs 69 cents in a supermarket, *just to avoid taking the extra five minutes* or driving the extra half-mile to go to the supermarket.

The evidence clearly supports the conclusion that even in a society of price-conscious, value-driven buyers, people will still pay a premium in exchange for *convenience*. The reason, of course, is that the value-conscious consumer is also a time-pressured consumer, valuing time even more than money savings.

In the convenience store example, I see that I am paying an extra 60 cents for my bottle of pop. I estimate that buying the pop at the supermarket instead of the convenience store would take another five minutes, not to mention the hassle of waiting in a longer line or walking farther to get the item.

Paying 60 cents to save five minutes puts the cost of this time savings at $7.20 an hour. I make the instant decision that *my time is worth much more than $7.20* and go ahead and pay the $1.29, even though the price-conscious consumer in me screams in silent agony at the waste of paying $1.29 for a 69-cent product.

Not everyone would come to the same decision. Some people might hate wasting money or overpaying. They might have lots of leisure time and not mind the longer trip to the market. Or they may have a limited income, so that the extra charge at the convenience store is significant to them. In any of these cases, this customer does not have a need for convenience sufficient to justify the premium price one must pay to obtain it.

Although customers vary, the trend today is for consumers to seek out convenience in all activities, including buying. And it's the same for business buyers. We want to deal with the pharmacy that's around the corner, the bank with extended hours, the video store with a drop-off slot, the supermarket that allows us to pay by check if we don't have cash, the catalog company that takes credit card orders over the phone so we don't have to waste time writing a check and filling out and mailing an order form, the restaurant that doesn't make you wait for a table, the auto rental place that drops off and picks up the car for you, the computer repair service that comes to your office instead of making you bring the machine in, and the department store that will allow your mother to return the gift you bought her without a receipt, for credit, exchange, or cash—whichever she prefers.

Depending on your business, you can construct a series of questions to determine the level of convenience each customer requires and whether that's compatible with what you can deliver. For instance, you might ask, "When your word processor breaks down, do you have someone to drop it off at our local parts depot, or would you need us to come pick it up for you?" Or "Are our standard reports acceptable to you, based on the samples you reviewed, or do you need customized formats or different information?"

The customer will tell you what conveniences she requires and what flexibility or responsiveness she expects from you as the vendor. Then you can alter your service to fit that requirement or determine that she is best served by another firm. The decision is yours.

7. Availability.   Availability refers to the hours during which you're open for business as well as the customer's ability to reach you or access all or part of your services after normal business hours.

Although the needs of each customer in terms of your availability to them will vary tremendously, the trend today is that customers expect you to accommodate the hours they keep and be available for business whenever they choose to conduct it.

If you're a catalog operation, for example, it's no longer enough to offer a toll-free number and take credit card orders over the phone: the consumer now wants to be able to call and place that order at any time of the day or night—preferably with a live operator or customer service representative or at the very least using voice mail or an answering machine.

The key point is that the consumer is busy during the day and will likely settle down with your catalog at 7 or 8 o'clock at night, make her selection, and pick up the phone to order right then and there. If the phone goes unanswered, many customers will lose patience, slam the receiver down, toss your catalog, and buy from a source which is more accommodating.

Answering machines and services first, then voice mail later, created the automatic expectation on the part of the customer that they can call your company at any time of the day or night to leave a message and voice a concern, with the responsibility for returning the call to be yours. It has reached the point where it is practically unacceptable for a business to have a phone that is not answered after hours.

The rising popularity of beepers and paging systems also attests to the customer's need for instant access to their vendors and suppliers. Once only doctors wore beepers; now field technicians, service people, delivery people, salespeople, account executives, and many others wear beepers so they can be reached within minutes if a customer wants to place an order or has a problem that needs immediate attention. On-premise paging systems ensure that the manager or executive is never beyond reach of his phone—or his customer—no matter where he is in the plant.

Cellular technology now allows businesspeople to have telephones in their cars or in their brief cases. Several of my clients even have fax machines in their cars for instant review of documents while driving (a trend that does not bode well for highway safety).

More and more companies are gaining a competitive advantage simply by being more *available* than their competition. Innovative Associated Air Freight, for example, will let you call its toll-free nationwide number to schedule a pickup of a package or shipment 24 hours a day, 7 days a week, at any time of the day or night—even on weekends and holidays. Federal Express, by comparison, has limited pickup hours during the week and does not pick up on Sunday.

You can, in conversation, gently probe to find out what level of availability the client expects from you. If your company repairs computer equipment, for example, ask straight out how quickly the client expects your field technician to be on site after placing a call for service.

Some clients do not demand extraordinary availability: they are happy to have you available during normal 9 to 5 business hours, and if you can't come for a day or two, that's okay. Others have requirements for faster response or longer hours of coverage. Some don't specify hours but simply expect a "beck and call" type of relationship where when they call, you come—no excuses, no other commitments or clients before them.

You must assess each client's level of need to see whether—and how—you will meet it. Few things frustrate today's customer more than not having you available when they expect you to be. Avoid this potential destroyer of client satisfaction by establishing, up front, what the client expects and what you can and cannot do for them in terms of availability and response time.

8. Choice.   Choice means options: How much freedom do you offer customers to choose between different products, different services, different methods of working, different payment plans and options, different models and accessories?

Conventional wisdom seems to be that the successful vendor is one who offers the widest range of choices to the customer. That's open to debate, but what *is* clear is that customers do indeed have more choices than ever before: more flavors of ice cream, more brands of laundry detergent, more makes and models of cars, more channels on TV to watch, more books and records released each year.

I'm not convinced, however, that offering the broadest range of choices is always the best strategy. It really depends on your business and the preferences of your customers.

In video rentals, for example, it's probably true that the more different titles available for rental, the more customers the store will attract. Deciding which video to rent, and having the ones you're looking for available, are important to VCR owners.

In the food industry, however, having more options is not necessarily better, nor does it ensure an advantage over the competition. There are lousy diners and restaurants that have dozens of items on the menu, all of them mediocre, that are not flooded with customers.

On the other hand, several of the top restaurants in my area feature smaller menus with only five to ten or so choices for main entree. Yet despite the lack of choice, these places are busy and successful.

Why? Superior food is the obvious reason. But another, maybe not so obvious, is that *many customers do not like to be overwhelmed with options*. They prefer to have the seller be selective in the presentation of options, and they find it easier to choose from a more limited selection.

For a while, Burger King tried to gain a competitive advantage over McDonald's by stressing the variety of choices available as toppings for their burgers, in an ad campaign with the theme, "Have it *your* way." But the campaign never really caught fire. What people want is a decent burger fast; offering a choice of lettuce or no lettuce is not a tremendous selling point.

While you should not go overboard with the choices you offer your customers, most do prefer to have some options rather than have you dictate that they do business with you only one way, buy one package of services, or buy only one type of product.

Unlike some of the other areas we are discussing, you usually don't have to ask customers what options they want; if you're not offering them, they will *tell* you. Listen when customers request services you don't offer or complain that they cannot get certain things from you. If it's only an occasional complaint, forget about it.

But if you hear the same request over and over again, take it seriously. The market is *telling* you what options and choices they want to be able to get from you. Ignore their requests at your peril: if you don't start offering these options, your competitors surely will.

9. Security. Customers want security. They want reassurance. They want to know they made the right choice.

However, there are degrees. Some people are extremely security-minded, conservative, and prone toward going with the tried and true, the safe choice. Others are risk takers. They too like security, but they are willing to go without it to be innovative, try something new, or get something that is potentially much better or offers a bigger payback than the safer alternatives.

For example, one of the first things any financial planner does when working with a new client is ask them to rate their tolerance for risk. You, too, must assess how important security is to your customer and make sure you deliver the "comfort level" required.

Why has IBM been so successful in selling computers to business? It's not just the product; many computer experts have told me that IBM is not the best or most technically advanced machine, and an IBM certainly costs more than a nonbrand name. But buying IBM offers a high level of security: it's a reputable company with the service resources to support the customer. And the firm is known for its commitment to making sure its machines satisfy business needs.

A nonbrand name, on the other hand, may run better and faster and cost much less. But you are taking a risk with that purchase: How do you know the seller won't be out of business six months from now, leaving you with no way to get your machine serviced or repaired? On the other hand, you can be pretty confident IBM *will* be in business six months—or six years—from today.

In business, making the safe choice also means job security. Among information systems professionals there's an old saying: "Nobody ever got fired for buying IBM." This means that, while IBM may not always offer the best solution, it's the most *defensible* purchase: if you buy an IBM computer and there's a problem, you can shrug and say, "How could I have known something like this would happen? I bought it from IBM!"

But if you had chosen to install "Bob's Computer" and there's a problem, your peers and superiors can say, "What a stupid choice; he should have gone with a better-known company."

Customers will indicate to you their need for security and their tolerance or lack of tolerance for risk in their actions and conversations with you. If, for example, a customer contracts with you sight unseen, they're probably not big worriers and are relaxed about doing business with a new vendor.

On the other hand, if they request a tour of your offices or plant, and meetings between their managers and your staff, this indicates a need to assure themselves that you're the right choice and capable of meeting their requirement—indicating a need for a higher level of comfort before proceeding.

You can tailor your service, presentation, and manner to the style of each customer based on their need for security and aversion to risk. As a rule of thumb, however, most customers like to have some level of comfort with those they buy from, and the more you can to do create an image of reliability, stability, professionalism, and trustworthiness, the better off you'll be.

You want to do everything in your power to make sure the customer is as comfortable with you as possible. A comfortable, secure customer is an easy-to-please customer. A nervous, frantic customer is more difficult to manage, more likely to generate conflicts, and more likely to become dissatisfied.

10. Support.   Support means that you not only deliver a product or service; but that you are there long after the sale is made to ensure that it delivers continued satisfaction to the customer throughout its lifetime.

On a product, support means having telephone support people available to answer questions or give help over the phone, and having technicians available to maintain and repair the equipment either at your own repair depot or the customer's site.

For a service, support means being available to give occasional advice and guidance over the phone; answering short, simple questions or requests from clients without charge; and offering follow-up services (for a fee) that address the needs of clients who require more of an ongoing relationship than originally provided.

The customer's need for support varies with the type of customer and the type of product or service you are selling. For example, support service for an office photocopier is more critical than is support service for the office music system. Support from the company that installed your roof is more important than support from the company that steam-cleaned your carpet—especially when the roof leaks. In the winter, if you live in the northeast, support service for your furnace is more important than is support service from the cable TV company.

The key aspect of support is that you must be able to offer it to customers who want it. Your product or service may be great, and the customer may have loved it, but if you're not there to help when they need you later, the original euphoria will vanish and you will have an unhappy, dissatisfied client on your hands.

Another key point about support is that, while not as critical as some of the other areas we talked about—service, speed, availability, convenience—the customer's desire for more comprehensive support is growing, not diminishing, putting a greater strain on your resources.

For instance, I recently met with a new consulting client. During our conversation, he discussed the graphic arts studio he was using to get his brochures designed and produced—and was telling how thrilled and happy he was with their service.

He told me how great their customer service was. He told me how whenever he called, there was an account person immediately available to answer his question or help solve his problem. He told how they had a network of couriers who were always in the area, enabling quick pick up and delivery of materials without his arranging for a messenger. He told me of their ability to respond to last-minute requests and changes pleasantly and efficiently while meeting all deadlines.

Not once, however, did he mention the *quality* of their graphic design work—excellent though it was. Obviously, he valued the firm's ability to *support his needs as a customer* much more than he valued the quality of the end product (though I am sure this too was important to him). He valued the firm's "can-do" attitude and their "being there" for him when he needed them much more than the style and look of their design work. Increasingly, your customers will value the same thing in *you*, and if you can't provide excellent support, you will be at a competitive disadvantage.

Business customers today want vendors to be their "partners." This can be as formal as forming a strategic alliance, or as informal as wanting to get some sense from you that you *care* about their wants and needs, and are not just out to make a buck from them.

I increasingly hear from new and prospective clients, "We are looking for someone to work in partnership with us." This does not mean a legal partnership; it refers to a spirit of cooperation, a level of loyalty, a can-do attitude, and a degree of service previously not requested by customers or rendered by most service providers. Now "exceptional" performance is becoming the "standard" in the customer's specification.

The level of support required by each of your customers can be easily assessed after a few dealings with the particular customer. Some businesspeople refer to this as the degree of "hand-holding" the customer requires. Some customers can manage nicely without frequent contact with you, and are able to put your product or service to use without a lot of daily contact and involvement on your part.

Other customers need lots of hand-holding: they have to be guided, reassured, and helped every step of the way. There may be some clients who are so "needy" that you are unable or unwilling to provide the amount of hand-holding being requested. It's important to know what you are and are not willing to do to support a demanding customer.

For example, I have one consulting client who is usually out of the office during business hours and wants to have his conversations with me in the late evening hours. I cooperate with him because I like him and value my relationship with him. However, I don't *enjoy* making business calls from my home at 11 o'clock at night and would probably refuse to take on another client who required that same level of support on a regular basis.

Here is where you must make hard decisions about business relationships versus life-style. Will you do anything the customer wants to keep the customer? Do customers and their needs come totally before your family or leisure life? How much are you willing to disrupt your day-to-day routine—not to mention your dealings with your other customers—to accommodate the support requirements of "needy" accounts?

These are questions that should be asked and answered before you continue serving that customer. A customer who demands extraordinary support will not be happy unless he or she gets it. Just providing an excellent product or service is not enough for this customer; he or she needs you to provide support above and beyond the norm.

Not only does the high-demand client require an extraordinary level of support, but they also expect you to give it with a smile. If every support request from this difficult account is an annoyance and is handled grudgingly, the customer will sense your negative attitude and will be put off by it. The net effect is you'll be doing all that extra work without building up the goodwill that is supposed to go with it.

Therefore, before you continue serving a high-need customer, take another look at the situation and make a decision. If you decide the customer is worth keeping, then resolve to put up with the extra headaches and stop complaining or feeling bitter. Just do the work and do it with a smile. It's not the customer who's forcing you to stay late—it was *your* decision, remember?

On the other hand, if you make the decision that the customer and the revenue he represents is not worth the extra aggravation, don't think you can retain the customer and keep them happy with a half-hearted effort.

It is better to explain to the customer what you can and cannot do, and then let them make a decision about whether they can live with the level of support you are offering to provide. If they can't, and they walk, don't agonize over it or feel let down. Realize you've made a decision to sacrifice income in exchange for peace of mind, and again, it was *your* decision. Do it and move on.

11. Expertise. Today's successful businesses generally don't sell just a product or service; they sell knowledge and information. And the more you are perceived as the expert in your field, the better. The more you help your customers succeed in their lives or their business because of your wisdom and advice, the happier they'll be with you.

A good example is computer stores. Recently, I was shopping for a new personal computer. In the first store I went to, the salesperson was unenthusiastic and not knowledgeable about his products. "I'm really not a technical person," he explained. "I used to sell office equipment."

In the second store, I got a person who was obviously a member of the computer generation. He knew his products, had definite opinions on what hardware and software options I should go with, and could quickly demonstrate the major features of the programs I was considering buying.

Both stores sold essentially the same computers, printers, and software packages. The difference was *knowledge*: as a customer, I want to buy not from a "salesperson" but from an expert—someone who can advise me and help me make the right decisions.

It's the same with your customers. Simply giving them your product and service and taking the money is not enough. They want advice on how to size, select, use, maintain, and benefit from that product. That's why customers would rather deal with someone they perceive as an expert.

A successful contractor in my area, Pete Johnson of Comfort Control, recognized this early in his career (decades before this book was written) and decided to do something about it. He wanted to position himself and his firm as the "experts" in home remodeling, to separate the company from the rest of the crowd. Pete's way of doing this was to write and self-publish a small book on home remodeling. The book focused on how to choose the right contractor and how to estimate the cost yourself so you know if you are getting a fair price quotation from your contractor.

Pete used the book as a premium, giving it to potential clients to impress them and convince them that he was the expert source. He also did a lot of local publicity, and with a published book, it was easier for him to get written up in town newspapers. He did in fact establish a local reputation and was successful to the day he retired, as far as I can tell.

Not all clients require the same level of expertise in their vendors, however, so you must appear to be at the right level for each client. For instance, an ad agency may position itself as "marketing strategists" in dealing with small accounts that do not have much in-house marketing expertise and need outside help. The more the agency seems to know about marketing and selling, as opposed to just "creating ads," the more attractive they appear to these smaller businesses.

However, that same positioning may hurt them when seeking work from some larger corporate clients. The corporate manager may feel *she* is the marketing strategist on the team and view the agency more as a support service that places ads, mails out press releases, writes copy, takes photos, and gets brochures produced and printed. If the agency comes on to this client too strongly in trying to establish their superior marketing knowledge, this customer may feel threatened—the attitude is probably, "Why should I hire a company that does marketing plans? That's *my* job." The customer may actually feel threatened by or in competition with the agency and not deal with them for that reason.

So it is important to realize how much your customers want to see you as the gurus or experts and to provide those customers who need information with good, solid advice. This means more time must be spent by you to keep up in your field and related areas—making you work even harder.

More and more today, clients want to deal with *informed* vendors. The knowledgeable supplier, the person or company viewed as the expert source or industry leader, is more likely to get and keep clients in the 1990s and beyond.

12. The personal touch.   In a dehumanized, computerized society, people crave human contact. One advantage you can give them, especially if you are a smaller business, is *personal attention* to their order or account.

Customers like to know that there is a caring human being (or team of people) doing their work, handling their shipment, arranging their program, or building their system. They want to be treated with politeness and something more: *attention to details*.

Ideally, you should operate your business as a time-sharing computer service bureau. This type of service, popular in the 1970s, offered computer services to companies that couldn't afford their own computer. The user tapped into the computing system via phone line. The time-sharing computer, a large mainframe, served many such users simultaneously, and its capacity was large enough so one user would not be aware of the many other users being serviced at the same time. It would appear to the user that he or she was the only one using the computer at that time, though this would rarely be the case.

Your customer wants that same feel to the relationship with you. They know you have many other customers, but when you deal with them, they want to be treated as if they were the only customer you were working with.

This means giving prompt, immediate attention to all their requests and doing so in an unhurried, pleasant, relaxed manner. The customer wants to feel that your attention is focused entirely on them and does not want to think you can't wait to get rid of them because you have many other projects to attend to.

Giving the business relationship a personal touch can be accomplished in a variety of ways: some people remember their customers with a birthday or anniversary card. Others buy inexpensive but tasteful gifts for special occasions, such as the birth of a child. One vendor makes it a habit to make donations to clients' favorite charities, and the client always gets a note from the charity saying a donation was made in the client's name by the vendor.

You'll add the personal touch to your business in the way most comfortable for you. The key is to recognize the customer's growing need for this highly personalized level of service and to respond appropriately.

ASSESSING CLIENT NEEDS BY USING DIAGNOSTIC TOOLS

Many service providers use questionnaires, surveys, needs assessments, spec sheets, and other written documents as an aid to assess the customer's needs and requirements.

For example, an infertility clinic requires patients to fill out a five-page medical history and questionnaire before the doctor will conduct an initial exam and interview. The written tool is superior to oral questioning in that it provides a formal mechanism for gathering information, ensuring that nothing is accidentally left out.

Another advantage of the diagnostic tool is that it raises the customer's comfort level with you. The customer is impressed if you take the time to ask questions first and assess their needs before trying to sell them something; a formal, preprinted survey form or questionnaire says to the customer that you consider this needs assessment important and have developed a proven method for conducting it efficiently. The questionnaire or survey form is, in effect, a selling tool, and you may want to include a copy with your brochure and other company literature you send to potential clients.

A third advantage of printed diagnostic tools is that they provide a clear starting point for your relationship with the customer. Often, especially in selling a custom-designed product or a service, the customer may want to work with you but doesn't know how or where to start. Handing them a form to fill out helps get them going.

Exhibit 3-1 is a sample two-page diagnostic tool, the Marketing Communications Audit, used by me in my consulting practice.

Exhibit 3-2 provides a simple diagnostic tool for evaluating your customer's needs based on the twelve criteria discussed in this chapter.

Exhibit 3-1.   Marketing Communications Audit

Bob Bly's
Business-to-Business
Marketing Communications Audit

In today's economy, it pays to make every marketing communication count.

This simple audit is designed to help you identify your most pressing marketing communications challenges—and to find ways to solve problems, communicate with your target markets more effectively, and get better results from every dollar spent on advertising and promotion.

Step One: Identify Your Areas of Need

Check all items that are of concern to you right now:

❏ Creating a marketing or advertising plan

❏ Generating more inquiries from our print advertising

❏ Improving overall effectiveness and persuasiveness of print ads

❏ Determining which vertical industries or narrow target markets to pursue

❏ How to effectively market and promote our product or service on a limited advertising budget to these target audiences

❏ Producing effective sales brochures, catalogs, and other marketing literature

❏ How to get good case histories and user stories written and published

❏ Getting articles by company personnel written and published in industry trade journals

❏ Getting editors to write about our company, product, or activities

❏ Getting more editors to run our press releases

❏ Planning and implementing a direct mail campaign or program

❏ Increasing direct mail response rates

❏ Generating low-cost but qualified leads using postcard decks

❏ How to make all our marketing communications more responsive and accountable

❏ Designing, writing, and producing a company newsletter

❏ Creating an effective company or capabilities brochure

❏ Developing strategies for responding to and following up on inquiries

❏ Creating effective inquiry fulfillment packages

❏ Producing and using a video or audio tape to promote our product or service

❏ Writing and publishing a book, booklet, or special report that can be used to promote our company or product

❏ Choosing an appropriate premium or advertising specialty as a customer giveaway

❏ Getting reviews and critiques of existing or in-progress copy for ads, mailings, brochures, and other promotions

❏ How to promote our product or service using free or paid seminars

❏ How to market our product or organization by having our people speak or present papers at conventions, trade shows, meetings, and other industry events

❏ Training our staff with an in-house seminar in:

_____
(indicate topic)

❏ Learning proven strategies for marketing our product or service in a recession or soft economy

❏ Other (describe): _____

_____

_____

– over –

Exhibit 3-1.   *(cont.)*

Marketing Communications Audit

Step Two: Provide a Rough Indication of Your Budget

> Amount of money you are prepared to commit to the solution of the problems checked off on page one of this form:
>
> ❏ under $500   ❏ under $1,000   ❏ under $2,500   ❏ under $5,000
>
> ❏ under $10,000   ❏ other: _____

Step Three: Fill in Your Name, Address, and Phone Number Below

> Name _____ Title _____
>
> Company _____ Phone _____
>
> Address _____
>
> City _____ State _____ Zip _____

Step Four: Mail or Fax Your Completed Form Today

> Mail: Bob Bly, 22 E. Quackenbush Avenue, 3rd floor, Dumont, NJ 07628
> FAX: (201) 385-1138
> Phone: (201) 385-1220
>
> If you wish, send me your current ads, brochures, mailing pieces, press releases, and any other material that will give me a good idea of the products or services you are responsible for promoting. I will review your audit and materials and provide a free 20-minute consultation by telephone with specific recommendations on how to solve your marketing problems, implement programs, and effectively address your key areas of concern. To schedule a specific date and time for your free, no-obligation phone consultation, indicate your preferred date and time below:
>
> Preferred date and time_____
>
> Alternate date and time_____

Mail or fax your audit form today. There's no cost. And no obligation.

Bob Bly • Copywriter/Consultant • 22 E. Quackenbush Ave, 3rd floor • Dumont, NJ 07628
Phone (201) 385-1220 • Fax (201) 385-1138

Exhibit 3-2.   Customer Needs Assessment Form

Rate the following needs of each customer on a scale of 1 to 5 as follows:

5 = Of utmost importance to the customer
4 = Very important to the customer
3 = Somewhat important to the customer
2 = Not too important to the customer
1 = Of no concern to my customer

Then go back and circle those needs rating a 4 or 5. These are the most important needs of the customer and the areas where your customer service efforts for that account should focus.

NAME OF CUSTOMER_____

Assessment of customer needs:

1. Quality

   [ ] 5 [ ] 4 [ ] 3 [ ] 2 [ ] 1

2. Service

   [ ] 5 [ ] 4 [ ] 3 [ ] 2 [ ] 1

3. Speed

   [ ] 5 [ ] 4 [ ] 3 [ ] 2 [ ] 1

4. Price

   [ ] 5 [ ] 4 [ ] 3 [ ] 2 [ ] 1

5. Reliability

   [ ] 5 [ ] 4 [ ] 3 [ ] 2 [ ] 1

6. Convenience

   [ ] 5 [ ] 4 [ ] 3 [ ] 2 [ ] 1

7. Availability

   [ ] 5 [ ] 4 [ ] 3 [ ] 2 [ ] 1

8. Choice
   [ ] 5 [ ] 4 [ ] 3 [ ] 2 [ ] 1
9. Security
   [ ] 5 [ ] 4 [ ] 3 [ ] 2 [ ] 1
10. Support
   [ ] 5 [ ] 4 [ ] 3 [ ] 2 [ ] 1
11. Expertise
   [ ] 5 [ ] 4 [ ] 3 [ ] 2 [ ] 1
12. The personal touch
   [ ] 5 [ ] 4 [ ] 3 [ ] 2 [ ] 1

RESOLVING CONFLICTS BETWEEN THE CLIENT'S REQUIREMENTS AND YOUR SERVICES

In analyzing the needs of your customers, you may find that there is not a perfect fit between their needs and your product or service. Your product may not have all the features they want. Or perhaps they require additional services beyond what you normally provide. What to do?

There are two questions you must answer:

1. Is this need or requirement so global, or the feature or service so essential, that I should modify my current product, service, or policies to meet the needs of the marketplace? Or is it an "oddball" request not likely to come up again?
2. If it's an oddball or one-shot request, do I want to customize to get this particular customer's business?

As for the first question, it's answered by the frequency of the request. If you hear a particular complaint or request only once or twice, it's probably just those customers and nothing to be concerned about.

On the other hand, if every other customer who wants to do business with you is put off by the fact you don't offer same-day delivery and *says so*, the market is telling you something: you may have to change your policies and implement a same-day service to stay competitive.

Degree of demand determines whether you need to make a particular change. If the demand is infrequent, business as usual will suffice. If the demand is strong and frequent, you may have to consider changing, redefining, or expanding your service.

As for the second question, that is, a special request for one customer only, the decision here is fairly simple: Do you want to do business with that customer strongly enough to change your policies, bend the rules, or offer something you do not normally handle? If you really want the business, and doing what the customer wants is the only way to get it, you'll do it.

On the other hand, if the time, expense, and aggravation of accommodating a special request outweighs the income and other benefits to be gained from a relationship with that customer, you should probably pass, even if you think you want the business. You may feel happy by saying "yes" and getting the contract. But you'll probably regret it once the work begins.

MAKING REALISTIC COMMITMENTS THAT CLOSE THE SALE BUT DON'T GET YOU INTO TROUBLE LATER ON

The rule here is simple: *Don't overpromise.* This means do not promise the customer you will do something you know you can't do (or are pretty certain you can't do) to get their business. You will lose the business and harm your reputation when you fail to deliver.

This sounds like easy advice to follow, but often isn't. As we'll see in Chapter 4, a powerful technique for creating satisfied clients is to promise the moon and give them the stars: that is, deliver *more* than the client expects.

At the same time, today's competitive marketplace has many businesspeople doing exactly the opposite: promising the moon and delivering mud, that is, promising a superior outcome and then delivering an outcome that is less than excellent.

It's understandable. You want to get the business. Every customer nowadays seems to be asking for miracles daily: faster delivery, better product, lower price. You try to be flexible and accommodating, because that's what clients want, so you say "Yeah, sure—no problem."

But if you make promises you can't keep, there *will* be a problem. And failing to deliver as promised is far worse in the client's eyes than is failing to take on an order because you can't handle it. The latter, although not meeting their immediate need, demonstrates honesty and integrity on your part. The former means you failed the client utterly and would be lucky to ever get work from them again.

When I have to turn down a consulting assignment because the deadline is too short and I already have other work scheduled, I tell the prospect: "I hate to say 'no' to a good client—especially you. But given my already heavy work load for the week, and the work involved in your project, I simply would not have been able to complete it on time.

"And, while you didn't enjoy having me pass on the assignment just now, *you would have liked it even less* if I failed to meet the deadline or rendered an inferior service. So, difficult as it was for me to turn you down, I feel I have done the right thing by you—and hope you will agree."

As I wrote this, I had a call from a new potential client. I examined the project, saw it was too much for me to do in too little time, and turned it away using the words just given. Hours later, the prospect called, thanked me for my honesty, and assigned to me essentially the same project in a format and time frame I *could* handle for her.

So while a can-do attitude is required in this "Age of the Customer," saying "no"—not too often, but once in a while—can, in some situations, actually help to enhance the vendor/client relationship and build your credibility with your customer. Try it!

Part II

KEEPING
YOUR CLIENTS
HAPPIER
LONGER

CHAPTER 4

Giving Clients More than They Pay For

$\mathbf{T}$oday's clients are fussier and more demanding than ever, which makes them a difficult bunch to satisfy. However, it's still possible, even in the "Age of the Customer," to keep clients happy and run a successful business based on *high client retention through continual client satisfaction.*

What's more, the secret to keeping your clients satisfied can be summed up in a single statement:

> To keep your clients satisfied, don't just give them their money's worth—give them MORE than their money's worth.

This premise is so simple yet so powerful that I repeat it: To keep your clients satisfied, don't just give them their money's worth—give them MORE than their money's worth.

I certainly didn't invent this principle, and it's been stated in different ways in many different places. Jerry Hardy, publisher of Time-Life Books, made that division fabulously successful by declaring, "Our policy will be to give the client more than he has any right to expect."[1]

What this means is that the vendor who merely fulfills the contract or proposal and does what the client asks is missing an *enormous* opportunity for creating a high level of client satisfaction. The secret to making your clients love you is not to give them their money's worth, it's to give them *more* than their money's worth.

---

[1] As quoted in Richard Benson, *Secrets of Successful Direct Mail* (Savannah, GA: The Benson Organization, 1987), p. 22.

MEETING CLIENTS' NEEDS: THREE PERFORMANCE OPTIONS

When asking a vendor to perform a task, render a service, or supply goods, there can be only one of three outcomes:

1. The vendor performs below expectation, failing to deliver all that was ordered or requested.

2. The vendor performs satisfactorily, delivering a product that meets the specifications or rendering the services called for in the contract.

3. The vendor performs "above and beyond" the call of duty, providing a superior product or more product than was ordered or rendering a superior service or providing more services than were contracted for.

Let's look briefly at the client's reaction in all three scenarios.

Scenario 1: The Vendor Performs Below Expectation

In this scenario the vendor's performance is subpar: he fails to deliver all that was ordered or requested or delivers but in an inferior manner.

The client's reaction? Dissatisfaction. In the "Age of the Customer," your buyers are far less tolerant of error than they were in the 1970s or even the 1980s. They demand more and are less forgiving of slip-ups, mistakes, delays, and defects.

When the vendor fails to perform as delivered in today's competitive marketplace, he is literally inviting his competitors to step in and take the business away from him. Clients are *much* less loyal to vendors today than years ago, so dissatisfied clients will be quicker to shop around for and try a new supplier when they get ticked off at you.

Worse, that client becomes dissatisfied easier and faster—it takes very little to incur a client's wrath or displeasure or make the client become unhappy with you.

A satisfied client is your most valuable asset, both in terms of repeat sales as well as referrals and favorable "word-of-mouth" advertising. The quickest way to lose that precious asset is to fail to deliver as promised. Why risk it?

Scenario 2: The Vendor Delivers a Product that Meets the Specifications or Renders the Service Specified in the Contract

This is the level where 80 percent of businesses aim: to do what the client asked—no less, no more.

It sounds logical. The client paid you for product X or service Y: if you deliver product X or service Y reliably, on time, courteously, and at the price you said you would charge, you've done everything they asked. So there is nothing for them to complain about or be unhappy over, and they *must*, by default, be satisfied.

Unfortunately, the truth is this: when you do merely what was asked of you—and nothing more or less—the client may be satisfied, but they won't be thrilled, delighted, or ecstatic. And the latter is precisely what you want. A transaction in which the client's expectations are met retains business and prevents client dissatisfaction, but a transaction in which the client's expectations are exceeded becomes *memorable* and "welds" the client to your company in a way ordinary transactions cannot.

Think back to your childhood. As a child, you were yelled at, scolded, and punished when you did not listen to your mother and father—that is, when you failed to do what was asked of you. Misbehavior on your part generated displeasure on theirs.

Doing as your parents asked eliminated this displeasure and may even have generated some praise or rewards: do the dishes as asked and get the allowance you were promised. But your parents didn't fall on their knees in gratitude when you did as you were told, after all, you were only doing what they expected you to do in the first place.

It's the same with clients. A client comes into your restaurant and orders a turkey sandwich. He gets a turkey sandwich on a clean plate. It isn't terrible, it isn't great. It's okay. Is he satisfied? If you asked, the answer would probably be an indifferent, "The sandwich? Yeah, it was okay, I guess. I've had worse meals, and I've had better. Here's your $4.95. May I have my change, please?"

Ten minutes later, he's back at work and has forgotten all about lunch, you, and your restaurant. He doesn't dream about your turkey sandwich. He isn't thinking about his next lunch at your place. He isn't telling his coworkers, wife, and friends all about you. The reason: you delivered only what you said you would deliver—and nothing more.

Scenario 3: The Vendor Performs "Above and Beyond" the Call of Duty

This is where you can rise above your competition and score points with your clients. Remember, 80 percent of the competition in your business seeks to do only what the client requested or provide the product the client ordered—and many times, they fail.

But not you. You can be one of the elite top 20 percent who render a superior service and give your clients *more than they have a right to expect*. By doing the unexpected, you delight and surprise the client. By giving them more than their money's worth, you elevate their level of satisfaction with you, build loyalty, and ensure that they'll come back to buy from you again and again.

For instance, do you remember your parents' reaction when, as a child, you did something *beyond* their expectations? Maybe it was cleaning up your room without being asked, or practicing the piano two hours instead of one, or getting straight A's on a report card, or winning first prize at the science fair, or vacuuming the whole house when you were asked only to do the living room. Whatever the event, it showed you that the real way to please people and make them extraordinarily happy with you is not to do what they expect from you, but to do *more* than they expect.

Or consider our luncheonette example. You obviously aren't dazzled when you order a turkey sandwich and get "just" a turkey sandwich. But let's say it came on hot, fresh-baked rye bread, with real, home-cooked turkey instead of turkey roll or "lunch meat" turkey, with free French fries smothered in hot gravy (even though it wasn't mentioned on the menu), and a whole bowl of crisp, fresh cole slaw instead of smelly old cole slaw in one of those dinky little paper cups. When the food is superior or more than you thought it would be, you sit up and take notice of the meal and make a mental note to have lunch there again—soon.

TWO EASY STEPS TO DELIVERING SUPERIOR CLIENT SATISFACTION

Giving your clients more than their money's worth involves not one but two separate steps:

> Step 1. Create an expectation on the client's part that is realistic, yet that is one *you* know you can not only meet *but actually exceed.*

Step 2. Consistently exceed expectation and deliver more than promised in a way delivers revenue to you, via increased client retention and repeat business, such that the revenue generated is far greater than the cost of creating that superior level of client satisfaction.

The two steps work in conjunction and are sequential. Let's look at how to do it.

Step 1: Instead of Promising More than You Can Give, Give More than You Promise

As I've said, most businesses promise more than they can deliver. Instead, to achieve a superior level of satisfaction among your clients, you should deliver more than you promise.

"But," you say, "if I promise spectacular results and then have to beat even that promise, I'll either fail to deliver *or* give the client so much 'extra' that I'll lose money on the deal."

The solution is to *underpromise* rather than overpromise. Now, in today's highly competitive business environment, *underpromising* is a tricky thing. Underpromise too much, and you won't appear as good as other companies who are promising your clients much more.

On the other hand, promising no more and no less than you are capable of giving, and then giving it, won't make you any enemies—but it won't turn the client into a fan for life, either.

As for overpromising, you already know what happens when you overpromise and then fail to deliver.

The key is to make promises to clients that are both attractive and accommodating, yet at the same time credible and realistic. For example, let's say you provide a certain type of service. Your service is superior, and that puts you in heavy demand. As a result, normal turnaround time is five days.

Now, a prospective client comes to you via word of mouth. She wants to know what you can do for her, and how quickly you can do it. You promise a *superior* outcome from your service than the competition provides, because you know that your service *is* superior and that your firm almost always does a better job. So far, so good.

Next is the issue of delivery. For this client, five days is too long. Her firm represents a big, potentially very lucrative account, and she is asking for overnight turnaround. What are you to do?

The immediate temptation is to promise your client anything to get the work and then hope she'll forgive you when you miss a deadline, because at that point you'll already have her business and she won't want to switch. Wrong. As we've discussed, there's *no* faster route to losing business today than to create a dissatisfied client. And there's no surer way to create a dissatisfied client than failing to meet a deadline or live up to some other promise you've made.

So what do you do? In this case, the best thing might be a very frank, face-to-face, sit-down discussion of the situation. You explain that while you want to help and give her the benefit of your superior service, the kind of quality you provide cannot be rendered overnight.

Tell the client the real, specific reasons why this is so. For example, you do certain quality checks that other vendors don't, and this takes extra time. And you are not willing to do without this extra time and these quality checks because of your reputation for doing superior work.

Also, probe the client's request. Does the work *really* have to be done overnight? What happens if it's done in two or three days instead of the one day they are requesting? Often you find that client demands are "artificial"—that is, the client has set a particular deadline or created a specification without any real thought to whether it's necessary or not. In nine out of ten cases, you find there is no real event or other concrete deadline driving the "rush" job and that absolutely nothing would happen if it were done a day or a week later.

By having this type of discussion with the client, you get them to see that not only are there legitimate reasons why the job shouldn't be done overnight but also that it doesn't need to be, anyway.

Still, five days is too much. She says, "What can you do for us?" Here is where you put the "art of underpromising" to work. You've agreed that one day is too soon, five days too long. You know, but do not say, that you could comfortably do the work in three days but could also turn it around in two days, if need be. The client says they would really love to have it in two days but could live with three.

The right move *is to promise three-day turnaround*. The client has indicated she can accept this, and because you've already established that your service is technically superior, she'll likely go with you on a three-day basis.

Now you have created a situation where the client has come to accept and agree to a three-day turnaround. It's not ideal, but it's been proposed and accepted. So now they expect to get it in three days. This puts you in a perfect position to deliver *more than is expected*—because, as we've said, you can do the work in two or three days.

What do you do? Tell her the first job will be ready in three days *and then aim to deliver in two days.* If you succeed, you will have exceeded the client's expectation, resulting in a pleasantly surprised buyer. If you fail to meet your internal, self-imposed two-day deadline (a deadline the client is unaware of), only you will know it, and the client will still get the order in three days, ensuring that no external deadlines are missed.

But let's say you can do it in two days. What if the client, instead of being euphoric, also get a little suspicious and says, "Wait a minute. You told me that this would take three full days. So what happened? Were you playing fast and loose with me?"

In response, you simply reconfirm your original promise: three-day delivery is what is realistic and what they will normally be getting, *but, because you knew it was important to them on this particular project,* you "pulled out all the stops" and delivered a day early. That makes you look like a hero without making you look like a fibber.

By now, you see the pattern: you promote all the superior aspects of the service you are going to deliver, while slightly *underpromising* on one small aspect. Then, when you do better than expected in this area, you exceed expectation and create the extraordinary client happiness and surprise that goes with it.

Here are some other examples of how businesses can score points with their clients by exceeding expectations:

- A restaurant tells you there is a 30-minute wait but then seats you in 10 minutes.
- A florist tells you it did not get a shipment and therefore will have to send your "significant other" pink roses instead of the red you ordered *but* delivers those pink roses in a beautiful vase thrown in at no extra charge.
- A shoe store giving balloons to children says only one per customer *but* then gives your two-year-old son one of each color when they hear him begging you for them.

- A photocopier company says it can't send a person to fix the copier today because it is short-handed *but* then phones 10 minutes later to say it has rearranged the schedule and a technician will be there within the hour.

- A doctor stays open late to see you on an emergency basis because you're worried about a lump on your body *and* when it turns out to be just an insect bite, tells you "No charge for the visit."

Step 2: Give Your Clients More Than They Expect

Okay. We've established that the best way to create satisfied clients is to give them *more* than their money's worth. I've also suggested a two-step formula for doing this in a way that makes the client happy while allowing you to still make a nice profit.

The first step, as just discussed, is to underpromise slightly rather than overpromise. That is, to get the client to anticipate and expect something slightly *below* the level of what you are actually capable of delivering.

The second step is to then deliver *above* that level, so that your clients now feel you are giving them *more* than they had a right to expect. This rendering of performance above the client's expectation level is what creates an extraordinary level of pleasure and satisfaction.

However, at this point you may object, saying: "All well and good. But if the client is paying for a Chevy, and I deliver a Rolls Royce, it's costing me extra money. Sure, if I deliver much more than I promised the client will be happy, but I won't make any money—and I'm in business to make a profit."

The solution is simple and straightforward:

> You can create an extraordinarily high level of pleasure and satisfaction in your clients by rendering them exceedingly small and simple favors.

The best example of this I know is the pediatrician, dentist, or barber who keeps lollipops on hand for children. The excellent checkup, dental exam, or hair cut provided is what the client—in this case, the child's mother—is paying for. But if that's all you give, she'll think you're good but not great: after all, you delivered only what she expected in the first place.

But it's that little extra gesture of a free candy for her little Bobby or Suzy that puts the smile on her face and warms her heart.

Ensuring the happiness of her children is perhaps the strongest emotional drive within her. When you help achieve that by consoling a crying child with a treat, you help her make the child happy again, and in that instant, you are the hero to her. You not only rendered your service; you were kind to her child. She knows you care and will come back to you again and again—and all it took was a 3-cent lollipop.

You can create an extraordinarily high level of pleasure and satisfaction in your clients by rendering them exceedingly small and simple favors. And that's the reason why giving your clients more than their money's worth—more than they have a right to expect—*doesn't* cost you a lot in money, time, or effort: The "extras" you provide don't have to be big. A simple gesture, a common courtesy, a faster response, a quicker completion time, a little extra topping on the sundae—these are the small things that will make the client's "satisfaction quotient" with you soar and bond you to them for a long and happy relationship.

This means we can amend our original "secret" for keeping clients happy, presented on the first page of this chapter, as follows:

> To keep your clients satisfied, don't just give them their money's worth—give them MORE than their money's worth—*but only a LITTLE more.*

MEASURING YOUR CLIENTS' SATISFACTION QUOTIENT

Although you can measure levels of client satisfaction by any scale you wish to use, the Client Satisfaction Quotient provides a quick, easy way of ranking how satisfied any given client is with you at any given moment. There is no "formula" or checklist; you simply use your judgment to rank the client's satisfaction level on a scale of 1 to 10 as shown in Exhibit 4-1.

When I ask you to assess how satisfied a particular client would or would not be with you in certain situations, you can refer to this scale and use the rating system to quantify your answer.

Exhibit 4-1. Client Satisfaction Quotient Rating Chart

CLIENT SATISFACTION QUOTIENT

Rank the satisfaction or dissatisfaction of your client on a scale of 1 to 10 according to the following guidelines:

10 = ULTIMATE SATISFACTION. Client is "in love" with you. Right now, you are a guru in their eyes. They love your product or service, buy frequently, refer all their friends and colleagues to you, and sing your praises all the time. The relationship is at a near all-time high because of something you recently did for this client that they absolutely loved.

9 = HIGHLY SATISFIED CLIENT. Same as a #10 except more time has passed since you pulled off that last great feat for the client. They still love you and all that, but that last super-success was a while ago, and soon they may start asking, "What have you done for me lately?"

8 = VERY SATISFIED CLIENT. Client overall is highly satisfied with you. They think your product or service is great and that you continually exceed expectation. They give you lots of re-peat business and referrals to friends and colleagues.

7 = SATISFIED. The client is still satisfied, but would probably give you a B or B+ at best instead of an A or A-. They like your product or service most of the time but have an occa-sional dissatisfaction with some minor aspects of dealing with you. Also, you meet expectation but don't really exceed it—nothing you've done has "dazzled" them lately.

6 = SOMEWHAT SATISFIED. The client finds your product or service satisfactory but doesn't get a "warm glow" dealing with you any more. They feel they get fair value for their money, but think that perhaps you are not really better than your competitors, and they may be talking to other vendors.

5 = NEUTRAL. The client is no longer fully satisfied with your product or service or their dealings with you. They find the product quality acceptable but not special, and they would say your service is sometimes okay but other times lack-ing. If asked, they could come up with a list of three or four things they like about you, but could also just as easily gen-erate an equally long list of complaints or things they don't like.

4 = A LITTLE DISSATISFIED. Similar to neutral except the client is becoming more aware of and concerned with the things they don't like about your product or service, while becoming less conscious of those things they like and you do right. Minor problems and slip-ups register more easily, stay longer in the client's memory, and annoy them more than in the past.

3 = DISSATISFIED. The client is at a point where they do not really think much of your product or service, or of the way you do business. If a friend or colleague asked what they think of your company, the client would reply, "Not great." They feel that quality has declined, service has deteriorated, and you no longer deliver what you once did.

2 = EXTREMELY DISSATISFIED. Not only does the client not like your product or service; they're now fed up with it—and you. They think your performance is poor and that you just do not "have it" anymore. They are already starting to buy from other vendors and are planning on doing much less (if any) business with you in the future—unless things improve radically.

1 = UTTERLY DISGUSTED. Same as #2, except the latest breakdown or disappointment has made the client totally unhappy with you to the point where they won't buy from you again (at least not in the near future).

SIXTEEN WAYS TO GIVE THE CLIENT MORE THAN THEIR MONEY'S WORTH

We have discussed the basic premise that a business can create superior client satisfaction by giving the client *a little* more than their money's worth. But how to do it? Here are sixteen methods you can use to give your clients those "little extras" that will win their hearts—and their loyalty:

1. Give Them an Unexpected Free Gift with Their Order

I recently bought several gift items in a local candy store. After packing my purchase, the clerk handed me a small box of chocolates taken from a basket on the counter.

"What's this?" I asked.

"It's a free gift box of chocolates for you," she replied cheerily. "We give it as a gift to every client who buys $20 worth of candy or more."

This put a smile on my face and put a "warm fuzzy" inside me. Why?

- It was a surprise. And most of us like surprises (good ones, anyway).
- It was free. I was spending a lot of money on gifts so hadn't bought any of their delicious chocolates for our own consumption. Now I could sample some without spending more money.
- It was a nice gift. We really enjoyed it.

However, from the seller's point of view, creating this unexpected surge in my client satisfaction quotient was easy and inexpensive because

- The gift was easy to offer. They make candy on the premises and probably made one large batch of this particular item just for giving away.
- It didn't cost them a lot of money, perhaps only $1 or $2 per box for a gift with a much higher perceived value.
- Also, they gave it only to those clients who spent a lot, ensuring that each transaction was profitable. Many who saw other clients getting it went back to buy more so their totals exceeded $20 and they could qualify for the gift.

Importantly, the free gift had not been *promised*. There was no sign in the store advertising it, nor had it been featured in newspaper ads. Therefore giving it had the added impact of *surprise*: It was a totally unanticipated and unexpected pleasure.

Had I come in response to an ad offering "free gift box with any $20 purchase," I wouldn't have been excited getting the box; after all, it was what I expected to get. Perhaps I would have even been disappointed, thinking, "Gee, I came all this way for such a small box?" But the fact it was not promised assured my satisfaction. I had expected nothing and was getting something.

Another example: A local printer I do business with printed a quantity of "Things to do" notepads. When he delivered my next print job, he gave me half a dozen of these large, attractive pads with my envelopes and cards—totally unexpected and at no extra charge. That's the kind of "little extra" clients like and appreciate far in excess of the actual value or cost of the gift.

Want to create delighted clients? Try a free gift. It can be given with purchase or just to every client who walks in or calls that week. The gift need not be elaborate. Indeed, the more unexpected it is, the less costly it need be to make the client happy with it.

2. Be Accessible

In today's fast-paced electronic age, many businesspeople use modern technology to juggle their busy schedules and put up barriers between themselves and their clients so they can manage what limited time they have more effectively. Problem is, while this practice may be convenient for *you*, your clients hate it.

Clients want to deal with vendors who are accessible and will take their calls *when* they call. They want to feel like their calls are welcome, not an annoyance. They want to feel that their concerns and problems are *your* concerns and problems, not an intrusion into your already crammed schedule or busy business day.

Many of us, pressured by too much to do and not enough time to do it, often seem agitated or distracted to our clients when we get calls from them. That's understandable, but not good: it annoys clients and puts them off. You may think seeming incredibly busy is a status symbol, but your client thinks you're just showing off and that you are more concerned with your other business than with their order or problem. And that's bad.

Also, most businesspeople behave hypocritically with their clients: They are always friendly, "up," and available when *making the sale*, but as soon as the contract is signed, all the client hears is "He's not at his desk right now; I'll take a message." The client senses the hypocrisy in this and is rightly offended. "I was important to you when you wanted my business," the client thinks. "Now that you've got it, you're too busy wooing other clients to return my calls, huh?"

Although they do not like this behavior, clients have come to expect it. So when you are more accessible than your client expects—friendlier, more helpful, quick to take and return calls—they become relaxed and happy. "Here's someone—at last—who treats me right," they think, and this elevates you in status head and shoulders above the other vendors they deal with.

How can you be more accessible? One possibility might be to answer your own phone, or, if that's not feasible, to at least reduce the amount of "grilling" callers are subjected to before your secretary or receptionist puts them through to you.

Think about it: Are you really so important that everyone who calls your office, even valued clients, must be put through "20 questions" before you'll do them the great favor of taking or returning their call? Come on! This kind of treatment annoys *you,* right? So how do you think it makes your callers feel?

And, since the people who answer your phone don't always remember the names of your clients, your clients often receive treatment equally as negative as the salespeople you want your assistant to screen.

Keep in mind that, according to a recent survey from *communication briefings* (reported in *Direct* magazine, April 1992, p. 5), 82 percent of 564 executives surveyed said the way employees answer the phone influences their opinion of the company. So better to do *less* screening and let an occasional telemarketer get through than to do *too much* screening and risk offending a valued client with such annoyances as "Does he know you?" "What company are you with?" and "Will she know what this is in reference to?"

Train your employees to be more courteous to callers, because many of those callers are clients or potential clients. Don't, for example, allow a secretary to say, "He's not in right now; can you call back at 2 p.m.?" You should *never* ask the caller to call back; you should always take a name and number and promise the caller the person will get back to them.

If you've installed or are thinking of installing a voice mail system, it might interest you to know that 42 percent of the executives surveyed by *communication briefings* said that automated business phone "menus" (e.g., "press 1 for billing, press 2 for account balances") is the phone practice that annoys them most. The second most irritating phone practice is being put on hold without first being asked permission to do so.

3. Fulfill Requests Promptly and Politely

This is the equivalent of "shock therapy" in business: it jolts the client into awareness because it's so sudden and unexpected. The client has come to anticipate poor attitudes, lousy service, impolite assistance, and slow, impersonal response. When you do what the client asks promptly and politely, they're shocked—and delighted.

The combination of *promptly* and *politely* is critical. An exceptional effort made on the client's behalf isn't enough to win their kudos—or their loyalty—in the fickle, client-driven business environment of the 1990s. To create exceptional client satisfaction, you not only have to do whatever the client asks, you also have to do it quickly and with a smile on your face.

The clients will not appreciate your efforts if you are slow, because they are impatient and hate to wait. They will also be put off if there is anything in your tone, manner, or behavior that suggests you are annoyed or unhappy about their request.

4. Fulfill Requests Beyond What the Client Requested

You create a high level of client satisfaction by fulfilling requests promptly and politely. You elevate that level of client satisfaction to an all-time high by doing what the client asked of you *and more*.

For example, we hired a painter to paint several bedrooms in our home. To save money, we decided we would paint the closets ourselves. In one walk-in closet, the ceiling was chipped and flaking.

While I can paint, I'm a lousy spackler. So I asked the painter if, when spackling the ceiling for that room, he could also do the walk-in closet ceiling. Several days later, when checking his progress, I saw that not only had he spackled the ceiling, he had *painted the entire walk-in closet*—at no charge. Did it cost him much extra paint, time, or effort to do it? No. Would I hire him again? You bet.

5. Correct Problems Promptly and Politely

Although you have certain policies that limit how far you'll go—or how much you'll give in—when dealing with clients, you should probably suspend most or all of these limitations when a problem arises.

Today's high-demand clients are totally intolerant of problems, expect you to do what they ask when they ask it, and will not continue to do business with a service provider who says "Sorry, but I can't help you."

When a problem arises, acknowledge it, apologize for it, and then move quickly to focus on the solution. Do everything you can to correct it. And do so quickly—and politely.

Did you ever ask a barber, waitress, repairperson, or any other service provider to fix or change something that was not quite to your liking and have them start *arguing* with you? Then you know the worst thing you can do with a client who is dissatisfied is to give them a hard time. When clients have a problem, they need to see immediately that you are "on their side" and dedicated to resolving it.

Part III of this book deals with how to handle problems and client dissatisfaction.

6. Correct Problems Without Charge

Even better than correcting problems quickly and courteously is to do it without charging the client *even if there is just cause for you to do so.*

We have a contractor who has done three large remodeling jobs for us and will soon do a fourth. His work is excellent; his prices are competitive but certainly not the cheapest. The main reason we will use him again, however, is that when he is in our home, he will frequently go through the house and fix minor things *and never bill us for it*. Even when we asked him to do a few simple repair jobs that did not involve things he had originally built for us, he did them (or had his assistant do them) and, in most instances, did not charge us.

You can imagine how delighted I was not only with this willingness to help us out but also with his invoice. The charges for the remodeling jobs were big enough as it was; it was certainly a pleasure not to have another few hundred dollars tacked on for the odd jobs he had handled. Obviously, if I had asked him to do something very time consuming, he would have billed me and I would gladly have paid it. But by giving me an extra hour of his time and labor free now and then, he has gotten repeat business from me worth more than $20,000.

7. Correct Problems and Pay the Clients for Their Trouble

You can prevent the client from becoming dissatisfied by correcting problems quickly and courteously. You can put a smile on their face by not charging them for it. But you'll really cement your relationship and build extraordinary loyalty by *paying them* for their time and trouble.

This, in effect, says to the client: "We believe that when you pay for our service, you have every right to be satisfied at all times. If there is a problem, and you become dissatisfied, this is our fault, and not only will we do everything in our power to correct the defect quickly and efficiently, without charge to you, but we will also *compensate you* for your 'pain and suffering.'"

You can "pay" the client through a refund or rebate on the invoice owed, but this isn't the best strategy. For one thing, it visibly reminds the client of the problems involved on this job. For another, it costs you money—unnecessarily, in my view—so that you have a loss instead of a profit.

A better way to compensate the client is to offer a credit, discount, price-off, fee reduction, or other cost savings on the *next* job you do for them. This is a better choice for you because:

- The client will be pleased and happy with such an offer.
- It shows fairness on your part.
- You still get your fee for the current job, so you don't feel upset or angry about the incident (as you would if you didn't get paid in full).
- You have now created a strong incentive for the clients *to use you again* for their next project because they have a "credit" with you—they do not "get paid" until they actually retain you and apply the credit toward your fee on that new job.

So not only is giving a credit or discount on future service a good way to resolve today's problem in a manner that makes the client happy, but it's also a selling technique for making sure you get the next job from them, as well.

8. Follow Up Unexpectedly One or More Times

A major mistake I have made repeatedly in dealing with my own clients—and it's an ongoing fault, I admit—is communicating with them only when necessary or only when they expect to hear from me.

Although we don't realize it, our clients are sometimes not as confident in hiring us as we may think. Perhaps they were burned in the past by a service provider whom they hired with great expectations, only to have the firm not deliver on time or meet expectations in some other way. So, while they may be trying an outside service again by retaining you, they're a little nervous about it, a little worried that their negative past experience may be repeated.

Communication between service provider and client is the solution. We've all gotten "How's it going?" calls from clients. Maybe you don't like such calls and think of them as an annoyance. I know I used to. My feeling was, "What is the point of such a call? I am a professional and deliver a professional service reliably and on time; the client knows that or they would not have hired me. Calling me to see 'How's it going?' is an insult—it means they don't trust me. And what business is it of theirs what progress I have or have not made at this time, as long as they get what they ordered on the date I promised?"

Today my attitude is different. And yours should be, too. You should respect the client's right to communicate with you to make contact or check progress from time to time. And you should treat such calls as an opportunity to build a positive relationship with the client. Act—and actually be—pleased to get and deal with such calls. Don't, as so many do, act as if the client is "bothering" you. How can they be bothering you when they are paying you and the primary reason your company exists is to serve them?

Taking it one step farther, don't wait for clients to call you and ask "How's it going?" Pick up the phone and call them *before they expected to hear from you* to say hello, touch base, and give them a quick update on progress. Clients appreciate this far more than you can imagine. It shows that you are concerned not only with the job but with their personal or professional stake in having you do the job well.

For consumers, how well you perform is important because it can affect their quality of life and because the money is coming out of their own pocket. For business clients, how well you perform determines how their supervisors and superiors will judge them. If you fail to deliver, people will say they made a poor decision in hiring you. If you do well, your performance makes them look good to their management.

Therefore, hearing from you is reassuring to your clients; it makes them feel better to know that everything is going smoothly and the project is on schedule.

So don't wait for the client to call you; if you let it go that long without communication, the client who feels compelled to phone and ask "How's it going?" is already experiencing mild anxiety and nervousness. You want your clients to feel relaxed and confident, not nervous and jumpy. So don't wait for them to call you—you call them.

9. Pay Personal Attention to Each Client

Although you have a business relationship with your clients, you can strengthen that business relationship by establishing a personal relationship as well. This does not mean that you need to become personal friends with clients or let socializing with clients impinge on your personal life. All it requires is to "be human"—to attend to the client as a human being as well as a buyer of services.

The best way to accomplish this is by rapport achieved through small talk. Find some common ground between you and the client and make that the ice-breaker that makes them think of you as a person, and not just a "consultant" or "contractor" or whatever it is you do.

You will find that, even if you and the client are very different and would not be compatible as friends, there is always some common ground that can be used to strengthen the bond between you. This might be sports, family, hobbies, likes or dislikes, similarities in life-style, or any one of a number of things.

For instance, I had an initial meeting with one client who had already decided to hire me but was a little difficult to deal with because he was stand-offish. After we got through the business portion of our meeting, we each had a couple of minutes to spare between appointments and decided to "shoot the breeze." As it turned out, we were the same age, each had one child, and our children were the same age. This resulted in a lively discussion about parenthood, which I feel established a stronger link between us and improved the working relationship.

Importantly, such bonding cannot be phony; you can't force it or fake it. Don't go looking for a shared interest or other common bond between you and the client; it will eventually come out naturally, in normal conversation. The important thing is, when you recognize it, encourage it, nurture it, and let it grow.

One important point: The area of shared interest should be a relatively safe and noncontroversial topic—gardening, for example. Avoid sex, religion, politics, money, or any other area where people who have conflicting views are likely to argue and fight passionately to defend their side. You don't want to state a strong political view you think the client shares, for example, only to discover they are diametrically opposed to your view and find it reprehensible.

What you're looking for instead is to find out that you and the client share an interest in jazz, or model rockets, or gourmet cooking, or something similarly safe. Then, whenever you call the client, instead of getting down to business you can first ask, "How about the game last night?" or "Did you know the Dukes of Dixie are coming to town?" or something else involving the shared interest between you. This shifts the client from all business to a more friendly mode and is also good for making the client easier to deal with on a day they may be agitated or frazzled.

10. Offer the Client Something Special

If you're an antique dealer, for example, and you come across a piece of beautiful carnival glass that's a real find yet reasonably priced, call your client who you know collects carnival glass and offer it to her first, before you display it for your walk-in trade.

If you're an innkeeper, and you're planning special activities and fantastic meals for a particular season or holiday, send a postcard to your past lodgers inviting them for this special event—and let them know it's exclusive for valued clients only.

If you sponsor public conferences or seminars, send a personal letter of invitation to past attendees of previous years' programs *before* your regular mailing goes out, and offer these past attendees a special "alumni discount."

You create extraordinary client satisfaction when you convey the impression that, even when you're not currently under contract or rendering service to that client, you're always on the look-out for things they would want or that can help them. For instance, even if I'm just writing sales letters and not handling any other aspects of the client's marketing, I'll still send them a copy of a new magazine I come across that might be a good place for them to advertise, *even though their advertising is handled by an ad agency and I am not involved with it.* The client appreciates that I am thinking of them and doing so with no immediate profit motive in mind.

11. Give Free Seconds

Several years ago, we made a pleasant discovery: a good restaurant in New York City that gives free seconds on any dish at any time. This policy costs them very little since few patrons take advantage of it (regular portions are more than adequate). But it makes them memorable and sets them apart from their numerous competitors (there are some areas of Manhattan where there are two to three restaurants or more on virtually every block in the neighborhood).

This "free seconds" idea can also be applied, with a slight variation, in ensuring client satisfaction in the service business. The basic principle is this: When selling a certain service to a client, include some additional *follow-up* service—which they can choose to use or not, at their option—included free with the original purchase.

For example, a friend of mine gives training seminars to corporations on business communications. He says to clients, "If any of the people you send to my seminar find they need more help or want more information, they can call my Business Communication Telephone Hotline for assistance—and, because they are alumni of my program, there will be no charge to consult with them or answer their questions."

This variation of "free seconds" adds to the perceived value of my friend's training programs and also to his credibility. Not only is he giving more value for the money than seminar providers whose fees include the training session only with no follow-up privileges, but he is in effect guaranteeing that trainees will get the knowledge they need when he is hired, since he will answer their questions long after the seminar is over.

This added level of service helps differentiate him from his competitors and has accounted for part of his tremendous success in the training field. Interestingly, while many new clients comment on how much they appreciate getting the use of the hotline included with their training courses, very few attendees actually use the hotline. So it costs him very little in time to offer this valuable extra.

12. Give Free Product or Service

This method is extremely effective as a "sales closer," especially when selling additional services to existing clients. Let's say the client is indecisive or unconvinced as to whether the fee you are asking for the service you are providing is justified. Probably, there's not a huge gap between what you're asking and what they are comfortable paying; more likely, you would have to do only a "little better" to make the client feel comfortable with the value they are getting.

Instead of lowering the price, you say to the client, "Okay, I tell you what: hire us today to do X and we'll also give you Y and

Z at no charge." X is the main job; Y and Z are small related or ancillary tasks that take very little time but have a high perceived value to the client. When the client feels they are getting three services—X, Y, and Z—and you are charging only for X, they grow comfortable with your fee and the level of service you are providing for that fee, which in turn helps build overall client satisfaction.

Sometimes, even if you don't absolutely have to, it's better to give the client a little extra service or, conversely, charge a bit less. Just because the client signed your contract doesn't mean she feels comfortable with it; perhaps she signed because of imminent deadlines or other pressing needs, but feels that you are "ripping her off" and are taking advantage of her situation by charging too much for too little. You may indeed by making a high profit on that job, but are you building client satisfaction and a long-term relationship based on maintaining that satisfaction?

Any contract you get a client to sign should be a win-win situation for you and the client. Giving a little extra service or a small "freebie" is a simple way to overcome client resistance or displeasure and create a client who's comfortable with the deal and feels you are being more than fair, even generous. "The challenge is to deliver results that exceed the client's expectations," writes Paul Vaughn, chairman of Hooven Direct Mail. "Providing clients with a service they hadn't expected is an excellent client retention strategy."[2]

13. Charge Slightly Less than the Original Estimate

Most surprises clients get are unpleasant: a botched job, a job that was not done as ordered, a missed deadline. So it makes an enormous impression on the client when you give them a pleasant surprise.

One easy way to do this is to send an invoice that is slightly less than the original estimate. Most service providers seek to do exactly the opposite. Reason: As the job progresses, and they have to do the actual work, they realize how much effort is involved and that they probably bid too low to get the job.

So they get "revenge" on the client by charging for every little expense, for every change in client direction, for every little extra

---

[2] Vaughn, Paul, *DM News,* "Vendors: You'd Better Go the Extra Mile," September 7, 1992, p. 39.

service that was provided along the way. The result is a bill 10 to 20 percent or more higher than the original estimate.

The problems? *Clients dislike receiving bills higher than they budgeted for or contracted for.* Everyone—the consumer and the business buyer—is on a budget today. Going over budget hurts the consumer because it's money out of their pocket and hurts the business buyer because it makes him look bad to his management.

A colleague of mine, who owns a small ad agency, told me as I write this that she had hired a new graphic artist to design an ad for a client. The artist bills $50 per hour. She loved his work, but when she got the bill from him, there was a $50 charge for one hour for *showing her his portfolio* and presenting his services and capabilities to her! This was completely unexpected—"I didn't expect to be billed for his sales presentation to me," the client said—and started the relationship off on a negative tone instead of an upbeat one.

You can be different by sending the client an invoice for an amount equal to or, even better, slightly *less* than your estimate. Your invoice should show clearly the amount of the discount, both in dollars and percentage savings, as well as the *reason* for the discount—e.g., you spent fewer hours than anticipated, or the cost of materials was lower, or you didn't have to do a certain phase or step you originally thought you would have to do when you gave the original estimate.

The client will see that you were able to achieve a cost reduction and then, instead of keeping it as extra profit, passed the cost savings directly on to them through a lower charge.

Taking a few dollars off an invoice now and then won't cost you a fortune, and there are few things as effective as a slight reduction in the final bill that will give your client such a pleasant surprise or make them think of you as favorably. It builds your credibility and, it's appreciated.

14. Complete the Job Slightly Faster than the Original Deadline

Next to getting it done cheaper, getting it done sooner is the thing that will "knock the socks" off your client. Everybody is in a hurry nowadays. If the original deadline is tight, beating it will make your client that much happier. If the original deadline is distant, the client will appreciate the extra time to review your work or use what you provide when you get it to them a week earlier.

Be careful, though: Do not complete the work *too* early; the danger is giving the client the impression that you rushed their job, didn't give it your best effort, and therefore did an inadequate job. As a rule of thumb, if you are going to deliver your work or complete the job early, don't beat the deadline by more than 20 to 25 percent.

So if today is April 1 and your report is due April 20, you can please the client by beating the deadline and handing it in any time between April 15 and April 19. Hand it in earlier than that and you risk the client taking your "hasty completion" into account when evaluating the work, and so the evaluation is likely to be negative.

Speaking of being criticized for handing work in too early, Milton, a consultant friend of mine tells a wonderful story.

His first job was as assistant to the circulation director of a magazine with a large circulation. On Milton's first day on the job, the circulation director handed Milton a stack of magazines and direct mail promotions and said, "Your first assignment is to come up with at least two dozen ideas for increasing the circulation of the magazine."

Milton went to his desk, studied the material, and by lunch handed in a typed four-page memo with the heading, "24 ways to increase the circulation of XYZ Magazine." His boss became furious. "I want you to *think* about it!" he shouted as he threw Milton's memo across the desk. "Go back to work and really *think* about this problem!"

Milton went to his desk and put the memo in his top drawer. Two weeks later, he pulled out the memo, changed the date, walked up to his boss's desk, and handed it to him. The boss scanned the four pages, turned to Milton, and smiling, said, "This is excellent! See—you can do good work when you really put your mind to it." Milton said nothing. He just smiled back.

15. Keep Complete, Well-Organized Records, and Have Them at Your Fingertips

Nothing annoys a client more when they call you up and ask you a question than for you to say, "Gee, I don't know" or "I have no idea."

We live in an age of instant information, a time when people are impatient with anything less than an immediate response to their queries. For this reason, many large companies have spent hundreds of thousands of dollars on computer and communications systems designed to help client service people gain fast access to client records, track projects, respond to inquiries, and resolve problems.

For the one-person office and other small businesses, you can achieve the equivalent by keeping well-organized and complete files on each job and storing those files in a place where you have quick and easy access to them.

If a client calls with a question or problem dealing with a current or past job, you should be able to access the information immediately while the client is on the phone or at least be able to find it so that you can call back with some answers or to discuss the problem further within the next five minutes. Keep a frustrated or annoyed client waiting for preliminary answers longer than that creates an impression of poor service and incompetence. Clients like to know you are in control of your information, are well organized, and have designed your office procedures to respond quickly to their needs.

In addition to keeping well-organized files, you can use your personal computer to put important client information within easy reach. Some people use popular database software to maintain client information; others use personal information management or client management programs more specific to their needs. Having the proper information immediately available when clients call with a query or complaint puts them at ease and creates a professional image for your business. Being unable to "find the papers" when clients call frustrates them and creates a negative impression. And the longer you force the clients to wait to get an answer to a question or a response to a problem, the more dissatisfied they will become.

16. Don't Be a Prima Donna

In the "salad days" of the 1980s, many freelancers, independents, and smaller service businesses could afford, to a degree, to indulge their egos and act like prima donnas. In those days, if you were a skilled craftsperson, carpenter, contractor, mason, photographer, graphic artist, software developer, or whatever, the demand for your services was probably greater than the supply, which meant you could call your own shots, be choosy about the clients you accepted, and casual, even gruff in the way you dealt with and treated your clients.

Clients would put up with prima donna service providers because they were willing to endure the less than exemplary treatment to gain access to the skills and services of these companies. But that doesn't mean they *liked* being treated poorly or indifferently.

The recession of the early 1990s permanently changed the situation. When buyers stopped spending, service providers, instead of having clients lined up and waiting to buy, had to go out and ask for—almost beg, in some cases—for work to keep their businesses solvent. Clients saw that they, not the vendors, are in control: the service provider needs the client's money, but the client can probably live without the service provider by going elsewhere.

As a result, a lot of service providers in many fields who were prima donnas are prima donnas no longer. Now they are humble laborers, competing—with many firms providing similar services—for a shrinking number of projects as clients cut back or do it themselves.

Being a prima donna was once an effective image for service providers in that it made them look busy, important, and in demand. But in the today's "Age of the Customer," I am convinced this image or approach no longer works.

The bottom-line advice: *Don't be a prima donna.* Clients want to work with service providers who are friendly and accessible and who have their egos in check.

Today, clients have no patience with—and no need for—snobs. You may think you're an original and that being stand-offish only makes you more desirable to the clients. In one case in a million that may be true, but for the majority, being a prima donna will bump you off the short list of vendors being considered for the job.

If you don't believe me, ask a plumber, contractor, or other home-improvement specialist for a quotation on a remodeling or other large project for your home. You'll find them happy to bid, patient, eager to please, flexible, and wanting to get the job.

When you tell the client how great and busy you are as a marketing ploy when it isn't really true, they'll see through it: they *know* what the economy is like today, and they simply won't believe your claims of glory. So be honest, accommodating, even a little humble. That's what will win you clients and their continued business in the decades to come.

CHAPTER 5

Ensuring Satisfaction Through Client Communication

Effective client communication starts with the realization that communication is not a separate activity from rendering service; communication is a *component* of how you render service. In essence, the saying "It's not what you say, it's what you do that counts" is inaccurate: it's what you say *and* do that counts.

Ways of expressing yourself, phrasing of sentences, nuances in verbal communication, tone, and body language can sometimes make the difference between pleasing a client and annoying a client; but most communications are tied to a related action. So, while communicating with clients in the right way is extremely important, it is not a substitute for taking appropriate client-centered actions to ensure client satisfaction. It's better to do a good thing for a client and not express it well than to do a terrible thing to a client and try to cover it up with sweet talk.

Case in Point: A Printer Loses a Customer

A printer had done three or four jobs for me, and the total of the jobs amounted to $354. Now, I normally pay bills on time, but I was swamped, and so the invoices sat for a few days beyond the due date.

To my surprise, I came in one morning to find the following message on my answering machine: "Bob, this is George from the print shop. What time can I come in today to pick up a check from you?"

Maybe I was in a bad mood, but this infuriated me. I had many things to attend to that day. How dare George presume that his invoice had to be my number one priority for that day or that I had to set up an appointment to *meet* with him to pay his bill? I had always paid my bills on time and he would get his money.

Had his first call been a gentle reminder, I would not have been angered. For instance, he could have said: "Bob, this is George from the print shop. We sent you bills for the three print jobs a few weeks ago, and they're a bit past due. No big problem, but please let me know if you didn't get them and I'll mail duplicates. Thanks."

In fact, I did drop by the print shop with a check later that day. When he saw me enter, George was immediately apologetic. "I'm sorry about the message I left you," he said, "We hired a new accountant, and he handed me a file of past due bills and told me they should all be paid up by the end of this week."

I replied, "Your accountant's advice makes sense from a cash flow point of view, but consider this: There are many printers in the neighborhood, each offering pretty much the same service you do at similar quality and price. It would be very easy for me to switch, and I almost did. Your clients are busy people and *don't need to take orders from vendors—including you.* Your first dunning notice should be a gentle reminder or query, not a demand or order for instant payment."

I had given George's print shop thousands of dollars worth of printing in a short period, and had much more to give, but gave serious thought to changing printers, just because of this single incident.

And that, I think, is the "thought mode" of most clients today. The old loyalty is gone, partially because increased competition gives clients more service providers to choose from and partially because in today's fast-paced society, clients are busier, more tired, more pressed for time, and therefore more irritable.

For example, an article in *Across the Board*[1] reports that American workers are putting in longer hours than they were a decade or so ago: 22 percent of the nation's 87 million full-time workers put in 49 hours or more a week in 1992 versus fewer than 18 percent in 1980. This means your client has less time for everything, including dealing with you. As a result, clients increasingly choose service providers not primarily based on the quality of their work but on *how easy they are to work with*; that is, clients do business with you because your service is good, not just because you're good at what you do.

---

[1] *Across the Board,* May 1992, p. 6.

Your clients expect their relationship with you to save them time and aggravation, not create additional work or responsibilities for them. You exist to make things easy for your clients, and alleviate their work load, not the other way around.

I already have too much to do in any given day; I don't need a printer telling me he wants to "schedule an appointment" to have me write a check for him. And I won't put up with it either—I'll just give my business to one of his competitors. Your clients and mine feel the same way.

Another reason loyalty to vendors is eroding is that there are more vendors to choose from then ever before, and this freedom puts the client firmly in control of the relationship: If you don't give them 110 percent effort, the client can simply go elsewhere. Public relations consultant Regis McKenna says that "choice has replaced brand as the primary consumer value . . . . Power used to be in the hands of the producer. It is now with the customer."[2]

TWENTY-NINE TIPS FOR MORE EFFECTIVE CLIENT COMMUNICATION

This chapter provides twenty-nine suggestions for communicating with clients in a client-centered way—that is, in a way that suits them rather than annoys them, and also encourages effective two-way communication in which they feel you are listening as well as talking. The result is conversations that help resolve important issues and leave the client feeling good about you and positive about their relationship with your firm.

1. Take the Responsibility for Making Contact

Don't ask clients to call you. If you need to talk with them, *you* call *them*. This sounds like common sense but is frequently violated. For example, many times I have called someone at a company and the person was not in. The assistant says, "He's not in, could you please call back?"

Wait a minute! That may be okay if I'm a vendor, but what if I am a customer of that firm? Is it right to tell a customer or potential customer to "call us back"? In many cases, I have gotten such a response when calling a company to get literature or prices

---

[2] *DM News*, April 6, 1992, p. 6.

on their product. My answer to the receptionist or secretary is, "I am a potential customer of your firm, so why don't you have *her* call *me* back?"

Since you *never know who might be a potential client or might be in a position to recommend your services to potential clients*, every caller should be treated *as if he or she is a client.* Your telephone staff should be trained to take a name and phone number so you can return the call, not tell callers they should call back later.

They should say, "Let me take your name and number and I'll have him call you back." Note that this is a firm commitment to have the call returned. Do not use the weaker "I'll be sure to give him this message." That doesn't contain a promise that he'll reply promptly to the message, which is what the customer is looking for. Instead, promise the callback. And keep that promise by returning all calls promptly.

Now, say you are calling someone who is *your* client, and they are not available. On routine matters, it's perfectly acceptable to say "Have him call me." But let's say it's an important call—for example, there is a big problem on the project, or the client's secretary told you he hated the latest set of drawings. You need to connect with the client as soon as possible so the difficulties can be discussed and the problem resolved; the longer it goes unresolved, the more it becomes a sore point with the client. The more it becomes a sore point, the more it threatens to disrupt your relationship with that client.

When it's important or urgent that you speak with the client *now*, you should take responsibility for making the connection. Instead of asking the client to call you back, say, "Betty, I need ten minutes of his time and it's rather important. Can we set up a time I could call him today for a 10-minute telephone conference?" You set a definite time for the call, treating it like any other appointment, and then call the client for discussion at the appointed hour.

Importantly, *you* want to be the one to take responsibility for making the call. If Betty says, "I'll have him call you at 1 p.m.," say, "Gee, I may be out on the road (or at the job site, or whatever) and I'll be hard to reach, so why don't I call him, okay?" If things are left so that the prospect is responsible for calling you, your chances of reaching them are diminished. They might not call—because they get busy, or forget, or don't want to talk with you. So you must initiate the contact and take responsibility for making it happen.

2. Communicate at Their Convenience, Not Yours

As discussed, people are busy and pressed for time. Families with children where both spouses work, for example, have crammed schedules and little time for conferences with service providers. Business executives may travel frequently or be tied up in meetings most days.

Therefore, you must arrange for in-person or telephone conferences to take place at the time that is most convenient for the client, not most convenient for you. For example, many people selling insurance, investment, and other financial services find that the only times consumers can meet with them is on weeknights and Saturdays. Parents are busy working or caring for children weekdays, and Sunday is the day of rest for most.

When dealing with corporate clients, preference for contact time will vary depending upon the individual. A client who is not overly pressed for time and not a workaholic probably prefers meetings and conferences during business hours, either from 9 A.M. to noon or 1 P.M. to 4 P.M. Meetings are not scheduled after 4 P.M. so the client can leave work promptly at 5 P.M.

Some clients like to be entertained or do business over meals. For them, a lunch meeting is best, although the trend today is for busier people to meet at breakfast.

A client who is a busy executive or entrepreneur under time pressure might be most reachable at off hours. They probably come in early, leave late, and eat lunch at their desk. So the best time to reach them is probably between 7 A.M. and 9 A.M., from noon to 1 P.M., and between 5 P.M. and 7 P.M. I have several clients who are successful entrepreneurs but so overworked that they request meetings after regular business hours (at 5 P.M. or 5:30 P.M.) and a few even on Saturdays.

If a client has a frequent and heavy travel schedule, he is going to be even harder to reach. To accommodate such clients, I offer to fax materials to the hotels where they are staying and arrange calls at night after they've returned to their room from a day of business. It's a mistake to force clients to talk or meet with you when you want, not when they want. For one thing, it annoys them. But also, if you engage a client in conversation when they are busy and have other things on their mind, they won't give their full attention—they'll be too busy thinking about the things they should or would rather be doing. So it's in your best interest as well as theirs to meet or teleconference at a mutually agreeable time.

It used to be that service providers were prima donnas, forcing clients to accommodate their wishes and whims. No longer. Now clients are busy and expect you to adjust your work schedule to accommodate theirs. Communication is a part of that. You should encourage clients to communicate with you at a time most convenient for them.

3. Schedule Long and Important Contacts in Advance

While it's all right to call up a client for a brief chat on the spur of the moment, longer calls and conferences should be held at a scheduled, mutually agreeable time.

Again, this goes back to people being time pressured. Thirty years ago, housewives were happy to get an unannounced visit from the Avon Lady or Fuller Brush Man. It was an "event," a welcome change of pace in a possibly boring day. They'd invite the door-to-door salesperson in, see the full demonstration, serve coffee and cake, and enjoy the experience.

Now the wife, working full-time and raising two children, doesn't have time for unannounced visits and interruption. Her reaction is to dismiss the salesperson and close the door or hang up on the telemarketer.

For this reason, any communication that is either important or lengthy, say, longer than five minutes, should be scheduled in advance. In such cases, your initial call is not to discuss the issue but merely to *set up an appointment* to have a discussion.

4. Get Permission to Proceed

Has this ever happened to you? You call a client on the phone. Instead of sounding happy to hear from you, she sounds annoyed or distracted, as if, for some reason, she is not happy to hear from you.

You have your conversation, with the client replying in monosyllables or speaking abruptly. After you hang up, you begin to worry that maybe you did something wrong or that the client is no longer happy with you.

That's a possibility, of course, and later in this book we'll discuss strategies for finding out what's bugging a client, and fixing the problem early, before it becomes a major threat to the relationship.

But in eight out of ten cases, the reason clients sounded annoyed or distracted when you called is that they were *busy* doing other things when you called. They didn't want to be rude, so they took the call, but they were only half-listening instead of concentrating on the problem or task immediately before them.

How can you solve this problem and have better phone contacts with clients? Easy. Before you begin talking, *ask for permission to proceed.*

I do this with a question that is simple yet powerful. Every time I call a client, when he or she answers the phone, I identify myself and then ask:

"Am I catching you at a bad time right now?"

Why is this so effective? If the client is busy and in fact does not have time for you, this gives them an opportunity to tell you so (most people won't unless you *ask*). So you ask when would be a good time, set an appointment for the callback, and call at the appointed hour. When you do, they'll be ready and receptive to talking with you, because you have *scheduled* the conversation.

On the other hand, if the client answers your question by saying that he is available and free to talk, he has given you permission to proceed. On that basis, he won't feel rushed or act annoyed, because you asked for time, and he freely agreed to give it.

Again, this sounds like a simple thing, but simple things are often the most powerful. When you telephone your clients today, start the conversation by asking "Am I catching you at a bad time right now?" If the client had seemed busy or curt answering the phone, watch her negative mood evaporate *instantly* after you utter this phrase, and feel how she immediately becomes more relaxed, receptive, and cordial. This *works*—try it!

5. Establish an Agenda and Time Span for Client Communication

Because clients are time pressured, it's a good idea not only to seek permission before proceeding to take up their time, but also to establish the amount of their time you will take and the agenda for your meeting or teleconference. Today people have no patience for those who take up their time when they are busy or who waste their time with things not of interest to them.

When meeting with or calling a client, establish in advance or at the appointment the approximate length of meeting. Even if you have established this in advance, make sure that the time frame is still acceptable to the client now. For example, when calling a client with whom I have scheduled a twenty-minute phone conference, I will say, "We had scheduled twenty minutes for this call. Is twenty minutes still good for you?" The client will have either remembered and set aside the 20 minutes for you, or forgotten, in which case you should either reschedule or conduct your business within whatever time the client *does* have for you.

When I call clients with unscheduled telephone calls, and I sense they are busy and hurried, I'll ask, "Do you have time for this now?" Some say yes. Others ask me to call back later, which I do.

A few are fence-sitters: they don't really have time now, but they feel they are too busy to schedule a call later. If the client tells you how much time he has, counter by promising to finish in a time period slightly under that.

For instance, if the client says "I have about five minutes," I will reply, "I'll keep it under four and a half minutes, okay?" This not only amuses them and lightens the mood; it also assures them I will not run over their available time.

If the client indicates lack of time but is not specific about how much time she has, I will suggest a short time period. For example, if the client asks, "How long will this take?" I will give a numerical answer, for example, "It will take seven minutes. Do you have seven minutes now, or should I call back later?"

This usually gains me permission to proceed. Note that I again give a specific number. I always quote an "odd" number like four and one half minutes or seven minutes rather than the conventional answer of five minutes, ten minutes, fifteen minutes, half an hour, a few minutes, "not too long," and so on.

Why? Because it's unusual, and therefore gets the client's attention. They realize it's a "technique" and that makes them smile, but it also makes clear that I understand and appreciate the value of their time.

I also use this technique when promising to return calls. If I am on the phone with client A, and client B calls, instead of just saying "I'll call you back," I say, "I'll call you back within seven and a half minutes." The former is a nonspecific and therefore vague promise; the latter is a firm, specific commitment that the client knows I will keep and that shows my intention to service him in a timely manner.

Again, these suggestions may sound simple—perhaps overly so. *But simple things are sometimes the most powerful.* Try using my "odd number" technique in conversations with clients today, and you'll see that it works beautifully.

6. Prioritize by Client Need, Not Your Need

Do what the client wants to do, not what you want to do. Work on what is important to the client, not what is important to you. Talk about what the client wants to talk about, not what you want to talk about.

Too many consultants, freelancers, and service providers in all areas focus on their own agenda when dealing with clients. For example, a graphic designer I know is constantly asking his clients what else he can do for them and what other projects he can help them with. He thinks he comes off as being helpful, but it is obvious to the clients that he is trying to get more business from them.

This is not a bad thing in itself, except he focuses so much on projects he'd like to do for the client that his clients perceive that he is not paying careful enough attention to current projects. "Harry is always asking what our plans are and what pieces we will be producing," one of his corporate clients confided in me. "Frankly, I wish he'd worry less about what's coming and show more interest in what we're paying him to do now."

Our tendency is to focus on future business, profitable projects, and ongoing selling of the accounts. Another tendency is to put the most effort into those projects that we find most interesting or challenging and give less attention to client work we think is routine, boring, or less important.

The client, however, wants to feel that you place his or her interests, needs, concerns, and goals *above* your own. This means giving your best on every job, not just the high-visibility assignments. It means finding out what the client needs and expects and then filling those needs and meeting those expectations.

In communication, we are inclined to talk about what excites and motivates us; we are usually more interested in ourselves than in the other person. If you don't believe me, pay attention to your conversation with your spouse or significant other when you come home from a busy day of work. Each of you is "bursting" with a flood of information and stories you want to convey to the other. You want to get it all out while it's fresh in your mind, so your focus is on your agenda—what you want to discuss—and you want the first opportunity to yak.

In a service business, however, part of your service is acting as counselor, advisor, friend, confidant, even therapist, father-confessor, or parent to your clients. They want to be able to transmit their wishes, concerns, problems, and information to you quickly and efficiently, without interruption, and then have you respond and address each issue in a problem-solving or supportive manner.

When you talk about what you want to talk about, instead of what the client wants to talk about, you step out of the "listening" role that is a large part of what your client pays you for. The client becomes unhappy and impatient, even annoyed. Not what you want.

For example, I recently hired a desktop publishing firm to do a number of jobs for me. One was urgent, and had to be handled quickly, and I was extremely busy that day.

I called to give the publisher some quick information she needed to finish and deliver the job. It should have taken thirty seconds. Instead, she began discussing five other jobs of mine which were *not* priorities that day, talking about small details of what typeface was used in the headline and how she solved a difficult layout problem using a certain software.

While she blabbed, I was anxiously waiting for a break and looking at my watch. Finally I interrupted and said, "Jean, that's great, and let's talk about it next week, but right now I need to get this package out and I have other calls to make. Do you have a pencil handy? Good. Here's the information . . . ."

Find out what is on the client's mind, and address those issues first. Then get to your agenda. The client will not listen or be satisfied until he attends to his most pressing concerns first. In his mind, yours can wait. And since he's the one paying the bills, he's probably right.

7. Make Sure One Problem Is Fully Resolved Before Discussing the Next Issue

A basic mistake in business communication is to attempt to handle too many issues or items simultaneously. People can take in only so much at one time. If you attempt to cover too many things in a single communication, you lose your listener or reader.

A big mistake many service providers make is not to give their full attention to the topic at hand. Because we're busy people, and our minds work faster than our mouths, we tend to jump ahead and think about items B, C, and D while we're still on the phone discussing item A with the client.

Have you ever tried to conduct a phone conversation with someone while you were, unknown to them, doing something else, like sending a fax, typing a letter, or proofreading a report? If you have, you know it doesn't work. You invariably lose your train of thought, or drift out of the conversation, or answer in incomplete "ums" and uhs." The person you are having the conversation with will sense this, realize you are not paying attention, and become annoyed.

Motivational speaker Dr. Rob Gilbert gives this advice: "Do what you're doing while you're doing it." What he means is that you should focus on one item at a time, handle it with your full attention and to the best of your abilities, resolve it or take it as far as you can go, and then—and only then—move on to the next item on the schedule or agenda.

Consider the rule of thumb: each client communication should ideally deal with only one major topic. A letter or report should have only one major subject, and a phone conversation should cover one concern or issue. If there are multiple items to discuss, you can cover them briefly at the tail end of your conversation, then schedule another meeting or phone conference to handle each of the items.

Sometimes, when handling multiple projects for a client, or complex projects with many parts and components, you are forced to cover more than one item in your letter, report, or call. That's okay, but be careful you don't overload your communication and confuse the client or take the focus away from what's really important.

Ideally, a letter, report, or phone call should have one major topic that takes 90 percent of the space or time, with the other 10 percent devoted to covering two or three other items in brief.

If needed, a meeting, call, or memo can cover two, three, four, even five items. More than that, though, and your listener or reader gets bored or confused. Better to say, "This is about issue A; we'll cover B, C, and D in a separate meeting/conversation/report."

What's the maximum number of items the human mind can deal with at one time? I once read about a scientific test to measure it. The researchers used slide projectors to flash dots of light against a black background. The dots were bright and appeared for only a fraction of a second; the subjects of the experiment (students) were then asked how many dots they thought had been projected.

The result? The average person could answer correctly when seven or fewer dots were projected. When there were more than seven points of light, the subjects could not accurately say how many dots had been flashed. The conclusion: The maximum number of items the human mind can handle at any one time is seven.

Is this true? I don't know if it's an accepted scientific fact, but it seems about right. So don't overload the client. Discuss one thing at a time. Discuss it thoroughly. Give it your full attention. Stop the discussion when the client is satisfied with the resolution or conclusion. Only then can you move ahead to the next topic.

8. Keep Your Communications Brief

I forget who said it, but there's a famous quote from a letter writer who said in a lengthy letter to a colleague, "I would have made this letter shorter, but I didn't have the time."

Clients value service providers who keep communication short and to the point, yet that's difficult to achieve. It's easier to ramble on and let the listener sort it all out. But part of your job is to save the client time by being an effective communicator.

People in service businesses tend to be talkers, because the service business is essentially a "people business." Most photographers can talk for hours about the finer points of their trade, as can landscapers, architects, engineers, graphic designers, and others in similar trades.

While the client values the information you provide, clients today want to get it concisely, quickly, in a compact format. Your communications should be concise. This means no wasted words, no unnecessary detours and sidetracks. Say what you need to say, tell the client only what they want and need to know—and no more. Today's clients want the bottom line, not the fine details. They simply do not have the patience or time.

How long can a meeting or conversation last? And when should it be ended? Look for body language or voice tone from the client as an indication. If they seem not to be paying attention, if their eyes glaze, you've gone on too long. Stop and shut up.

According to Dr. Gilbert, you should not swamp your clients with excess information or details, but should give them just what they ask for or what is essential for them to know. Reason? When you present more information than you have to, you risk saying something that the client will find disagreeable, wrong, or annoying.

"Most businesspeople worry too much about always saying the right thing," says Dr. Gilbert. "The important thing is not to worry about saying the right thing, but to avoid saying the *wrong* thing. And the less you talk, the less chance there is of saying that wrong thing."

When it comes to meetings and telephone conversations, is there a limit to human endurance? Each person is different. For example, while I often have lengthy telephone conversations with clients, I have very brief personal conversations; at home, I rarely speak on the phone for more than five minutes. My wife, on the other hand, takes a half hour just to say "hello" and has had marathon phone chats with close women friends ranging from one to two hours or more, something that would be inconceivable for me.

There is no rule of thumb for how long to make your communication; let the client's patterns guide you. Some clients like long meetings and phone conferences; if that's the case, you know you can schedule lengthy sessions with them.

On the other hand, if the client is quick to get off the phone, break your communication into smaller segments, because a single long teleconference will not hold his attention or be an effective way to deal with him.

My personal experience is that I start to fade out after about forty-five minutes on the phone, and my maximum endurance for a single in-person meeting is about two to three hours. You and your clients may feel differently, of course. Get a feel for the client's pattern, and act accordingly. When in doubt, however, it's better to keep the conference shorter rather than longer.

9. Listen to the Client More Than You Talk

The late Howard Shenson, a well-known consultant, once told me that to have a successful conversation or meeting with a prospect or client, you should listen 60 percent of the time and talk only 40 percent of the time.

Another rule of thumb for establishing a talking-to-listening ratio is based on our "equipment": We have two ears but only one mouth, so logically we should listen twice as much as we talk.

I would take this even further and assert the 80/20 rule applies to any successful client conversation: The service provider should talk only 20 percent of the time and listen 80 percent of the time. Or to put it another way, the client should do 80 percent of the talking.

The percentages aren't as critical, however, as the concept that in a successful client conversation—that is, a conversation that is productive, achieves its goal, and leaves the client feeling well served and satisfied—you should listen rather than talk, and when you talk, it should be to address the concerns and needs voiced by your client or to help the client communicate their concerns and needs to you.

As you know, the best way to learn what your client wants from you is to ask questions. So even during the 20 percent of the conversation when you talk, you aren't there to lecture: you're there to help the client define their requirements and communicate their needs to you. You give information, suggestions, advice, or recommendations primarily in response to what the client asks you for. You are there to uncover need and solve problems, not show how bright you are or how much you know or to "dazzle" the client with your expertise.

I used to have some dealings with a public relations firm led by a brash young consultant who was the opposite of what I am recommending to you here. In client meetings, he would hold forth like a professor lecturing a college class, and he obviously couldn't wait to show off his expertise, give his opinion, or demonstrate that his knowledge was superior to that of anyone else in the room.

In fourteen years in business, he was the *only* service provider I've ever known who took this attitude with clients *and was successful* (in spite of it, not because of it, in my opinion; despite his boastful manner, he really is tops at what he does). In *every other case I have observed*, the service providers who are successful—who have long, profitable relations with their clients—are focused on the client's needs, not their own egos.

10. Ask Questions and Listen to the Answers

The best communications tool for focusing on the client's need is to ask questions. "Would you agree that if you could read your client's mind, you would be outrageously successful in business?" asks Dr. Gilbert. "Well, you can. I have a four-word formula that will enable you to read any client's mind. It's this: *Ask questions and listen.*"

Asking questions is a powerful communications tool, for a number of reasons. First, it demonstrates to the client that you are focused on the client and his problems, not on yourself.

Second, it is an essential method of diagnosing the client's problem. You are in business to fill needs and solve problems. You cannot do this if you do not understand the real need or problem the client wants addressed.

Third, it impresses clients. Asking the right questions is fairly easy; doing the problem-solving work—rendering your service—is harder. Yet in my experience, asking the right questions, and being thorough in your diagnosing of the client's problem, impresses the client and immediately boosts their confidence in you. Ask good questions and clients will say to you, with genuine admiration, "Boy, you sure are thorough in your questions."

Fourth, it makes your work with the client easier. Sitting there and having to say something smart all the time is difficult, yet some clients think that's what you are there to do. Asking questions takes the burden of "thinking on your feet" off you and makes the *client* do the thinking. Once again, this advice—"Ask questions and listen"—may sound simple-minded to you. But simple techniques are often the most powerful techniques. Try it. It works. Exhibit 5-1 lists some questions that you can use as is or adapt to your own conversations with clients.

11. Show Empathy and Understanding

Your clients want to believe that you truly, genuinely care about them. Perhaps you do. Then again, you may, like some service providers, dislike your clients and only want their money.

I think you'd be better off and happier if you did like and care about your clients. But you don't have to—what's important is that you consistently *act as if* you care about and like your clients, regardless of how you feel. Clients are extremely sensitive to your "attitude" and how you come across to them. In the past, clients would take a fair amount of abuse, even scorn from vendors, because good vendors were hard to find. Clients felt they had to be "nice" to you, for fear you would cut them off from service or dump them from your client list.

In the "Age of the Customer," things have changed. Clients no longer have to "take guff" from vendors; the supply of vendors outweighs demand, and clients are firmly in control of the client/vendor relationship.

Exhibit 5-1. Questions to Ask Clients During Meetings and Conversations.

"What are you trying to accomplish?"

"What is the purpose of this meeting today?"

"What do you want to do?"

"What are your goals?"

"What do you want to happen as a result of our work together?"

"What are you looking for?"

"What do you need"?

"What do you want to happen next?"

"What's the next step?"

"Where do we go from here?"

"What exactly is it you want us to do for you?"

"What should we be doing for you that we are not now doing?"

"That's interesting. Tell me more about that."

"What do you mean by that?"

"Could you explain what you mean by that?"

"Which of these things is most important to you?"

"What are your priorities?"

"What have you been doing to handle this problem up until now?"

"What is it we would have to do for you to be ecstatic with our work on this project?"

"What are the benefits you are hoping to get out of this?"

"What else have you done to try to address this requirement?"

"Who else have you worked with or used in the past?"

"What is the biggest problem your company is facing right now?"

"What else do you want to cover today?"

"Is there anything you want to ask me that I haven't told you?"

"Is there anything else I should have asked you that I didn't ask you?"

This means clients can be choosier about vendors, and they are. For example, if you are uncaring and inconsiderate, the client doesn't have to put up with it anymore: they can simply go elsewhere.

You want to "bond" with the client, or more important, you want the client to "bond" with you. To accomplish this, you must care about the client, or at least behave as if you do.

This takes several forms. It means empathizing with the client and their problems. It means listening even when you're not getting paid to. It means caring more about serving the client and meeting their needs than about collecting your bill or taking more money out of the client's pocket. It means helping and supporting your client in any way you can, not just in the way you were hired for.

Clients often vent frustration and anger to service providers, and in many cases you may not agree with what they say. It is not necessary for you always to agree with the client; this would be phony. You merely have to demonstrate understanding and empathy. You want to communicate to the client that you are listening, you hear what they are saying, and you can sympathize with their situation.

May I give you another magic phrase? These two words are amazingly effective in responding to client "venting" and communicating clearly and directly that you empathize. The two-word magic phrase is:

"I understand."

Suppose the client says, "I hate dealing with my supervisor, Joe Blow; he's always doing things in a last-minute, disorganized fashion, and it's bad for the company."

You want to acknowledge the client's position, but at the same time, you don't agree: you think Joe Blow is a talented manager, and besides, he too is a client. What do you do? Simply reply, "I understand." If you were to disagree with the client, you would in essence be arguing with him, and it is never beneficial to you to argue with a client. If you agree with the client, then you too are calling Joe Blow an incompetent. You risk this getting back to Joe Blow and offending him. Worse, the client may only be temporarily angry with Joe, and the next day, when he and Joe are good buddies again, remember that you made a negative remark about Joe . . . and think poorly of you for it.

On the other hand, the reply "I understand" does *not* mean you are agreeing that Joe Blow is a boob. It simply means that you are acknowledging how the client feels and how difficult this problem is to handle. And that's all the client is really looking for: another human being to listen and nod in sympathy to his tales of woe; the service provider is merely assuming the role once reserved for friendly neighborhood bartenders—that of the sympathetic ear.

Simple? maybe. Effective? definitely. Try "I understand" in business conversation as a substitute for "yes" or "no," or "I agree" or "I disagree." It works!

Have you ever hired a babysitter? If you have, you know you want to feel as if the sitter really cares about and likes your children. If the sitter acts caring and loving, that's all that matters—it's not important that she'd rather be out on a date and is watching your kids only for the money.

It's the same with you and your clients. Act as if you like and care about your clients, and your clients will like and care about you. If you are understanding, kind, and sympathetic, that's all that matters—it's not important that you'd rather be golfing and are doing the client's taxes or painting their garage only for the money.

12. Be Enthusiastic

Enthusiasm is the next step above understanding and empathy. The *American Heritage Dictionary* defines it as "(1) interest or excitement, (2) eagerness or zeal."

Clients are naturally enthusiastic about what you are doing for them or at least about the end result of what you are doing. For example, a homeowner who is adding a large addition to a house is probably ecstatic about doing so and is excited about how it will transform the house, improve the family's standard of living, and give the family more space. It's the only addition they're doing to their home, and so, during construction, it becomes the focus of their life. As the contractor, the addition is just another job, one of many you have this month or this year. So you can approach it in one of two ways. You can treat it as "just another job," which to you, it is. Or you can *act as if* it's as thrilling and exciting to you as to the homeowner.

Let me tell you, doing the latter will go a long way to enhance client satisfaction with you and your contracting firm. Yes, the most important aspect of rendering your service is to do a good job—in this case, to build a nice room. But almost as important is how the client *feels* about what you've done, and sharing in their enthusiasm will make them feel more pleased and happy about your work and the decision to have hired you.

13. Keep Arguments and Disagreements with Clients to a Minimum

Do not give the client a "hard time." Always communicate that you are working with the client to achieve what they want, not what you think is best.

The service provider rarely profits from arguing or disagreeing with the client. You've heard the saying, "The client is always right." Unless what the client wants risks failure of the project or job, that's true. And really, it's true even if doing it the client's way will result in a less than perfect job.

Remember, the judging of the end result of most services is on subjective criteria. You may think your opinion should count for more because, after all, you are the expert, and expertise is what the client is buying from you.

But the client's opinion counts more, because it is the client's money you are spending—and ultimately, they must be happy with what they are buying from you. You earn your fee and repeat business by *pleasing clients*, not by being right. My experience is that service providers who feel they are right all the time and must constantly prove it to their clients are usually going broke.

For instance, I recently hired a graphic arts firm to design a newsletter masthead for a client of mine. The firm submitted several designs, all of them excellent.

After reviewing the designs, the client pulled out a masthead from an old newsletter he used to have, pasted it onto the designer's layout, and said, "Let's go with this."

The art studio was indignant and ready to fight. "That design is no good!" they complained. I countered, "It's a masthead for a promotional newsletter. The client is paying for it and must be happy with it. Picking a design is subjective; you cannot really *prove* that yours will make the newsletter get noticed and read more or generate greater reader response. Besides, laypeople don't look at it with the same discerning eye as a graphic arts pro, and most won't know the difference." I did not argue with the client but instead moved ahead quickly to produce the newsletter, which is the result the client wanted and was paying for.

Does this mean you should be a mouse and never have an opinion? No. The client is paying you for advice, and so you should give it, freely and honestly. But then respond in a cooperative and pleasant manner if the client disagrees and wants to do things another way.

When should you fight—and when should you back off? David Ogilvy, founder of Ogilvy & Mather advertising agency, compares dealing with clients in a service business to a game of chess: "Fight for the king and queen; don't argue over the pawns," he advises.

In other words, if you must argue (and therefore engage in conflict) with a client, do so only when it's critical to the project's success. Fight over major issues only—those that really make a difference in the end result.

Do not quibble and quarrel over every minor point or argue every time a client wants to change a word or delete a comma. If you do, clients will quickly become frustrated and feel that you are too argumentative and difficult to work with.

Although client conflicts invariably create tension, the tension can be temporary and even beneficial rather than long-lasting and harmful, as long as you follow these simple steps:

Warn clients in advance that a disagreement is coming. The discussion will not offend or annoy the clients nearly as much when they expect it and know it's coming.

So if you're going to disagree with a client, don't jump in with your argument right away with an abrupt "You're wrong—and here's why."

Instead, use a warm-up sentence to let the client know the two of you are going to have a short, friendly discussion about the matter. I typically say something like, "Walter, I understand what you are saying, but on this one point we are in slight disagreement, and I'd like to give you another option to consider." This says to the client, in effect: "We're about to have a small conflict, but I respect you and I'm doing it to serve you, not to give you a hard time, okay?" By preparing the client in advance, your disagreement comes as less of a surprise, and they are better able to handle it.

Agree to disagree. Not only should you tell the client you are about to disagree with him, but you should also seek permission to do so. You might say, "Can we spend five minutes now discussing the pros and cons of redesigning the widget as you've drawn it, or keeping the twin manifold, as I've suggested?"

If the client says yes, you proceed knowing they'll at least be somewhat receptive—after all, they agreed to let you plead your case.

If the client says no, you should probably accept their argument and move on—they've told you they want it their way, and don't want to discuss it.

Assure the client that the argument is not personal and pervasive.   Like you, the client does not enjoy conflict. For one thing, they don't have the time for it. For another, they are afraid that if they argue with you and you lose or get angry, it will adversely affect your relationship and the quality of the work you are doing for them.

Assure them that this is not so. One consultant I know uses this line very effectively: "We are about to discuss something of major importance to your company. These are important issues, so it's only natural that we will get emotional about them and have a discussion that is passionate, probably heated. It's okay to argue—that's what will help us get the best result." By saying this, he makes the client feel comfortable about the discussion, and it becomes productive rather than awkward.

Let them know you are doing this for their benefit.   If clients resist discussing something you think is important, let them know that you are bringing it up for their benefit, not yours.

For example, if the client acts annoyed that you would dare disagree with him, or indicates you are being uncooperative, say, "Paul, I know it seems like I'm arguing with you. But in addition to my service, you are paying for advice on how to do this best. I am bringing this up for your benefit, because I think doing it this way would be better for you. You know, I don't like arguing with clients, because it gets people like you mad at me. From my point of view, the easiest thing would be for me to shut up and not bring this up. But from your point of view, you at least want me to let you know if a design change may hurt the final product, right?"

Clients will be much more receptive to your arguments when they perceive that you are making the argument because you are genuinely looking out for their best interests, rather than fighting because of your ego or pride.

Assure them they are the final judge.   The client will be much less bothered by a heated discussion or disagreement if she is assured in advance that, no matter what is said, she is the final decision maker and you will happily and cooperatively abide by that decision.

Explain your role to the client in this way: "I know we disagree on this. You pay me for advice, so I feel obligated to let you know my opinion on this. But my job is to make suggestions and recommendations only, not decisions. The final decision is yours, and we will do it the way you feel is best."

The client already knows in advance that she can win any argument at any time simply by insisting, but when she hears that *you* know it too, she relaxes and feels more inclined to at least listen to you. After all, what could it hurt?

14. Say What Is Good Before You Say What Is Bad

Aside from arguing with the client, the worst thing you can do is to criticize them—to say that something they did or like or bought is bad or wrong or inferior.

But during the working relationship, there will be times when criticizing the client or telling them something is wrong becomes necessary to performing your task. To do this in a way that is most palatable to the client involves this simple principle: *praise before you criticize.*

For example, let's say you are a marketing consultant. You walk into the client's office, and the client says, somewhat sheepishly, "We wanted to save money on the new product launch, and so, eh, um, we wrote the brochure ourselves instead of having you do it." And then the client hands you his copy, beaming, "And to tell you the truth, we're happy with it and think it's pretty good. What do you think?"

You read the copy, and it's terrible. What do you do? There are two ways to handle it.

THE WRONG WAY: "This is awful," you tell the client. "Poorly written, badly organized, sloppy, and boring. I'm glad you showed it to me. It proves you need a professional service like mine, and can't do these important jobs yourself. I'll redo the brochure for $3,000. When do we start?"

This is a terrible approach—for several reasons. First, you are telling the client he has made a poor choice. This makes him feel inept as a decision maker. Second, you are saying the client has poor writing skills. Obviously, from what the client just told you, the client thinks he's a good writer. And people don't argue with their own beliefs and opinions. Instead, they reject the contrary opinion, in this case, yours.

Third, no matter how right you are, your argument seems driven by ego and self-interest. The client expects you, as a professional copywriter, to naturally say amateur copy is no good. The client expects you, as a service provider, to do or say anything that will win you back the assignment, and the revenue it will generate for your firm. So your objections seem self-centered and lacking in objectivity and therefore not valid.

How should you have handled it?

THE RIGHT WAY: "Hmmm . . . say . . . this is pretty good. Reads nicely. Good headline. Wait a minute, though. Wouldn't we get more orders if we gave our toll-free customer service phone number, maybe highlighting it on the cover? Also, there's no mention of the optional Heavy Duty Sweeper, and didn't you say that was an important new feature? Tell you what . . . you've already got the copy, and it's basically fine. Let me read it more carefully, give it a thorough once-through. If there are minor changes, I'll make them—no charge. If we decide we need to expand, rewrite, or add any copy, I'll give you a price for doing the work, fair enough? That way, we'll have the best brochure possible, and you'll have produced it at substantial savings over my regular writing rate. Okay?"

Why is this approach effective? Because (1) you said what was good about the client's work before you brought up anything negative about it; (2) when you did bring up the negatives, you did it as a suggestion, not as a criticism; (3) you did not personally criticize the client or something he had done; and (4) you made him feel smart and good about his decision to do the work in-house rather than make them feel stupid, wrong, or guilty.

Whenever you have something bad to say, say something good first. Always find one positive aspect, point it out, and praise it. People react negatively when you totally shoot down whatever they've done. People can handle criticism when they feel that they were basically right and that you are only offering to improve upon what they did or thought.

And when you do get to the bad part, state the negatives in the gentlest, most positive manner possible. Do it in a way that is constructive, not in a way that is mean or hurts feelings. Remember, profitable relationships with clients occur when the client feels pleased, happy, helped, and supported by you and your service. Being right all the time may give you a temporary satisfaction, but it turns clients off and takes money out of your pocket.

15. If the Conversation Is Negative, Follow Up Quickly with a Positive Fax

The fax has given service providers a marvelous tool for enhancing client communication and satisfaction. Here's why.

Previously, if you had a bad encounter with a client in person or over the phone, you would leave the encounter on a negative note. The client would be dissatisfied, unhappy, or angry. You would be nervous and fearful that you had done something wrong and that you would lose the business.

Typically, as you drove home, or sat at your desk, ways you could have handled the situation better would begin to occur to you. You wished you could go back in time and do the meeting again, using these ideas, but of course, you can't.

You would think about calling the client back, but you didn't. Perhaps you were afraid, or perhaps you judged, rightly so, that a phone conversation would precipitate another confrontation and only make things worse. So the phone was out.

What to do? You could write a letter, but that doesn't work: By the time the client received the letter, the negative encounter has done its damage, and your letter won't help; at worst, it may even remind them of that day and make them experience their anger and frustration all over again.

The fax has solved this problem. With the fax, you now have an instant way of recontacting the client after a negative encounter in a dignified, professional, well-thought-out, nonconfrontational way. I say "nonconfrontational" because with a fax, unlike a phone call, the client does not have to respond on the spot. Nor are you exposed to more of the client's wrath. Instead, the client can receive your fax, then read and consider it at his or her leisure.

If their response is still negative, at least you've taken your shot at making it better, and the client doesn't have to tell you to your face that it didn't work. If the response is positive, you'll know it next time you talk with the client from their mood and tone of voice.

While the ability to "think on your feet" is usually lauded as a critical factor to business success, the fact is none of us thinks on our feet as well as we'd like to; we think only as well and as quickly as we can. Most often, the best ideas and solutions occur after the incident, not during.

Well, with the fax, you can immediately communicate these superior solutions and problem-solving ideas to their clients as they occur to you and *while the need to resolve the problem is still fresh in the client's mind.* You can send the fax within minutes of a negative phone call or as soon as you return from a less than successful meeting.

The fax gives you a "second chance" to set right what went wrong earlier in the day. The instant nature of the communication is what makes it work. Even an overnight letter or express package will take twelve to twenty-four hours to reach your client; a fax can be there in thirty seconds or less.

For example, a potential new client and I could not come to agreement on a fee for me to write a brochure for her company. I knew that she wanted to have me work on the project and that she was disappointed I was not being more flexible about my fee.

After I hung up, I thought, "How could I have accommodated her needs better?" And the solution came to me: Offer her a "copy rewrite" service where she did the first draft, then had me polish it. I would charge an hourly rate, so could guarantee that my fee would not exceed her budget, for example, if her budget was $500, I would sell her four hours of rewrite service at $125 per hour.

I didn't call her back with this information, however. Why not? If for some reason she found this solution inappropriate or not to her liking, she would just become further annoyed, and our phone conversation would go from bad to worse.

On the other hand, a fax would allow her to review the proposal in privacy, without the need to formulate an immediate—and therefore possibly adversarial or negative—response. If she liked the proposal, she could call me and let me know. If not, she was not obligated to reply to me.

As it turns out, she called within the hour and went with my solution. "I really appreciate that you took the time to think of a way to solve the problem after we talked," she said, "and then let me know about it right away. If you hadn't, I don't know how we would have handled this."

Should you follow up your fax with a phone call? It's up to you. Follow up if you think the client would appreciate it, or if you want to get the issue resolved one way or the other. If you think it's better to let it pass, just send the fax and wait for the client to take the next action.

16. Follow Up in a Few Days to Ensure Satisfaction or Resolve Unresolved Issues

Unless your instincts tell you to do otherwise, it is usually best to resolve conflicts or problems with clients rather than let them fester. When a problem between you and the client is unresolved, you risk having it cloud your dealings or cause the client to become unhappier and unhappier as time goes on.

Send your letter, fax, or proposal. Wait a day or so. Take your cues from the client's mood. If the client is friendly and relaxed, you know he is eager to "make up" with you, resolve the problem, and move on to more productive issues.

On the other hand, if the client is stiff, unfriendly, or distant, you know you have a problem. What to do? You need to get the client to acknowledge it directly and head on, before you proceed. For example,

You:

"Scott, I sense you're angry or unhappy with me. Is it still about that widget report?"

Client (tersely):

"Yes."

You:

"You're still unhappy that we couldn't deliver the cost estimates along with the consulting report, aren't you?"

Client (a little more human):

"Well, yes, that's what I wanted, and I was unhappy I didn't get it."

You:

"Well, I have to take the blame. I did say in advance the cost estimates might take longer to get from the suppliers than I originally thought, but I should have let you know earlier."

Client (even more human):

"Yes, you should have. But I understand about these things."

You:

"Great. What I would like to do today is update you where we are on the vendor bids, then see if we can work to get this moving and resolved in a way that enables us to continue productively and get the result you want. Of course, if you're really unhappy and want to drop the project, I understand."

Client (sympathetically):

"Oh, no, no, I don't want to do that. I just wanted you to know how upset I was. But we'll live. Tell me where you are now and let's see if we can get this thing going . . . ."

You simply cannot go forward with a client who starts out in a foul mood or unreceptive state, because he is likely to stay there unless moved, by your skilled conversation, into a better mood or a more receptive state. Remember, the key to successful client communication is not what you say to the client but rather how they receive it. In a negative mood, the client will be unreceptive. You have to correct the mood and get "good reception" before you can communicate effectively with your client.

17. Do Not Allow Yourself to Be Treated in a Dismissive or Inferior Manner

While I do think that in this "Age of the Customer" we service providers have to "kow-tow" to clients a bit more than in years past, this does not mean you need to put up with abusive, rude, inconsiderate, or unprofessional behavior.

Most clients are reasonable people, but some are not. Do not allow a difficult or unreasonable client to bully you. Should you be respectful? Of course. Should you follow orders? Yes. Should you let other people treat you badly or make you feel bad about yourself? In my opinion, no.

Consultant Howard Shenson once told me that for a client/service provider relationship to be effective, the relationship must be one of equals, of peers. While that sounds good, I'm not sure it's accurate and viable anymore.

In today's marketplace, the clients are in the driver's seat, and clearly, they know it. No matter how good you are, no matter how big your reputation, the client controls the dollars and therefore controls you.

You exist to serve the client. Therefore the client/service provider relationship is more "boss/employee" than "peer/peer." And I believe service providers who think otherwise are, for the most part, fooling themselves.

As one professional speaker told me, "Most speakers have huge egos. They think they're this great expert that everyone is in awe of and impressed by. I know better. As a speaker, I am basically a hired hand, there to serve the client in whatever way I can. That is the attitude which, along with giving an excellent performance, gets me great testimonials and repeat bookings."

However, just as employees have a right to expect some basic level of human decency from their employers, we service providers have a right to expect the same level of decent treatment from clients.

How do you know if a client is treating you badly? Dealing with them will create anxiety, fear, and nervousness. You'll find yourself avoiding contact with them. You'll spend time fretting over thoughts like, "I wonder what I did to get Betty mad today" or "I haven't heard from Diane; she must have really hated the work again." Finally, when coping with this client keeps you up at night, affects your appetite, and gives you stomach aches or migraines, you know things have reached a critical level.

At this point, you try to change client behavior by bringing up the subject of their behavior with them. This naturally will be a confrontational conversation, but you should strive to do it in a constructive and positive way. For example,

"Joann, I really like working for you, but there are some things in our working relationship that make me uncomfortable and affect what I do for you. I'd like to spend a few minutes discussing them to let you know the story and see what we can do about it. Is now a good time?"

In many cases, clients do not realize that their behavior has been abusive or makes you feel uncomfortable or unhappy, and when you tell them, they say, "Oh, sorry"—and stop. In some cases, the client may become indignant; let them fume, and see if you can resolve it later. Or they may deny that they are treating you poorly and refuse to acknowledge your feelings or the conditions of the relationship.

Keep in mind that when a client treats you badly, it's not *you*—it's them. Do you think the client has just singled you out? No. More than likely, they treat *everyone* this way. So don't let it bother you; *they're* the one with the problem, not you.

If their behavior does not change, you have one of two choices: You can continue in the relationship and accept the abuse or aggravation, or you can put an end to the relationship and move on to better, happier, more productive relationships with other clients.

Are you staying in a bad relationship with a client because of economic need—money? In today's economy, many do. But understand that you don't *have* to stay in that relationship; no one is forcing you—it's your choice.

You would survive, and your family would not starve, if you lost that client tomorrow for another reason, say, because they went bankrupt—something over which you have no control and that could happen at any time with any client. Therefore, if a bad ongoing relationship with a client continues to drain your enthusiasm and self-esteem, it is ultimately not the client's fault. It's yours, for not putting a stop to it, which is something that is within your power to do and do immediately.

18. Ask Clients to Tell You How You Are Doing

Ed Koch, former mayor of New York City, made famous the phrase, "How am I doing?" Whenever he was on the streets, or in a public forum, he would ask people in the city for their opinion of his performance as mayor—"How'm I doing?" You also should constantly be asking your clients how you are doing. This is the only way to determine whether they are satisfied.

Just because a client is not complaining doesn't mean he or she is totally satisfied with your service. Many clients who have some level of dissatisfaction won't tell you *unless you ask them*. In fact, some may take your *not* asking them as a sign of your lack of attention to client service.

Packaged goods manufacturers discovered this principle when they began putting 800 numbers on boxes and can labels. Suddenly, manufacturers who had received very few complaints about their products were getting phone calls by the hundreds. Apparently, many consumers did have problems with these products, but they just didn't bother to complain. Perhaps they were too busy, or it just wasn't that important to them, or they didn't feel like going to the trouble of writing a letter. But with the toll-free 800 number right there on the cereal box, it suddenly became easy to let the manufacturer know that his crunchies didn't stay crunchy in milk, or that the surprise toy was broken.

Is this bad? Many service providers do not ask their clients whether the clients are satisfied, and one of the main reasons is they are afraid to find out the truth! It's like someone who has a lump in his neck but doesn't go to the doctor for fear of being told he has cancer. This person has convinced himself that if he ignores the problem, it will go away or turn out to be nothing. But of course, we know that isn't so.

It's the same with you and your clients. You may think that if you don't hear any complaints, everything will be okay and nothing is wrong. You may feel that asking clients "Is everything all right with our service?" will cause the client to *think* of problems so they can answer you meaningfully, thereby generating complaints that would not have otherwise existed.

The truth is, however, that communicating with customers to assess their satisfaction with your service is a positive act, not a negative—beneficial to the relationship, not harmful. The dissatisfaction is there anyway. When you don't know about it, you can't fix it, and it can become more serious as time goes on. When you ask what's wrong, and the client tells you, you can do something about it to repair the damage and get the relationship back on track.

"The best way to find out whether customers are satisfied is to ask them," says Ann Wiley, writing in *Technical Communication*.[3] "Conversations and interviews are the best method to use with small audiences."

For example, such a conversation might begin like this:

You:

"Tony, this is Jane Smith calling. Am I catching you at a bad time?"

Client:

"No, Jane. Go ahead."

You:

"Tony, I'm calling just to check in with you and see if you are satisfied with the projects we have done for you to date and with our progress on the current assignment."

Client:

"I think so. Yeah, pretty much so."

You:

"Tony, I appreciate your telling me that, but let me ask you: Is there anything about our service that you *don't* like, or that could be improved, in your opinion? Any way we can do even better for you?"

Client:

"Well, there is one small thing . . ."

This quickly identifies the dissatisfaction so you can fix the problem and make the client even happier. And Tony will be impressed and grateful that Jane took the time to make this call, even though he hadn't voiced any complaints about the service.

---

[3] *Technical Communication*, Second Quarter, 1992, p. 308.

If you want, you can get feedback from clients using a specific type of letter I call a *combination testimonial/feedback letter*, as shown in Exhibit 5-2.

The testimonial letter was developed by marketing people as a way to get testimonials from satisfied clients for use in ads, brochures, and commercials. But I have added a new twist that converts the letter from merely a testimonial-gathering tool to a client-satisfaction-assessing tool as well.

Exhibit 5-2. Sample Combination Testimonial/Feedback Letter

Date

Ms. Jean Client
Anytown, USA

Dear Jean:

I have a favor to ask of you.

I'm in the process of putting together a list of testimonials—a collection of comments about my services—from satisfied clients like yourself.

Would you take a few minutes to give me your opinion of my service? No need to dictate a letter—just jot down your comments on the back of this letter, sign below, and return to me in the enclosed reply envelope. (The second copy is for your files.)

I look forward to learning what you like about my service, but I also welcome any suggestions or criticisms too.

Many thanks, Jean.

Sincerely,

Bob Vendor

YES, BOB, YOU MAY USE MY TESTIMONIAL IN ADVERTISING PAMPHLETS AND OTHER MATERIALS USED TO PROMOTE YOUR SERVICE.

Signed_____ Date_____

I've done this with the last paragraph, which says, "I look forward to learning what you *like* about my service, but I also welcome any suggestions or criticisms, too."

Asking for suggestions and criticisms serves two purposes. First, it makes the letter seem less self-serving: you are not asking for praise but for an honest opinion, which may or may not be flattering. Clients respond well to this and in fact may give a nicer testimonial because of it.

Second, you now get the both the flattering testimonial *and* the valuable feedback which is the truth about how the client *really* feels about you and your service.

Mail the client the original letter plus a copy for the client's files along with a stamped, self-addressed reply envelope (it is rude to ask the client to do you a favor and then make them pay for it by requiring them to supply their own envelope and stamp).

A "customer satisfaction survey" is a more formal way of soliciting client feedback on your service and the client's satisfaction with your performance. Ideally, the survey should fit on one or two sides of an 8½-by 11-inch sheet of paper. Exhibit 5-3 shows a typical customer satisfaction survey, this one for a firm that prepares technical documentation. You can easily adapt the format to fit your service.

The only addition I would make to this form is, at the bottom, give instructions telling the recipient to complete and return the survey to you (don't forget to supply your address and fax number). Also, there should be a space where the client has the option of filling in their name, if they are willing to be identified.

19. Communicate to Show Appreciation, Not Just to Conduct Business or Make Requests

When the only time the client hears from you is when you call to discuss an ongoing project or to sell them on something new, how do you think that makes them feel?

Our tendency is to contact the client only when we want or need something, or when it is necessary to transact business or attend to a task we are performing on the client's behalf. While this may be efficient, it does not show the client any level of consideration above the ordinary. Therefore, you should take time out to contact different clients to say "hello" or to let them know how much you appreciate their business.

Exhibit 5-3. Customer Satisfaction Survey for a Technical Documentation Firm

CUSTOMER SATISFACTION SURVEY

Documentation of:_____

Date survey was completed: _____

For the following items, please indicate if you:
1-Strongly disagree
2-Disagree
3-Can't say
4-Agree
5-Strongly agree

	1	2	3	4	5
1. I am satisfied with the documentation.	[ ]	[ ]	[ ]	[ ]	[ ]
2. I can find the information I want.	[ ]	[ ]	[ ]	[ ]	[ ]
3. I can find information at exactly the time I need it.	[ ]	[ ]	[ ]	[ ]	[ ]
4. I can find information easily.	[ ]	[ ]	[ ]	[ ]	[ ]
5. The information is in the order of importance.	[ ]	[ ]	[ ]	[ ]	[ ]
6. The information is complete.	[ ]	[ ]	[ ]	[ ]	[ ]
7. There is no extraneous information.	[ ]	[ ]	[ ]	[ ]	[ ]
8. The information is stated in as few words as possible.	[ ]	[ ]	[ ]	[ ]	[ ]
9. The information is reliable.	[ ]	[ ]	[ ]	[ ]	[ ]
10. The information is correct.	[ ]	[ ]	[ ]	[ ]	[ ]
11. The information is consistent.	[ ]	[ ]	[ ]	[ ]	[ ]
12. The source for the information is clear.	[ ]	[ ]	[ ]	[ ]	[ ]
13. Any additional information I need seems readily available.	[ ]	[ ]	[ ]	[ ]	[ ]
14. If I don't find information or a reference, I am sure no relevant information exists.	[ ]	[ ]	[ ]	[ ]	[ ]
15. The format is correct.	[ ]	[ ]	[ ]	[ ]	[ ]

16. The documentation is free from errors in spelling, punctuation, and grammar.   [ ]   [ ]   [ ]   [ ]   [ ]

17. The documentation was delivered on schedule.   [ ]   [ ]   [ ]   [ ]   [ ]

18. The documentation was delivered within budget.   [ ]   [ ]   [ ]   [ ]   [ ]

Does the documentation provide everything you need? Please comment:_____

_____

Other comments:_____

_____

Thank you for your time!

Source: Ann L. Wiley, "Customer Satisfaction: The Quest for Quality," *Technical Communication*, Second Quarter 1992, p. 309.

When was the last time you got a letter from a department store, plumber, doctor, lawyer, electrician, or accountant that said, "No special reason for this letter, other than to say thanks for your continued business, and I value you as a client"? It's rare, very rare. Therefore, here's an opportunity for you to stand out from your competition and strengthen your relationship with your clients. This type of communication was actually quite popular years ago, and many businesspeople sent thank-you and "cordial contact" notes to their clients and customers on a regular basis. As the world became more hurried, this polite, almost quaint practice diminished and virtually disappeared. But that means it will be even more effective today, because no one else is doing it.

How to make the contact? A typed letter, a handwritten note, a Post-it™ note attached to an interesting article. It doesn't have to be slick or formal. In fact, the more personal it looks, the more effective it will be.

The telephone is also effective for this purpose. "Call good customers to say 'thanks,'" advises ad agency president Judy Finerty[4] noting that the thank-you phone call is an excellent tool for keeping customers sold on your company and your services.

---

[4] *Target Marketing*, January 1992, p. 23.

Many office supply catalogs and printers sell preprinted thank you notes. These are convenient because you can simply sign your initials and drop them in an envelope, and if you're pressed for time, these may be the best option. Another method is to write or have your ad agency produce a thank you letter or several cordial contact letters that are mailed periodically to your client list. If you serve a smaller number of clients, a personally typed or short handwritten note is a nice touch.

20. Be Polite

Because of the increased pressure and stress in our society, many people have a short fuse today, with tempers quick to flare. If you don't believe me, take your car on the highway, get in the middle lane, and drive at or slightly below the speed limit. People will flash their lights, swerve around you in their rush to get ahead, and otherwise communicate to you their annoyance with your slow driving.

My observation is that people have gotten ruder, not more polite, over the past decade or so. Do you agree? Do you feel the stores you patronize, the service providers you hire, are nicer or nastier than in the 1980s? And when a clerk or service person is rude to you, how does it make you feel about giving that store or company more of your business?

Because politeness is vanishing, you can gain an enormous competitive edge over the competition *simply by being polite at all times.* "Be nicer to people," advises marketing consultant Bruce E. David[5] "I guarantee, if you don't give me the kind of attention I desire, you won't have my repeat business. People remember the niceties . . ."

This strategy of "be polite" sounds simple in theory, but it can be difficult in practice, for two reasons. First, although many service providers are "people people," some of us are not. We went into our profession because we love our craft, be it photography, design, computer programming, or whatever. And we went into business to make money and be our own boss.

Neither of these necessitates a love of people, and many service providers have confided in me, "I'd love this business—if it weren't for the clients." So if caring about and being nice to people does not come naturally to you, it's a habit and skill you will have to develop.

---

[5] *Starting Smart Newletter*, June 1992, p. 8.

Second, even those of us who are inclined to be nice have bad days. And when a client initiates contact with us in the middle of one of those bad days, our control over our veneer of politeness becomes thin. For example, to find out that your child has just flunked out of college, and then deal successfully two minutes later with a phone call from a client who's yelling at you because he didn't get your Federal Express package, takes enormous self-control. The tendency is to get angry and explode. And since we're only human, there will be times when this happens, much to our regret.

A simple strategy for preventing this is to not be accessible to clients during periods where you are overly busy, annoyed, pressured, or for some other reason in a foul mood. Have your secretary or assistant pick up the phone and take a message. Put on the phone machine. Or switch on your voice mail.

When you have someone or something else take a message, this gives you time to calm down and prepare for the call, no matter how annoying or bad it may be. By calling back, you initiate the contact when you are in control of your emotions, which prevents slips of protocol and lapses in appropriate professional behavior.

There are some days, of course, when no amount of preparation will put you in the right mood. At these times, it's better not to return the call, if you can avoid it. Perhaps your assistant can say you're out of town and will return the call tomorrow. Or you can send a fax saying you are in a seminar or meeting but will get back to them the next day.

Just as rudeness can quickly cause a client to be angry or unhappy, politeness, provided it is sincere and not faked, is a valuable asset in client communication.

How do you ensure politeness? One technique sales trainers teach is to "put a smile in your voice." When the phone rings, you pause, put a big smile on your face, and then, still smiling, pick up the phone. Some sales trainers even suggest putting a mirror in front of your desk so you can see yourself smile, but to me, that's overkill.

I know this smiling idea sounds ridiculous, but *it works*. As one psychologist explained to me, the physical act of smiling does something biologically or psychologically which makes it *impossible* for us not to feel better and in a lighter mood, not matter how harried or upset we are.

Don't believe me? You're probably frowning or expressionless right now. Okay, smile. *Big* smile. Do you feel the difference as the corners of your mouth move up? See? It works!

21. Be Professional

No matter how you behave, act, or dress at home, you should behave, act, and dress in an appropriate professional manner when dealing with clients. While some service providers feel odd dress, long hair, or nontraditional behavior identifies them as quirky and are seen as endearing qualities or signs of individuality, these behaviors turn most people off.

When communicating with clients face to face, how should you dress? You should dress at the level of your client, or better—never worse. If your clients wear suit and ties, don't go in with a sport coat and open collar; put on a jacket and tie. Even when giving seminars where attendees are wearing leisure clothes, I wear a suit and tie, because I want to behave in an appropriate professional manner.

Let me give you an example of a service provider whose behavior was *not* professional. I called this person at 5:05 P.M. on a weekday at the number on his business card.

"Hello?" he answered. (That's wrong, of course. You should always identify yourself when you pick up a business phone, e.g., "DEI. Steve Schiffman speaking." "Hello" is appropriate only for a home telephone.)

"Hi, is this Frank?" I asked

"What do you want?" he snapped.

"Oh, I was calling in response to your mailing," I explained, a bit puzzled at his manner.

"It is dinner time and I am eating," he said stiffly. "Could you call me back tomorrow, please?"

What's wrong? Simply this: It's not *my* responsibility to know or ask whether his office is also in his home; if he doesn't want business calls after 5 P.M., he should say this on his answering machine or voice mail. If he wants a line open for personal calls, he should have a business number separate from his home number. The assumption that a client or prospect cannot telephone you after 5 P.M. Eastern Standard Time is wrong and a good example of unprofessional thinking and behavior.

22. If You Are Doing the Client a Favor, or Doing a Good Job, Let Them Know It

Let's face it. In today's world, you have to toot your own horn. Clients are not as appreciative of all the extras and favors you give them as they should be.

You do a good job for your clients because that's what makes them give you repeat business and referrals (not to mention payment for your invoice); you do extras and favors because you want the client to consider you for future projects.

But sometimes clients don't realize what a wonderful job you've done, or that you've given them more than their money's worth. So you have to communicate to them the value of what you have provided and the level of service they are getting.

You don't want to come right out and say, "Look at what a good job we are doing," because it sounds self-serving. You don't want to say, "I hope you appreciate all the extras we are giving you," because it sounds as if you are trying to make the client feel guilty. You need to be more subtle.

One excellent method of letting the client know, in a subtle way, that you have given some extras or "freebies," is the "courtesy discount" invoice. Here's how it works:

Let's say you do a small extra task for a client, at his request, and you decide not to charge him but rather to do it as a freebie so the client will be happy and delighted.

You should do the work and not charge, but you should *send the client an invoice for it* anyway. This invoice should show the dollar amount that you would normally charge for the service, and the fact that you are giving it free. Exhibit 5-4 shows a model courtesy discount invoice you can copy.

This invoice can also be used when you do something not for free but for a reduced rate. For instance, if you charge the client

Exhibit 5-4. Sample Courtesy Discount Invoice

INVOICE FOR SERVICES   Date

TO: Client name, address
FROM: Your name, address
FOR: Service you rendered

Service fee	$100
Less: 100% courtesy discount	-$100
Total	$ 0

AMOUNT DUE: NO CHARGE

THANK YOU!

only $50 but would normally charge $100, the courtesy discount would be 50 percent off.

This invoice requires no response or payment, but it serves two purposes. First, it reminds the client of what you did for them. (They may not even be aware of what you did or that it is something you normally charge for.)

Second, it creates a higher perceived value of the service rendered. If you spent an hour repairing the client's cracked foundation while painting the home exterior, he might take it for granted. If your invoice shows this free service as having a normal charge of $150, then the client sees you have given him something worth $150 at no charge. He'll appreciate it more and remember it longer.

23. Notify Clients Early About Any Problem That Arises

Clients hate surprises, if they're bad surprises. So if you are going to miss a deadline, or not provide something you promised to provide, or the paper stock or molding the client wanted is not available, tell them as early on in the process as you can.

This isn't necessarily as soon as you know there's a potential problem—that may be too early, since with some legwork, the problem can possibly be resolved, but problem notification should occur as soon as you are reasonably certain that you will be unable to meet all or part of your original commitment to the client.

The tendency is to delay notifying clients or not tell them at all, since we are quite rightly anxious about the clients' response to the bad news. But from the clients' point of view, they'd rather find out sooner than later. With enough advance notice, the damage of any problem can be minimized. It's only when clients find out about the problem at the eleventh hour that the damage is maximum.

24. Avoid Taboo Topics

Some of us keep our distance from clients, operating professionally but in a detached manner. Others have warmer relationships. And some service providers actually become close personal friends with their clients.

The advantage of forming a closer personal relationship is that it bonds you to the client more closely than if the relationship is strictly professional. The disadvantage is that when you feel the client is a friend as well as a colleague, you tend to talk too loosely. As a result, you increase the risk of saying something that will offend or anger the client.

As a rule, it's better not to say too much, and let the client do most of the talking. In any event, there are certain topics that you should *never* discuss with any client:

- Sex
- Religion
- Politics

These are the most sensitive and emotionally charged issues and should therefore be avoided.

You should also not express strong opinions about nonbusiness-related subjects, since the client may have the opposite opinion, and the difference in opinion can serve to distance you from the client. For instance, when dealing with a Florida client by telephone, don't complain how humid it is and that you hate the hot weather; in Florida, it's always hot, and therefore your comment is critical of the client's chosen life-style and residence.

Of course, if a client says he likes pizza, and you love pizza, by all means talk about that mutual interest, share your tips on making pizza at home, or where the best pizza joints are, and so forth.

As a rule, avoid telling jokes or ribald stories. Gentle, self-effacing humor? Fine. But yuk-yuk punchline jokes? No. Why not? The problem with humor is that it's highly subjective: What is funny to one person may be offensive to another. So don't be a clown.

25. Be Genuine

By the same token, don't be a phony and agree with everything the client says or like everything they like just to butter them up.

For example, the Monday after Superbowl Sunday, I had a telephone conference with a client. He was excited about the game—which had been close—and asked tentatively, "What did you think of the game?"

I replied politely but without shame at having violated a male tradition, "I didn't see it. Why, was it good?"

"It was exciting," he replied. "I was going to talk about it with you, but I gather you are not a football fan?"

"No, David, I'm not," I replied. And then we got down to business. He wasn't offended. And I didn't lose my dignity. Years ago, I probably would have tried to fake my way through it, or at least feign interest—and sweat the whole way thorugh it. But today, I believe people value people who are genuine and sincere. So I don't try to be something I am not.

On the other hand, if I were in a business were virtually every client played golf, and where most business was conducted on the golf course, I'd probably give some thought to taking up golf, or at least trying it to see if it was something I could like or even tolerate.

26. Plan Frequent, Regular Communication with Your Clients

How frequently should you contact the clients you work with? It depends on the ongoing nature of your work with them, your relationship, your type of business. Obviously a public relations firm on monthly retainer communicates with its clients much more frequently than does a contractor who performs an occasional job for the client every year or so.

As a rule of thumb, however, you should probably keep in touch with the client *more often than you think, and more than you do now.* If you had the urge to call and say hello, but didn't act on it, you should give that client a call now. Your instinct to call was probably correct.

Here's another tip. Do your clients interrupt you at work with calls and ask you "How's it going?" If they do, it's because they need to hear from you more than they do. This need to hear from you may not be required to do the actual work, but it's important from a client service point of view: they want to be reassured that you are forging ahead and making progress on their work, and this is their way of letting you know that a periodic "progress report" via phone or fax would be welcome.

So take their cue. Don't wait to get a "How's it going call?" Call them before you think they will call you.

27. Be Available for Instant Access

The rule of instant access is simple: The client should be able to deliver a message to you at your office twenty-four hours a day, seven days a week, fifty-two weeks a year. This doesn't mean you have to be sitting at your phone night and day but that your business line is always set to receive calls and take messages.

Why is this important? Because the client is busy, part of your role is to shift burden from the client's shoulders to yours. And that includes communication. If the client calls your office but no one answers, that forces them to post a note to remind them to try you later. That's extra work, and it's annoying. The client would much prefer it if she could leave a short message and have *you* get back to *her*. This puts the burden of a return call on your shoulders—where it should be.

Another thing clients find extremely annoying is to call you and get a busy signal. If you have only a single line, ask your telephone company about the "call waiting" feature that lets you take two calls simultaneously on your line instead of just one. This cuts way down on the probability of any client getting a busy signal.

Even better is the new electronic voice mail offered by the telephone companies in many states: if you are on the line, the second incoming call is automatically routed to a voice mail box which takes the message. Again, a busy signal is avoided.

Despite the advances in telephone technology, numerous small businesses I deal with still have not invested in a phone machine (which you can now get for under $70), and when you call them before or after business hours, the phone rings with no answer.

As for faxes, my feeling is that business clients prefer a fax machine that is switched on and ready to receive around the clock with a dedicated (separate) phone number for fax calls.

Some businesses, to save the cost of a second phone line, have phone and fax on the same line. When you call to send a fax, a person picks up. They tell you to hang up and call back. In the interim, they switch on their fax so you will get a fax signal when you reconnect with them.

This is wrong, and don't you do it! Provide your clients with a dedicated fax line they can call to send you a fax at any time of the day or night. Why should the client have to make and pay for two phone calls because you're too cheap to install another line? It's a pain for them, unprofessional for you. Also, it makes you look cheap and small time.

One other way service providers cement their relationship with their client is the giving out of the home telephone number. It impresses clients when you say, "You know, I want you to feel free to call me any time if you have a question or problem or need to discuss a project. Here is my home telephone number." This conveys to the client the impression that you value his business success above your personal life.

Whether you are actually willing to give your home number out to clients is another story, and I cannot make that decision for you. It is not mandatory to do so, and if your privacy and leisure time are important, you may not want to volunteer it.

Be aware, however, that a client who brings up the matter and suggests a swap of home numbers probably will be a bit put off at your refusal. A possible solution is to install two home numbers, one for client use and a second, unlisted number for friends and relatives. If you want to shield yourself from client contact, you simply turn on the phone machine attached to the home number you give to clients, and let the machine take messages.

28. Respond to Clients Promptly

Another simple rule: When a client calls and you are not in, get back to them promptly. How quickly must you return calls? Again, it depends on your client base, your business, your industry, and the nature of your work. A problem with landscaping, for example, is not as urgent as a problem with a kidney dialysis machine, so quickness of response is less urgent. Every service provider has a somewhat different philosophy on how accessible they want to make themselves to clients and how promptly they return phone calls. One successful consultant's voice mail promises a return answer within forty-eight hours, but gives the name and number of an assistant to call if the need is urgent. A local printer, also successful, wears a beeper, has a car phone, and promises instant return of a call at any time of the day or night—something his competitors do not do. A successful ad agency executive I know has a telephone *and* a fax machine in his car.

Two rules of thumb for how quickly you must return phone calls. First, by the caller's tone of voice and the content of the message, you can usually assess whether it is routine or urgent. If it's routine, it can probably hold overnight until the next business day; if it's urgent, be sure to return the call on the same business day, preferably within three to four hours or sooner.

Second, it's especially important for you to be accessible, reachable, and available and return calls promptly if you are a subcontractor and your client is hiring you to perform a service which he in turn must deliver to *his* client; for example, a computer programmer who is writing part of a larger system as a subcontractor to a large systems development firm producing a new application for a major client.

In such a situation, the prime contractor is trusting in you, the subcontractor, to help him serve his important client, and he is likely to be juggling many responsibilities. He needs prompt answers to questions and requests and will be displeased and uncomfortable if you are never in when he calls, constantly play "phone tag," or don't return calls. When the prime contractor calls, you should as a rule always return the call within three to four hours (half a business day) or less.

29. Select the Method of Communication Appropriate to the Client and the Importance of your Message

There are many different options for communicating with clients at various times: phone, in-person visits, letter, fax. Choosing which to use is largely a matter of common sense, but if you are uncertain, consider the advantages and disadvantages of each method:

- Drop-in visit—*Advantages:* Spontaneous acts add warmth to relationships. In-person visits remind client of your existence and value. *Disadvantages:* Client may resent unscheduled interruption in their day.

- Scheduled in-town visit (seeing client B when in town to meet with client A)—*Advantages:* Client appreciates your going out of your way to see them even though there is no immediate ongoing assignment. *Disadvantages:* Client may feel you view them as secondary in importance (because you only see them when in town for other purposes).

- Phone call—*Advantages:* Easiest, least time-consuming method of keeping in frequent contact with clients. *Disadvantages:* Clients may not like interruption of "trivial" or nonessential communication.

- Fax—*Advantages:* Allows you to communicate with client instantly and in writing, without two-way communication. Ideal for situations where you want to give the client time to consider your message before replying, or where you want to give the client information to review in advance of a phone discussion. *Disadvantages:* Client may perceive fax as impersonal or as a way to avoid direct contact with them.

- Letter—*Advantages:* Appropriate for nonurgent, routine communications. Can be made powerful by enclosing article clippings, photos, or other items the client may find of interest. *Disadvantages:* Letters are not as immediate as phone or fax, and you do not know when the client received it, if they read it, or what their reaction to it was.
- Survey—*Advantages:* A more formal way of measuring the level of client satisfaction. Gives you in-depth, accurate feedback on their perception of you and the service you render. *Disadvantages:* Client may resent being asked to do the work of filling out and returning the survey form.

Performing Services Above and Beyond the Clients' Request

What does it take to keep your clients satisfied?

In Chapter 4, we saw that the fundamental rule of client satisfaction is "Don't give your clients their money's worth—give them *more* than they paid for, more than they have a right to expect."

In Chapter 5, we learned that it's not only what you do that affects your relationship with your client; it's what you say—and we explored more than two dozen specific strategies for enhancing client communications.

In Chapter 6, we return to the actions necessary for maximum client satisfaction and consider a potpourri of proven client satisfaction techniques and tips for your use.

BE DILIGENT; DON'T RELAX

If you've already put the principles expressed in previous chapters to work and are getting good results, you may think, "Things are pretty okay with my clients at this point; now I can relax." Not so. One of the key secrets of ensuring client satisfaction I haven't shared with you yet is this: *diligence.*

Client satisfaction is not something you practice one month, then coast on when things are going smoothly. It is an attitude, and a way of doing business, that must be diligently applied every waking moment, every minute of the business day.

It takes months, even years, of excellent client service to form solid, lasting relationships with the most profitable, lucrative clients. And all that can be destroyed with one slip, one mistake, one lapse, one error that gets the client ticked off at you enough to make them walk. Therefore, you can't "relax" when it comes to applying the principles of maximum client satisfaction expressed in this book. You have to do it every week, every day, every hour, every minute. Tiring? Possibly. Doable? Yes. Rewarding? I guarantee it.

Another reason why diligently practicing maximum client satisfaction and never "letting your guard down" is important is that, in this "Age of the Customer," only those firms that create maximum client satisfaction will survive and prosper.

"Let's make sure that our customers are satisfied," suggests Lois Geller, president of Lois Geller Direct, in an article in *Target Marketing*[1] "Lack of customer service can break all of our efforts. If we are to cement buyer loyalty in the '90s, customer satisfaction must be a key objective."

Low levels of client satisfaction can cost your business a lot of money. According to investment consultant and author John M. Cali, Jr., 91 percent of unhappy customers who have been treated discourteously will not buy from the offending business again.[2] And, just as bad, says Cali, the average unhappy customer will complain about the poor treatment you gave them to nine or ten other people, and 13 percent of these unhappy customers will tell more than 20 other people!

According to the American Productivity and Quality Center (as quoted in Towers Club USA Newsletter, September, 1992, p. 6):

- 68 percent of customers stop doing business if they receive poor service
- customers are five times more likely to leave because of poor service than for product quality or cost
- customers who receive poor service tell nine to twenty other people
- losing a customer costs five times the annual value of the customer account
- the average happy customer tells five other people
- 50 to 75 percent of customers who have their complaints solved quickly return and buy again, and

---

[1] *Target Marketing*, January 1992, p. 13.

[2] *Tower Club USA Newletter*, September, 1992, p. 6.

- if the complaint is solved very quickly, 95 percent of customers return.

SUCCEED BY BEING BETTER, NOT BY BEING GREAT

Many business authorities say the only way to succeed is by being great at everything you do. The book *In Search of Excellence* inspired a new breed of business authors, speakers, and seminar leaders proclaiming that only "excellence" will win customers and profits in the 1990s.

While striving for excellence is a laudable goal, there are two problems I have with experts telling you you have to be great or excellent to stay in business. First, it puts tremendous pressure on you. It's hard enough today to juggle all your client responsibilities and still get all your work done on time. To have to be great in *everything* you do as well? It's too much!

Second, it's not true. You see, to stand head and shoulders above your competition, you don't have to be "great" or "excellent," you just have to be significantly *better* than the competition.

And in giving excellent client service, that's fairly easy, because, despite all we read in the business press about the importance of customer service, most service providers are *lousy* when it comes to client service. So you don't have to be great, you just have to be better than they are. And because they're so mediocre, it's easy for you to beat them.

"You beat 50 percent of the people in America by working hard," says A. L. Williams, the self-made millionaire life insurance salesman, in his book, *All You Can Do Is All You Can Do*.[3] "You beat another 40 percent by being a person of honesty and integrity and by standing for something. The last 10 percent is a dogfight in the free-enterprise system."

GET YOUR CLIENTS TO TRUST YOU

"Your professional relationships with your clients and employees require complete trust," says Mark M. Maraia, a Colorado-based management consultant. "Trust, not time, is your most valuable stock in trade."

---

[3] *National Home Business Report,* Summer 1990, p. 27.

Mark has identified a number of practices which many service providers or their staff engage in which undermine their clients' trust in them. These include

- Failing to identify yourself by name when answering the telephone.
- Failing to perceive pressure experienced by your clients.
- Failing to listen with the intent of understanding; for example, cutting off sentences "waiting for your turn to speak."
- Failing to keep a promise no matter how small or insignificant.
- Failing to offer a satisfaction guarantee to your clients.
- Talking down to your clients.
- Failing to educate clients on ways to reduce their dependence on outside services like yours.
- Making clients wait more than a few minutes in the reception area for appointments with you.
- Failing to act consistently with your stated values.
- Failing to act in your clients' best interest at all times.
- Acting without humor in your interaction with others.
- Making excuses; failing to accept 100 percent responsibility.
- Showing little discourtesies and unkindnesses.

I agree with all these points. Most are self-explanatory; I elaborate on a few of them briefly in the following paragraphs.

Use Good Manners in All Interactions with Your Clients

Be polite, cool, calm, collected. In today's society, acting busy and harried has become almost a status symbol. Yet clients resent it when you are curt with them, or act as if their call is an annoyance or interruption, or make them feel you don't have time for them.

The *Record*[4] reports that in a survey of two hundred businesspeople, bad manners were the number one complaint among those surveys. People don't like to be treated rudely. So don't. *Take the time* to be polite and give each client your full attention, acting as if their concern and problem is your number one priority and the only thing you have to deal with that day.

---

[4] January 6, 1992, p. B-2.

Listen to Your Clients

Failure to listen is usually caused by eagerness to be speaking. As Mark says, when you find yourself cutting off the other person's sentences, and not listening but sitting there waiting for them to finish so you can talk, you're not really listening. And that's bad—for two reasons.

First, if you don't listen, you don't know what the client really wants you to do; therefore, you can't do it. And if you don't do what the client wants, you don't have a satisfied client.

Second, it annoys the client. If they see you are not listening, they will feel you are not interested in them and their problems.

Equally as important as listening is to *let the client know* you are listening. This is done by making eye contact, by sitting in an attentive position, leaning forward slightly to signal your intense interest; by brief verbal responses that show you are paying attention ("I understand," "That's interesting," "Really?" "Uh-huh," "Tell me more," etc.).

Another useful technique is, after the client is done speaking, to pause for a full second or two before you begin your reply. If you jump in too soon, the client may get the false impression that you weren't really listening and were just "waiting for your turn" to speak. By pausing for a second or two, you convey the impression that you have listened carefully and are still formulating your response.

Reduce Your Clients' Dependence on You

This advice may sound contrary to common sense; after all, the more dependent a client is on your service, the more he'll use you, and the more money you'll make, right?

But if you deliberately attempt to make a client dependent on you, limit his growth, and not teach him to do for himself, he'll resent it. He'll see that you are trying to maximize your profit and take as much money out of his pocket as you can. And this will cause unhappiness, dissatisfaction, and distrust of you.

Doing the opposite—helping clients become less dependent on your services, not more—makes good sense. If you can show the client how to do more for themselves, you save him money, and that's one of the primary benefits a client looks for from any service provider. The less he has to spend on outside services, the more he saves; the more he saves, the more he'll be grateful to you. And that gratitude translates to loyalty.

What's more, reducing client dependence on your services can actually increase use of services rather than decrease them and raise revenues instead of lower them. How? By teaching the client to do more on his own, he saves money by handling routine and less critical tasks in-house. With the savings, he will have extra money to spend on more important projects and goals and is likely to think of hiring you to handle those assignments in return for your good service and honesty.

Guarantee Your Work for Your Client

A guarantee helps build sales and buyer satisfaction. Observe that when you get a direct mail solicitation for a book, magazine subscription, or product, it usually offers a 30-day money-back trial period. Do you see why this is necessary? Without such a money-back guarantee, many consumers would not buy the product sight unseen, fearing that if they didn't like it once they received it and looked it over, they'd be stuck. A guarantee of satisfaction removes that barrier and increases sales.

As service providers, we have an extra difficulty: unlike manufacturers, who if they refund money can resell the products that are returned to them, once we render a service, we can never get back the time we spent performing the task for the client.

For this reason, many service providers reject the concept of a guarantee, saying, "If I give a money-back guarantee, clients will take advantage of me. They will ask me to do the service, get the benefits of the service, then say they are not happy, ask for their money back, and rip me off. So I won't do it."

Yet experience contradicts this belief. The facts are that (1) most people are honest and won't abuse a guarantee privilege, (2) having a guarantee is becoming increasingly important in getting people to buy services, and (3) clients like service providers who give a guarantee.

A guarantee shows that you are dedicated to delivering the best service possible and that you have confidence in your ability to do so. When the client sees you are confident enough in yourself to guarantee your service, the client becomes much more confident in—and comfortable with—you.

What types of guarantees can service businesses offer? Here are just a few of the ways to structure a service business guarantee.

Feel free to use these as is or adapt them to your particular business and service.

> SPECIAL NOTE: The one thing you cannot ethically do is absolutely *guarantee* a result or service unconditionally. For example, if you are a roofer, you can guarantee the roof against leaks for twenty years, saying that if it does leak, you will repair it at no cost. But you cannot guarantee that the roof will never leak. That is simply impossible. John Cali says it best: "It's true you can't guarantee a service you provide. But you *can* guarantee customer satisfaction."

Offer a money-back guarantee based on tangible results.   The strongest guarantee is to tell the client you guarantee a good result and that if it is not achieved, the client doesn't pay.

For example, in my seminar business, corporations hire me to do in-house training seminars in client service, sales, marketing, and writing skills. Sometimes a potential client says my fee seems high, and how do they know they will get their value for that kind of money? My guarantee to them is simple: if the seminar is not everything I promised, and if 90 percent or more of their attendees do not rate it "excellent," they don't pay me. Period. This eliminates any hesitancy or fear they may have about my not living up to what I promise—because I am removing the risk from their shoulders and putting it on mine.

A variation of this "guaranteed results or you don't pay" offer is the service firm whose fee is a percentage of the profits or revenues generated, or money saved, by the service. For example, yesterday I met an inventory management consultant whose services cut costs and whose fee is 3 percent of the money saved. Under this arrangement, of course, the client does not pay a penny unless money is actually saved; thus again, there is no risk.

Offer a money-back guarantee based on satisfaction.   This is similar to the previous guarantee, except instead of pegging the money-back guarantee on a specific result (e.g., "90 percent of participants will rate it excellent," "roof will not leak," etc.), you peg it to more subjective client criteria. A company that specializes in logo design makes this offer: it will come in and do three preliminary logo designs for you at no up-front cost; if you like one and want to use it, the company negotiates a fee based on use. "If you don't like it and don't want to continue with us, we shake hands, part as friends, and you do not owe us a cent," states the owner.

The client's satisfaction is guaranteed, and even better from the client's point of view, *they* are the only judge of whether the service was satisfactory—no ands, if, buts, or conditions.

Offer a money-back guarantee based on performance.   If you are unwilling to offer a money-back guarantee based on results achieved or client satisfaction, a weaker but still effective pledge is to guarantee performance of service. This works especially well in industries where service providers routinely do not perform everything they promised, do not keep to schedule, or have lots of cost overruns added to the final bill (examples include defense contracting and home remodeling).

Such a guarantee might be: "We promise to do what we said, when we said it, at the price we quoted. If not, if we don't do what we said, fail to meet our deadline, or don't stick to our original estimate, then you don't pay us. Period."

Offer a money-back or replacement or service redo warranty.   A warranty is a guarantee of satisfaction for an extended period—typically one year—after the service has been performed and the bill has been paid. In a money-back warranty, the service provider guarantees the quality of the work for the warranty period, with a refund of all or part of the money if the work doesn't stand up.

For example, an exterminator might say, "We guarantee your hotel to be free of bugs for one full year. If at any times pests reappear, we will re-treat at no charge and refund part of your exterminating fee in proportion to how long you had the reinfestation."

We recently had our tiny front lawn landscaped, for the sum of $5,500. The landscaping came with this simple guarantee: All plants guaranteed to thrive for one year or replacement is free. In fact, three bushes did die within the warranty period and were promptly replaced.

But that's not the end of the story. One of the replacement bushes died a few months after planting, and by that time, the warranty period of one year had passed. We called the landscaper to tell him the bush had died, and he said, "No problem, we'll plant something different and see if it does better; no charge, of course."

Although he had a legal right to charge us, he didn't. Isn't that what you'd want from your landscaper? Isn't that what your clients want from you?

Offer a double-money-back or bonus guarantee. Some companies offer to give back to the customer *more* than the customer paid if there is a problem or defect. This might be a refund fee larger than the fee paid for the service ("double-your-money-back") or a refund plus bonus ("full refund plus an extra month's service FREE").

I don't think this is necessary in service selling, and it's probably overkill. The guarantees already discussed are more than sufficient to make you shine head and shoulders above your competition, simply because more than 95 percent of service providers do not guarantee their services. Therefore, even a limited guarantee puts you ahead.

DELAY BILLING SO YOUR CLIENT CAN FIRST APPRECIATE YOUR WORK

This is a small matter, but sometimes, it's little things that make the difference. I feel you should not be too eager to push a bill on a client after service is completed and the money is due. Why is this?

The service—and especially, the completion of service and the result provided—is a very positive thing. It's what the client wanted, and if you have delivered it, they're going to be happy. But the bill—the money they have to pay for the service—is a negative thing. It's the one part of the deal the client would love not to have to keep if this was possible. Money is in short supply these days, everyone is on a budget, and people don't like to part with it. So getting the final bill, and seeing that big number under "AMOUNT DUE," converts the smile into a frown.

As a result, I recommend you do not rush to bill the client, but instead wait a short period, for several reasons.

First, the waiting period gives clients time to enjoy the fruits of your labors before having to get to the reality of paying for it. Letting them "live" with the completed project or job for a bit allows them to enjoy it and therefore raises their satisfaction level to a new high.

Second, if you bill too quickly, you risk having clients receive an invoice before you know whether they are pleased and happy or whether they want some adjustments or alterations. If clients get billed immediately, and the job is not 100 percent to their liking, their attitude will be, "I'm not going to pay one penny until she gets back here and does it right!" Having the bill will act as a magnifying glass, focusing the client's attention on what's wrong (versus what's right) and making any minor dissatisfactions seem larger than they are.

Third, when your bill arrives two seconds after the job is done, you convey the impression that you don't really share in the client's interest in the project or enthusiasm for the work; you remind them that you're just a hired hand, in it for the money and waiting with your hand out to be paid.

Of course, you don't want to hold up billing too long; this deprives you of cash flow and may be problematic for the client's accounting department. But it's better to err on the side of billing too slowly than billing too quickly.

How long after the service is performed should you bill? In my consulting work, I send the bill about a week to ten days *after* I have handed in the report, given the speech, or presented the seminar to the client.

If your "deliverable" to the client is a report, drawing, sketch, design, computer disk, or other material to be mailed or delivered to the client, do *not* enclose your invoice with your completed work. Instead, mail it in a separate envelope, and mail it *after* the client has received your completed assignment. Getting your work, if it's good, will make the client happy. Don't weaken that moment of peak client satisfaction by adding a negative element (the big bill he must pay) to the package.

If your work is done on-site, don't insist on a check before you walk away; just bill the client net thirty days (or whatever your terms are). And don't, as so many contractors do, hang around awkwardly without saying anything, hoping the client will "get the hint" and cough up a check. Clients resent this behavior; it seems petty and annoying. My advice is to let them praise you for a job well done, thank them, go back to your office, write out an invoice, wait a few days, then put it in the mail.

Your accountant or bookkeeper will tell you that this advice is nonsense and will weaken your cash flow. But accounts receivables are *not*, contrary to what your accountant tells you, your firm's number one asset. *Satisfied clients are.* It won't kill you to wait another week for your money or contend with an occasional slow-payer. It will harm you far more to leave every job on a negative note and have your clients report your money-grubbing, self-centered behavior to other potential clients.

NOTIFYING THE CLIENT OF CHANGES IN POLICIES, RATES, BILLING PROCEDURES

When you notify a client of a change in policy, procedure, or fees, do it in a way that implies this is a *suggested* change only, and subject to discussion or negotiation. For example, if you are sending out an announcement saying your billing procedure is changing from net 30 to net 15 days, add a paragraph to the notice that says something like:

> We are putting this policy in place because slow payments from large corporate clients to small vendors like us put us in a cash flow crunch, makes us end up being your "banker" (a business we're not in), and would force us to raise rates to compensate. We feel the new net 15 days is a good solution for us and for you. But, of course, our policies are flexible and tailored to each client's needs; if net 15 days is a problem for you, let us know and we'll work out an alternative.

When you send a policy or procedure change notice to a client and write it as a commandment etched in stone rather than a desired request that can be negotiated, you risk having clients who do not like the policy or cannot comply with the procedure leave you, without even telling you. You want to keep the lines of communication open and let the client know you are flexible and are willing to accommodate their requirements.

ACT IN YOUR CLIENTS' BEST INTEREST
AT ALL TIMES

Mark Maraia says failure to act in your clients' best interest at all times undermines their trust in you. And he is right.

Clients resent it strongly when they hear or even sense anything in your manner, behavior, or conversation indicating (1) that their interests are not your number one priority or (2) that your self-interest, schedule, profit, problems, or concerns should in any way be of concern to the client or have any affect on the work you are doing for that client.

Says Dr. Rob Gilbert, "The Golden Rule—Do unto Others What You Want Them to Do for You—is wrong." To achieve maximum client satisfaction, Rob continues, you must do unto others what *they* want you to do for them.

Whenever you are faced with a decision whose outcome favors either you or the client, choose the action that benefits the client, not you, most. In the short term, they will be the winner. In the long term, you both will.

For example, I bought a bag of shrimp at the local supermarket, along with many other items. When I opened the shrimp, it stank—it was spoiled. I went back to the store, found the assistant manager in the aisle, and asked for a replacement.

"Do you have a receipt?" he asked. I told him I did not; I do not save grocery receipts and had thrown it out after unloading the groceries. But I showed him that the printout from his store's digital scale, with the price of the purchase, was still on the bag.

"That could be from another store," he protested. "No refund without a receipt!" he snapped and walked away.

I went home, called the supermarket, got the name of the manager, and wrote him a letter. It said: "I don't know the exact figure, but our family spends well over $150 a week in your store in groceries. That's $7,800 per year; $39,000 in the five years we've lived in this town. As we plan to stay here at least ten more years, our continued business is worth at least $78,000 to you.

"I bought a $13.99 bag of shrimp from your store, which was spoiled before the expiration date. Can I come in and get back $13.99 or a replacement bag of shrimp? Please let me know. If not, I will be spending our $78,000 at the supermarket next door to you."

I mailed the letter. Two days later the manager called, apologized, told me a refund would be waiting, and I could pick it up the next time I came into the store. Aren't you glad that the assistant manager who would not pay $13.99 to retain a $78,000 customer is not *your* employee? Three years later, we still do our food shopping at that supermarket.

THE MAGIC OF BEING COOPERATIVE

More than almost anything else, the client wants you to be cooperative, not difficult; easy to work with, not hard to get along with; a team player, not a prima donna.

Lou Weiss of Specialty Steel & Forge in Leonia, New Jersey, says, "What works today is a 'can-do' attitude—what the client wants to hear you say is, 'Yes, we can do it,' not, 'No, we don't do that.'" The can-do attitude has helped Lou build several successful businesses.

In terms of communicating to the client that you are cooperative and flexible, not difficult or unwilling to extend yourself on their behalf, there are two words that are pure magic: *No problem*. Here are some examples of how to put these magic words to work making your clients happy with you:

Client:
"We need it by Tuesday."

You:
"No problem."

Client:
"Our budget is limited on this project."

You:
"No problem."

Client:
"I'll be in meetings all week, but this is important. Would it be possible for us to have a short phone conference over the weekend?"

You:
"No problem."

The one thing a busy and harried client does not want to hear when making a request is you telling him you can't do it and then going into a long explanation of the reasons why. Will there be times you cannot agree to a client's request and legitimate reasons why you cannot do so? Of course. And at those times you will have to say no and explain why.

The idea is to *reduce to a minimum* the number of occasions on which you tell a client "no." You do this by being flexible, by putting the client's interests above your own, by being client focused, and by realizing you are in a service business, and service (according to the *American Heritage Dictionary*) means "work done for others," with the emphasis on *others*.

Often doing all the things you agree to do for your clients means working harder and putting in more hours. Many service providers complain to me, "It's not fair; I have to work *much* harder now than in the 1980s." Well, if it were easy, *everybody would being doing it*. So quit complaining, buckle down, and get to work!

It is *others*—your clients—you must please to succeed in your service business. You *want* to be saying "yes" to client requests if at all possible; those repeated "yesses" and "no problems" are what make clients love dealing with you.

While an occasional "no" is sometimes necessary, turning down a client is something you want to avoid almost at any cost. As one sharp service provider said to me, "Every 'no' to a client initiates a search on the client's part for another vendor to do the job you turned down, and that gives your competition a prime opportunity to get their foot in the door and show the client what they can do—which is often as good as what you can do, only faster and at lower cost."

So have the can-do, no-problem attitude. Make "yes" your routine response to client queries; get "no" out of your vocabulary. This is one of the most important points in today's "Age of the Customer" and one of the elements most vital to your success.

HOW TO HANDLE "UNEXPECTED" REQUESTS, SURPRISE INCIDENTS, AND OTHER "CURVEBALLS" CLIENTS THROW AT US

The one area where most service providers fall down is when clients hit us with the unexpected. Most of us can give reasonably good service when dealing with clients on a "business as usual" basis. But when the client asks us something out of the ordinary, we often make mistakes and end up infuriating rather than pleasing the client.

Why is this so? It's simple. When the client makes an unexpected request, it is usually something we don't want to do, don't know how to do, or don't know whether we can do. We don't know how to respond.

But, because it's our client and we are his vendor, we don't want them to think that we've never encountered this situation before or that we don't know what we're doing. We also believe they are expecting a response on the spot.

As a result, we feel compelled to answer immediately, without giving the matter any thought. Since we don't know the answer, and haven't thought about it, we have to make up our answer as we go along. In doing so, we give a poor answer—one that doesn't adequately address the question.

The client indicates that the answer isn't satisfactory or doesn't make sense. We become defensive, and argue back, trying to support a solution to a problem which we hadn't given five seconds thought to. By arguing, we engage in an adversarial, confrontational conversation with the client, which is always a losing proposition for the service provider and a turn-off for the client.

How do you avoid this awful situation? The technique is simple. Instead of trying to answer the unexpected question, solve the unfamiliar problem, or handle the unusual situation on the spot—*don't*. Instead, do this:

First, tell the client you want to make sure you understand the question or the request. Ask them clarifying questions. Then repeat back their request to them in your own words, and ask if you have it right, for example, "Is that what you are looking for?"

When they say yes, you say, "That's an interesting challenge. I don't have an answer for you off the top of my head. I've had similar requests, but nothing exactly like that. Tell you what. Let me give it some thought and get back to you first thing tomorrow morning (or later today, or whatever). How does that sound?"

Then, you get off the phone or out of the meeting, go back to your office, work through the unusual request, come up with a solution and some alternatives, then call, meet with, or fax the client to go over your proposal, and find a solution that meets her needs. The advantages of this technique?

First, it produces a superior solution to the client's problem.

Second, rather than make you look dumb because you couldn't answer on the spot (as many service providers fear), it makes you look smart. The client respects that you care enough about her to handle a difficult request and quickly formulate some solutions and alternatives.

Third, it eliminates the pressure of having to give an immediate answer to a request you don't know how to handle. It buys you the extra time to do it right.

Fourth, it comes across as cooperative and helpful, eliminating the confrontational, adversarial situation of not answering correctly, proposing something off the top of your head the client doesn't like and then having to defend it—or saying "no" to the client when you really didn't have to, just because you didn't see a way to handle the request within two seconds after you heard it.

LOOK AT YOUR SERVICE FROM THE CLIENT'S POINT OF VIEW

One strategy that saved me a lot of anger and frustration and made me feel better about clients (as well as treat them better) was this simple philosophy:

Always look at things from your client's point of view.

Doing this is easy, but most of us don't, because it takes a deliberate effort. For example, when faced with any decision involving our work for a client, we tend to make an instant decision, because we're pressed for time.

Before making any decision or responding to any request involving the client, do this. Stop, take a breath, hold it for a second, exhale slowly, and then repeat the process two more times.

Now that you are relaxed, say to yourself, "Let me look at this from the client's point of view. If I were the client, how would I want to be treated in this situation?" Once you have the answer, you know what to do:

Do unto the client what the client *wants* you to do.

For example, a few days ago a client asked me to fax short write-ups of seminars I was scheduled to present for her. Yesterday, under extreme deadline pressure, I got a call from her. "This isn't what I asked for," she complained.

My immediate reaction was to get testy; it was *exactly* what she had asked for. These were the "boilerplate" write-ups I send to everyone who hires me to speak, and no one else complained. Instead, I took a breath, and thought to myself, "If I were in her shoes, I'd probably be frantically trying to pull a big conference together in a short time, and under that enormous work load, I'd need total cooperation from vendors, no speakers giving me 'grief.'"

I said pleasantly and apologetically, "I'm sorry, Fran, that these weren't what you needed. Tell me what you need and I'll fax it over to you. Would noon be soon enough?" This put her at ease, made me look good, and made her feel good about having hired me. What she wanted was simple and easy to do, and I did it.

As another example, I sell business books, audio cassettes, and special reports by mail. On the shorter reports, there is no money-back refund, and this is stated on the order form. The other day, I received a letter from a buyer saying, "I like the books but not these two reports. I am returning them. Please refund my $14. I apologize about the dog-eared condition, but this is how they arrived."

My immediate reaction? (I was having a bad day.) "If he doesn't realize the tremendous value of these reports, and how he could put this information to work, he'll never succeed at his venture. And besides, there's no refund on reports." I wanted to send a letter saying "No refunds on reports; sorry."

But that would have created a dissatisfied customer who might tell ten to twenty other people, and would never buy from me again. Who wants that? Instead, I thought, "If I were him, and I didn't like the reports, of course, I would want my money back; $14 is a lot of money to waste on something you don't want."

I wrote back that I was sorry he did not like the reports, would happily give him a refund, and would give him, in addition, one free report of his choice for his trouble.

How do you think that made him feel about me and my catalog?

RESPECT THE CLIENT'S TIME

We've discussed throughout the book how busy people are and therefore how you must respect their time. One important way to communicate this respect is always to show up on time for meetings.

Because being on time is important, plan your travel so you will arrive early for your scheduled appointment; you might leave even earlier if you expect heavy traffic or don't know the area and might get lost. Ideally, you should arrive five to ten minutes before your scheduled appointment. This benefits the client, because they can start on time with you. It benefits you, giving you a few minutes to get yourself together and mentally prepare. When you arrive with seconds to spare or minutes late, you often lose your composure and start the meeting in a highly agitated state.

If you think you are going to be late, call and let the client know before you leave or from the road. If you're going to be very late, explain why and offer to reschedule at the client's convenience (most will tell you to come anyway).

PERFORMANCE ABOVE AND BEYOND THE CALL OF DUTY

The rule here is: When there is a problem or crisis with a job you are doing for a client, your normal rules, procedures, and business policies do not apply, and you should do *whatever it takes* to solve the problem, meet the deadline, and set the situation right.

Jack Gribben, retired founder of Sun Graphics, a successful printing company, tells this story:

"I had kept part of the order off a shipment, because the quality was not quite right. However, I wanted to meet my promised delivery date, so I chartered a plane for $64 (this was many years ago) to deliver the material in person from our plant to the client the next day—even though the fee we were charging the client to do this portion of the printing job was only $3.50."[5]

Joe Vitale's Five Tips for Providing Better Customer Service

Joe Vitale, coauthor of *The Joy of Service*, offers these five tips for building client satisfaction with superior service:

---

[5] *Record*, January 6, 1992, p. B-3.

1. Show your appreciation to good customers. Tell the client you appreciate their business.
2. Reward your customers. Give them something free. They may hire you for one service, but toss in something else.
3. Be friendly with your clients. And treat them well.
4. Don't let your clients wander away. Keep them loyal. If you give them everything they want, and more, they won't leave.
5. If your clients are complaining, check it out. Don't hush them. They probably want you to take care of something.

Now let's discuss two ways you can do Joe's first suggestion of showing appreciation to clients: thank yous and business gifts.

Showing your Appreciation with Thank-Yous

Sending "thank-you" notes to clients is a wonderful way to show your appreciation and to get them to think well of you. You can send thank you notes to show appreciation for:

- Ongoing business and the client's steady, regular use of your service
- A kindness or favor the client did for you
- Awarding you a specific job or contract
- Referrals to potential clients within their organization or at other firms
- Their friendship (if you consider them a friend)
- Their praise of your work or nice treatment of you
- Anything else you think is appropriate to thank a person for

Your thank you note will make a big impression on your client simply because he gets so few of them: it's quite possible no other vendor he deals with sends thank-you notes.

To ensure that you send thank-you notes or letters to your clients on a regular basis, set aside twenty minutes every week, at a regularly scheduled time (say, from 10:00 to 10:20 A.M. on Monday morning), to write thank you notes to your clients. Exhibit

Exhibit 6-1.   Model Thank You note to a Client

date

Mr. Joe Client
ABC Corp.
Anytown, USA

Dear Joe:

Just a short note to say "thanks" for all the business you have given us this year.

In the rush to get work done, we rarely take time to thank clients. Yet thanks are in order—we appreciate your trust in us and the opportunity you give us to work with you on the many exciting projects we handle together.

So again, "thanks." I appreciate the business, and I value our relationship.

Regards,

[signature]

6-1 shows a model thank you note you can use as is or adapt to suit your needs.

"Appreciate your existing customers," writes Jo Anne Park, editorial director of *Target Marketing*.[6] "Let them know it. Not a one of them is expendable. The attitude, 'There are more where they came from,' is both naive and dangerous. Markets have limits."

Showing Your Appreciation with Business Gifts

Bulova Watch, a company that sells watches to be used as business gifts, premiums, and incentives (as well as direct to consumers), published a study of the gift-giving habits of businesspeople. The

---

[6] *Target Market*, January 1992, p. 6.

most interesting finding: approximately 75 percent of business gifts are given at Xmas time; 25 percent are given on birthdays, anniversaries, for promotions, spontaneously, or at other times of the year. Therefore, a simple but effective technique to improve the impact of giving business gifts is to give them at times *other than the holiday season.*

In fact, I go a step further and recommend that you *not* give gifts to your clients at Xmas time. A card? Of course. (Make it "seasons greetings" rather than "Merry Christmas" so as not to offend those who do not celebrate Xmas.) But I am against giving clients Xmas gifts, for several reasons.

First, because 75 percent of business gifts are given at this time, your gift will be lost in the shuffle. And it competes with all the gifts the client is getting from other vendors (and larger vendors have probably outspent you).

Second, once you give a nice gift at Xmas, the client expects it every year; absence of the gift may make the client feel you are treating them cheaply. The Xmas gift-giving becomes a mandatory obligation that, in rough economic times, can quickly become too expensive, especially as you add more and more names to your Xmas business gift list.

When is the best time to give a gift to a client? Many advocate keeping files on clients indicating birthdays, anniversaries, children's birthdays, and other occasions on which a tasteful gift can make a big impression. Although I don't do this myself, I agree it's smart thinking. And by the way, if the client has young children, they'll appreciate a gift for the kids more than a gift for themselves.

My practice is to give gifts "spontaneously," almost randomly throughout the year. Some of the best times to give a client a gift are

- Thanking them for a specific project or assignment
- Thanking them for being patient and understanding if there was a problem on a job or project
- Thanking them for a referral
- As a get-well gift for a client who has been ill
- Strengthening your bond with the client at a time where the relationship seems in danger of weakening for any reason or for no reason

For example, I called a client to discuss a project. Her assistant said she had fallen off a horse, wasn't hurt seriously, but was laid up in bed at home for two to three weeks. I knew this person loved baked goods, so I sent her a large tin of gift muffins and cookies. Not only was it gratefully appreciated, but since she had the leisure to enjoy it at home, it stuck in her mind for many days that I alone of all her vendors cared enough to make her a bit more comfortable during her recuperation period.

In another case, a client's office was destroyed by a broken water pipe in her building. She had to move to another office within the building. When she got to her desk, she found a vase of cut flowers welcoming her to her new office—courtesy of me. After the annoyance and headache of sorting through soaked files and papers, and moving boxes, this put a smile on her face. If you have a client who travels too much and is tired out from it, find out from their assistant where they are headed. Call ahead to the hotel, ask for the concierge or the catering department, and arrange to have a snack delivered to the room that night, courtesy of you.

Here's a time-saving tip on the logistics of giving gifts to business clients. Don't go out, shop, buy the gift, wrap it, and mail it yourself—that's too time consuming. Instead, shop by catalog from any of the many fine mail order companies that specialize in gift merchandise. They will wrap the package, send it for you, even enclose a note from you.

You probably receive many such mail order catalogs each year, especially at Xmas. Just save them in a file folder marked "MAIL ORDER BUSINESS GIFTS." Whenever you need to send a gift, open the folder, pick out a nice item from one of the catalogs, call a toll-free 800 number, and order using your credit card. Remember to keep the catalogs on file so you have the information handy when you need it.

Do Your Clients Small Personal Favors

From time to time your clients will ask for small personal favors that really do not relate to your business relationship or the work you are doing for them. My feeling is, as long as the favors aren't illegal, immoral, unethical, or unreasonable, you should do them if you can.

For example, after a meeting, a client, knowing I write books, said, "Bob, I hope you don't mind me asking, but I have an idea for a book and I think it would really sell. Do you have any advice on how to get it published?"

I mailed him several how-to reports I've written on how to get books written and published and also gave him half a dozen names of agents, editors, and publishers. Did this increase my business with them? Not visibly. Did it increase my goodwill with this particular person at the client organization? I hope so, but don't know. Would ignoring the request and not responding have been noticed and created negative feelings from this person? I strongly believe so.

So when a client asks, "Can you do me a favor?" don't ignore it, and don't say yes and then not follow through, hoping they will forget. They won't. Instead, say yes, then follow up immediately— as if this were a paying assignment—and do the favor you promised.

Even those favors that do not seem to pay off immediately for you create goodwill that cannot possibly hurt and that may pay off handsomely in the future. For instance, I did several favors for one client who never reciprocated, gave me little business, and ultimately left the company and took a job out of state. But a year later, he referred two people to me, both of whom instantly became paying clients. So what goes around does come around.

SEPARATING BUSINESS FROM PERSONAL LIFE

In TV situation comedies, employees frequently get involved in the personal lives of their bosses and clients. Must you? No. Some service providers enjoy mixing their personal and business lives and have very little separation between them. One friend, for example, works at home and has a telephone extension for his business line on the nightstand next to his bed, so he can take calls from clients or the media (he is a publicist) at any time of the day or night (with no advance notice he once did a half-hour interview on a call-in radio show at 4 A.M. from his bed). Another has so intermixed business and social life that at his thirtieth wedding anniversary party, 90 percent of the guests were business clients, associates, or colleagues.

By comparison, my business and personal lives are completely separate. I have an outside office and separate phone lines for business, and do not socialize with clients.

Is it necessary to allow clients into your social life? Or is it better not to? My conclusion after ten years as a service provider and seminar leader is this:

1. It is not necessary to socialize with clients to do extremely well in your business. You want to be *friendly* with clients, but you don't have to "hang out" with them evenings and weekends.

2. You can be successful without mixing your business and social life, and many people are.

3. Many other successful people do mix business and personal life, and this is effective for them in forming strong relationships with clients. But most do it because it's *natural* for them—they have an outgoing personality and generally enjoy hanging out with clients.

4. Therefore, socialize with clients only if you are so inclined. Don't force it or go against your nature if it's not for you.

How to Handle "Small Talk" With Clients

As discussed in Chapter 5, some small talk helps to strengthen the bond between you and the client. But keep the small talk to fairly safe, neutral subjects, and don't let it go on too long. After a few minutes, move on to business.

The longer you engage in small talk, the more relaxed your mind becomes, the more you "let down your guard," and the more likely you are to talk too much and say the wrong thing. So small talk is okay, but keep it to a minimum, and always be in control, thinking before you speak and aware of what you are saying and who you are saying it to.

Attending Client Functions, Parties, and Meetings

If a client invites you to a hospitality suite, holiday party, company family day, or other company-sponsored event, it is nice to attend and stay for an hour, but it is not necessary: the client understands you have a business and a life, and their invitation is more of a courtesy and a way to say "We think of you as a friend" than a mandate saying, "You better come—or else."

So if you are in the neighborhood or at the trade show, by all means put in an appearance. But don't go out of your way or rearrange your schedule to do so.

LESSONS FROM SUCCESSFUL SERVICE PROVIDERS

According to James L. Heskett, writing in the *Harvard Business Review*,[7] many successful service providers have strategies in common that offer lessons to other companies. These include:

- Close coordination between marketing and operations
- A strategy built around elements of a strategic service vision
- An ability to redirect the strategic service vision inward to focus on vital employee groups
- A stress on the control of quality based on a set of shared values, peer group status, generous incentives, and where possible a close relationship with the customer
- A cool appraisal of the effects of scale on both efficiency and effectiveness
- The substitution of information for other assets
- The exploitation of information to generate new business

---

[7] *Harvard Business Review*, March 1987, p. 125.

How

TO HANDLE

PROBLEMS

AND COMPLAINTS

---------------- **CHAPTER 7** ----------------

Handling Price
Complaints

In today's economy, with consumer confidence low and business budgets limited, your clients are looking to spend less, save money, and get things as cheaply as possible.

At home, the consumer is experiencing a kind of "downward mobility." The new generation is the first that will probably have a lower, not higher, standard of living than their parents. People are strapped for cash, afraid to spend money, and price conscious. Some are downright worried about keeping their jobs or their homes.

At the office, the business buyer has a smaller budget than in years past, and for some products and services, the budget has been eliminated. Business buyers frequently "look good" to their managements when they can buy cheap and save the company money.

Since they don't want to sacrifice quality or take the risk of dealing with unproven vendors to accomplish these cost savings, they put pressure on existing vendors to reduce prices. In situations where acceptance of your price would have been routine years ago, now clients are haggling and sending more and more jobs out for "competitive bids."

Their intent is not necessarily to switch service providers, but to get *you*, their preferred vendor, to *feel as if* the client has many options and would go elsewhere if necessary. The idea is to make you more flexible and willing to haggle and negotiate, so they can get your service at a lower fee than you normally quote. If you subcontract to other service firms, you'll feel the pinch even more. As the prime contractor is forced to bid lower and lower to win contracts, their profit margins shrink. If they can buy a subcontracted service at significantly less than they were budgeted to pay,

177

the difference is money in their pockets. So prime contractors are especially looking to get the "lowball" price.

Does this mean people buy on price only and that service, quality, and value no longer matter? On the contrary, more than ever clients not only want, but demand and *expect to get*, the best service, quality, and value *with* a low price. As Joseph Balaban, vice president of Database America observes, "For a service provider, there's the difficulty in keeping a client happy who wants to get it faster and for less, and whenever possible, wants more of it."

Handling price complaints and coping with the objection "Your price is too high" is not, as you well know, restricted to selling new accounts. In the service business, virtually every job or project is a new assignment that requires a proposal, recommendation, or at least a simple cost estimate. For any job that is not "standard" or quoted off a fixed rate card (and even for many that are), price can be an issue and a client can object and ask for a lower price at any time.

How you handle and resolve the price objection is extremely important because:

- It determines whether you get the work or not.
- It determines at what price (and therefore at what profit) you get the work.
- The manner in which it is handled can strengthen or weaken (even destroy) your rapport and relationships with your clients.

HOW SERVICE PROVIDERS TYPICALLY RESPOND TO PRICE-CONSCIOUS CLIENTS

Because of the weak economy, many service providers are more flexible and end up working for lower rates and fees than in the past. The benefit is that it helps them hold on to their most valuable asset—their customers. The negative is that you end up working twice as hard and making half as much money as you used to.

What to do? Get used to it. The "golden years" of the 1980s are gone forever, and the tough, competitive "Age of the Customer" has replaced them. You are going to have to work smarter and harder and give better service than ever to get and keep clients.

And you'll have to do it at competitive prices. That's the way it is—no words of comfort for you here. The service providers who are successful change with the times, accept it, and move ahead. Those who still think they can be prima donnas or charge outrageous fees are in for a rude awakening.

Of course, this does not mean you agree to provide whatever service the client wants at whatever price the client wants to pay. Rather, you must learn to negotiate so that it is a win-win situation: the client is able to hire you at a price he or she can afford; you get hired at a price that gives you a decent profit.

As I write this, a client called about a large job consisting of many individual tasks. I had given prices for each task and a total; she wanted to negotiate a lower total if she gave me the entire job as a package.

She suggested a figure; I countered; we split the difference. I added the condition that I would do the job at the reduced rate only if it was not a rush and I was given plenty of time. She agreed to that also; then she said, "I'm glad we were able to hammer this out. I wanted you to do the whole thing, but your original total would have busted my budget. Now I feel I'm not being squeezed as much. Thanks."

She gets the service she needs at a price she can afford. I get a large assignment, several thousand dollars in revenue, a happy client, and a good relationship that continues without disruption. However, most service providers are not very good at negotiating prices or responding to clients who say they want to pay less—for two reasons.

First, we're not used to it. In the 1980s, many of us tended to quote fairly high fees and, because of the high demand for our services, could pick and choose, working only with those clients who met our price. So we did not have to negotiate fees or respond to the client who balked; we simply worked for those clients who instantly said "yes."

Second, in many service firms, the person selling the service is also the person rendering the service, so any challenge of fee is taken as a personal affront (though it should not be). In product selling, if the customer says the price is too high, the salesperson may negotiate, but is not emotionally involved in the cost negotiation—after all, it's the TV set the client doesn't want to pay $799 for, not him.

In a service business, however, many of us tend to interpret the client's objection to our price as an insult or attack on our self-worth. After all, if the client says I'm not worth $500, isn't he demeaning my worth as a professional and a human being?

For these two reasons, most service providers react poorly and ineffectively to clients who object to the price for a particular project or assignment. The resulting confrontation usually loses the job and generates ill will that can damage or destroy the client/vendor relationship.

The rest of this chapter presents strategies for dealing with price-conscious clients effectively, meaning:

- You maintain your dignity, "cool," and self-respect.
- You do not offend, put off, or in any way argue with the client.
- The client comes away with the impression that you are flexible, reasonable, and interested in helping them and that you have their best interests in mind.
- You work out a mutually beneficial arrangement concerning fees to be paid and services to be provided for those fees.
- Both you and the client are pleased, happy, and comfortable with the agreement, its terms, and the manner in which it was arrived at.

Let's get started.

HOW TO NOT TAKE PRICE NEGOTIATIONS PERSONALLY

You must respond to the price-conscious client who attempts to get you to lower your fee in a professional and not an emotional manner. The best way to do this is to look at things from the client's point of view. When clients ask, "Can you do it for less?" they are not looking to force your fee down for the sake of "beating" you in a negotiation or bragging about how they hired a top-notch firm like you for a bargain-basement price. Nor are they saying that you aren't good at what you do or that your service is not worth what you charge.

Rather, they are indicating that, they cannot or will not pay the fee you quoted, for one of several possible reasons,

- They don't have the money.

- They have the money but want to hold on to it because business is slow or money is tight.
- They are cheap and always like to pay as little as they can get away with.
- They don't understand exactly what you do or why you are the tops in your field and can command the type of fees you do (this would apply only to new clients; existing clients, of course, already know you and what you do).
- They think they might be able to do it themselves.
- They think one of their other vendors might do it cheaper.
- Another vendor has submitted a lower bid; the client would prefer to retain you, but needs your bid to be closer to the lower bid to engage your services.
- They have been told by management to freeze spending.
- The particular problem this project addresses is not, in their minds, bad enough or major enough to warrant the kind of money involved in hiring you.

In all these situations, can you see how reasonable it is for the client at least to inquire whether you can do it for less or reduce your fee? And do you see how, if they rely on you and trust you for advice, it's your duty to at least explore other options and see if you can meet their needs within their budget constraint?

Also, look at the list of reasons. Are they an insult to you or your skills as a professional? No. The client's haggling over fees should not be taken as a negative or an indication that they do not value you; on the contrary, you should be flattered that they came to you and want to seek a workable arrangement because you are their number one choice for performing this type of service for them.

To become less emotional and more professional about cost estimating and fee negotiations, take the attitude that it's an opportunity rather than a problem—an opportunity to help the client meet a particular need cost effectively. After all, that's why you exist: to help your clients.

DON'T GET ANGRY—BE EMPATHETIC

Don't get angry with the client who is trying to get more for less. We all are. Do you instantly agree to pay the $14,000 the dealer is asking for a new car when you know full well he can be negotiated down to $13,000 or $13,500? Of course not. And neither does your client. You're not a car, but it's the same principle: the client attempting to buy at a lower price is seeking to solve a problem and save money, not demean you or your trade.

Let's say the client says, "I can't pay that much." You can respond either rigidly in a noncooperative manner or flexibly in a problem-solving manner.

> RIGID: That's what it costs! I'm the number one person in my field and I am worth what I charge.

> PROBLEM SOLVING: I understand. Can you tell me what budget you do have, so we can see whether we can get this work done within those constraints?

The first response would probably be given in anger, or at least in a terse, stiff tone of voice. What's wrong with it? First, it is haughty. You come off as having an inflated opinion of yourself or being arrogant, which turns people off. Second, it's so final that it leaves you and the client absolutely no room to maneuver.

For most services, coming up with the initial fee you quoted the client is a matter of educated guesswork anyway, and the price could easily have been lower or higher, depending on who estimated the job. When you are completely rigid and unyielding, and unwilling to consider even the possibility of being flexible about fees, you make it extremely difficult for clients to continue to do business with you.

Most products are standard, off-the-shelf items with no difference between them: TV set number 500 rolling off the production line is pretty much the same as TV set number 499. But services are much more flexible, and you succeed in selling services and satisfying clients by tailoring your service to their needs. The price you charge is one aspect of your service, so why not be flexible about that as well?

As you'll see, I don't mean working for $10 an hour when your regular rate is $100 an hour or doing a $5,000 job for $2,500. There are easy ways to make a profit equal to or just slightly less than your normal margin on these fee-negotiated jobs, and you can cut costs by *tailoring the package of services* you sell the client, not selling yourself short.

HOW TO EVALUATE WHAT THE CLIENT SAYS IN RESPONSE TO YOUR COST ESTIMATE

Many sales training programs teach you that the client is lying and your job is to uncover the real reason why they are trying to get you to lower your price. My experience is to the contrary, as the following scenarios illustrate.

"We Don't Have the Budget"

When the clients say this or tell me "I can't afford it," nine times out of ten they are telling the truth or at least the truth as *they perceive it*, which is really the same thing.

You can't change factual circumstances restricting the client's purchasing power. For example, if a large corporate client stops hiring you because management has put a halt on all spending for outside services such as yours, there is nothing you can do to cause that company to unfreeze the budget. Therefore it's pointless to argue or plead your case.

"Our Budget is Frozen"

When a client tells me this, I express empathy; then I ask how long the budget freeze will be in effect. Usually they will give a date or time frame after which they expect to have money to spend again. I make note of that date and recontact them to discuss the project at that time.

"The Project Is on Hold"

Another client comment many service providers take as a threat to get them to lower prices is to say, "The project is on hold" or "We can't move forward until such and such happens." Service providers tell me, "The client is just saying that, so when you thought the job was a 'done deal,' you're suddenly unsure whether the project will come through at all. That unsettles you, and the client can say you have to be more flexible or lower your price if the project is to get back on track."

Again, baloney. When a client says "The project is on hold" or "We can't move forward," they mean just that. Your price is not the issue. The best strategy is to ask what the cause of delay is, and whether you can do anything to help move things forward. The client will say there is nothing you can do to help, but appreciates that you care enough to try to solve their problem.

"I Have to Get My Manager's Approval"

Another thing clients say that many service professionals think is a ruse to induce lower fees is "I think the price is okay but I have to run it by my manager." The service provider believes this is an imaginary "good cop/bad cop" scenario where the client says, "I feel your price is fair, but my boss hit the roof. Can you do it for $750?"

Again, my experience is that clients are not lying. Most corporate people have to run a price by at least one other person, if not an entire committee, before signing off. And with consumers, you can sell one spouse only to be told when you come by to close the deal, "My husband/wife thinks it's too costly/doesn't want it" and so on.

If the decision is made by committee, it's desirable to meet or talk with each individual on the committee. That way, you can find out who has the objection to your price and deal with that person individually; once he or she is sold, the rest will sign off.

WHY CLIENTS SOMETIMES SUFFER FROM "STICKER SHOCK"

"Sticker shock" is the shock the consumer experiences when shopping for an item, looking at the price tag, and discovering it costs much more than he or she thought it would. Clients getting estimates on your services can also suffer from sticker shock when your quote, although fair and reasonable, is more than they had imagined it would be.

Do not be offended if the client exclaims "That's too much!" or says "That seems awfully expensive" immediately after you quote your fee. They have made the very human mistake of giving you their gut reaction instead of thinking about it and phrasing their objection in more agreeable, less confrontational terms.

Keep in mind that money's tight and you're expensive. Many of us are well paid, and our clients are sometimes jealous, offended, or even outraged at what we charge—not because the service isn't worth it, but because we seem to be making "too much money."

Often, it isn't so: The client, hearing our fee, immediately translates this into pure cash, not realizing that we have overhead, expenses, rent, sales and marketing costs, research and development, computer equipment, bills to pay, and all those other expenses to cover out of the check, and what is left is not such a princely sum as she thought. But remember, the client does not think in these terms, so the *perception* is that you're making "too much money"—*too much money* being defined by most people as more than they make or think they can make (or more than they think someone in your profession should be paid).

The key is that when the client expresses shock or voices an immediate objection to the price quoted, it is an emotional response, not necessarily a refusal to pay or signal that they want to haggle. So there is no need at that point to stammer or apologize or say "Well, what do you want to pay?" as so many do. Instead, you answer politely, "Yes, it takes many hours of hard work plus years of experience to [do whatever it is you do]." Then let them make the next move. (You want them to respond. If you talk first, you lose the negotiation.)

HOW TO GUARANTEE THAT YOUR PRICE FITS WITHIN THE CLIENT'S BUDGET

The easiest way to make sure your quotation or cost estimate is in line with what the client can afford is to ask in advance what they are willing to pay.

For example, suppose an existing client calls you in for a meeting. They say, "We want you to do so-and-so for us. What will it cost?" How do you respond?

Some service providers advocate asking the client their budget up front. When you know in advance what the client is looking to pay, you can tailor your proposal and quotation to fit that budget.

For instance, if a client wants you to landscape his property, you might ask if he has a budget for the job. Based on that response, you can do your preliminary sketch and proposal to create a design that the client will be pleased with and can afford.

As with many services, a landscaping job can vary enormously in price, depending on budget. The factors which raise or lower price include rarity of plants; density of plants; regrading of property; construction of walls, walks, or ponds; and so on.

It makes sense to get an idea of the budget and tailor the proposal accordingly. A client who says "My budget is $2,000" should get a nice basic design with some ground cover and small but tasteful bushes and plants. On the other hand, the client who says "My budget is $9,000" can have a lusher design with some exotic trees, a stone wall, perhaps even a pond with waterfall. It is a perfectly legitimate action and not at all unethical to ask a client, "What is your budget?"

When should you ask what the budget is, and when should you not? On small jobs, routine tasks, and other items that are fairly standard, you should probably just quote the price without asking the budget. When asked what your law firm charges for a simple will, you should respond, "$300," or whatever the charge is. The client understands the fees on smaller and more standard jobs don't have much if any room for negotiation and will either hire you or look elsewhere.

On large jobs, customized work, and projects that cannot be easily priced off the top of your head, it's your choice. You can ask the client, "What is your budget?" Or you can defer the issue of budget until after the quotation is submitted. On small to medium-sized jobs and standard jobs I tend to quote directly; on large, complex, and nonstandard jobs I tend to ask what the budget is.

Once in a while a client will object to your asking the budget question. "Why do you need to know that to quote a fee?" they may ask. I respond, "It is going to take a lot of time and effort on my part to work up the estimate and write the proposal. I don't want to waste your time or mine if the budget is not large enough for you to retain me, so could you give me a rough feel or range of budget? If it's too low, I'll tell you so immediately; if it's within the ballpark, I'll go back to my office and work up an estimate as you requested." That's extremely reasonable, and clients will not find it objectionable.

You will, however, have some clients who respond, "Gee, I really haven't bought this kind of thing before and have *no idea* of what it's worth. I really can't give you a budget; I want *you* to tell *me* what it costs. Then I'll decide." In such a case, you have to just go ahead and work up an estimate based upon the work involved.

GIVE THE CLIENT A PRICE RANGE RATHER THAN A FIXED, LOCKED-IN FIGURE

If you are afraid the client will find your estimate too high, you can quote a range of fees. By doing so, you have a greater chance of presenting a number that is within the budget. You also indicate flexibility, whereas quoting a single fixed figure ($5,499) indicates lack of flexibility.

The range you quote can be narrow or quite broad. It's up to you. An example of quoting a narrow range would be, "We can program your computer to do so-and-so for between $4,000 and $4,500." Some clients may say yes to the range and allow the final quote to stand as a range. You charge the low end if the work is easier than expected and takes less time than anticipated; the high end if numerous changes, revisions, and extra work are required.

An alternative is to quote the fee as a *choice* of ranges from which the client can select. The client calls you in and says, "We want you to produce a thingamabob for us. What will it cost?" You are unsure as to whether their budget is big or small, but really want the job and are afraid a high quote will blow them away. You respond, "Well, we recently did something similar for several of our clients. Here's what it cost. Company A wanted us to produce a top-of-the-line, premium-quality thingamabob for them, with all the bells and whistles and complete service from start to finish. That type of job costs about $4,000 to $5,000.

"Company B chose a middle-range option. They still got a high-quality job, but without the bells and whistles, and we didn't do X, Y, and Z for them. This costs about $2,000 to $3,000.

"Company C was on a limited budget and wanted the plain vanilla thingamabob—no options, no extras; a good job, but nothing fancy. We did this simple job for them and they were happy. That basic, no-frills job costs about $1,000 to $1,500.

"Mr. Client, which of these seems within your budget?"

My experience is that seven out of ten clients, when given this scenario, choose the *middle* range rather than the low end or high end. So if you want to get $2,000 to $3,000, quote that as your mid-range job.

The big advantage of this is that it eliminates price complaints because here, you are not telling the client what it costs. Instead, you are letting them tell *you* what they *want* it to cost.

The way most service providers quote fees—a fixed, nonnegotiable price—is like going to a restaurant, being handed a menu, and opening it to find there is only one item on it. You have no choice—you either order it or eat nothing—and if you don't like that dish, you'll probably leave.

Restaurants succeed because they offer their customers a *menu* of items and prices to choose from, so that the taste and budget requirements of the customer can always be satisfied.

That's why you never hear a patron ask a waitress, "$19.95 for steak is more than I can afford; can you serve me one for $10?" If the customer has only $10, they can order the spaghetti and meat balls instead.

To avoid pricing conflicts that cause confrontations and arguments between you and your valued clients, run your service business like a restaurant. Offer a "menu" of different services and different price ranges and help your customers select based on need and budget. As I've said throughout this book, flexibility = success in the "Age of the Customer."

NEGOTIATE BY ADJUSTING SERVICE RATHER THAN BY CUTTING PROFIT MARGIN OR BASE RATE

How can you be flexible about price without underpricing yourself? Simple. You negotiate by adjusting the *amount of service* you provide rather than cutting your hourly rate, profit margin, or base fee.

For example, let's say you are a management consultant. The client asks for a cost proposal to do a certain type of consulting program. Your proposal breaks down the tasks and steps involved, shows the number of hours required for each, and gives the total number of hours; the fee is based on the number of hours multiplied by your hourly rate. Since the total was 100 hours and you charge $200 an hour, the project fee is $20,000.

The client balks. "That's way too much!" they object.

"I understand," you reply calmly. "$20,000 is not an insignificant sum. Yet we know the potential pay off of doing this work is a cost savings of many hundreds of thousands of dollars per year over a period of ten to fifteen years. Does it seem sensible to invest $20,000 to save $500,000 or more?"

The client doesn't buy it. "That may be the case, Bob, but I just don't have the money in the budget."

You reply, "Well, give me an idea of what your budget is for this project, and I can try and tailor the scope of work to fit that budget and still deliver the result you want."

The client thinks. "I don't know, I suppose we can afford $15,000."

You reply (either on the spot or after a more considered study of the problem back at your office), "Okay, here's the solution. On phase II we eliminate the two days of training the support staff; their managers can do that for them, and you will save $3,200. On phase IV we will elimimate the second audit survey; this was an extra safety check, and we live without it. That saves 9 hours of work and an additional $1,800. This gives us essentially the same job and result, with two steps elimimated, at your budget price of $15,000. How does that sound?"

Note what was done: you accommodated the client's budget constraint not by lowering your rate or profit margin (e.g., dropping your fee from $200-to-$100 an hour) or by simply agreeing to do the same work for whatever the client wants to spend.

What would have been wrong with those options? It's bad to lower your fee for two reasons. First, you'll be earning less. Second, there's no logical reason for it. Why should a $200 an hour consultant suddenly work for $100 an hour because someone says the price is too high? If you do that, the client will suspect that you really do not earn $200 an hour, as you claim.

As for the other option, it is also wrong to say simply, "Okay, what do you want to pay?" in response to a client who objects to price and then agree to the lower fee with no adjustment in scope or level of service. Why is this bad?

If you immediately jump to a lower price with no negotiation or adjustment, clients conclude that your original estimate was inflated and will therefore assume *all* first estimates you present also have a lot of "fat" in them. As a result, they will form the habit of objecting to your price and negotiating you down on every estimate *whether the initial estimate is too high for their budget or not*. It also makes them feel you are not forthright and honest in your pricing, and so reduces trust and credibility.

As we've just seen, the best way to give clients a lower price when they need it is to *reduce the scope of service proportionally to the reduction in price*. This makes the job affordable for the client, gives you the profit you want to earn, keeps your credibility high, makes the client appreciate your fairness and flexibility, and is a reasonable, sensible method the client can understand and accept.

Reducing Services by Eliminating Removable Options

A variation of the technique of reducing the scope of service to accommodate a restricted budget *after* submitting the original estimate is to submit the price bid or cost estimate in such a way that such reductions in service are built into it as "removable options," allowing the client to choose their level of price and service from the oral or written estimate you present.

In such a scenario, the primary estimate is the full job at the full price. Below that, you show different elements as options which can be removed from the total job, along with the cost reduction resulting from removal of that item.

For example, a construction estimate for adding a room to our home showed the removable options as follows:

TOTAL FOR ADDITION OF NEW ROOM: $25,000

SUBSTITUTE BRAND X FOR PELLA WINDOWS: Subtract $1,000

SUBSTITUTE CARPET FOR OAK FLOORING: Subtract $1,800

ELIMINATION OF SKY LIGHTS: Subtract $1,500

ELIMINATION OF TRACK SPOTLIGHTS: Subtract $700.

This way, if $25,000 is more than I had planned on spending, I see by subtracting the options that I can still get a room for only $20,000, if I am willing to go without the extras.

At this point you may object, "This sounds good, but my clients are going to want the $25,000 job, with all the extras, and want me to do it for the $20,000!" What about that?

It depends on so many factors: how much you need the work, how flexible you are willing to be, whether your prices are in line with what others are charging, and whether you rarely or frequently lose jobs based on price.

Let's examine some of those factors.

HOW THE NEED FOR WORK AFFECTS YOUR PRICE NEGOTIATIONS

Ideally, you should approach every negotiation as if you do not need the work or care whether you get the job. This gives you the inner strength and confidence to be accommodating and cooperative but not frightened or weak-willed; you will work with the client, but not get pushed around or bow to unreasonable demands.

Unfortunately, while this advice sounds good in theory, it doesn't always work so well in real life. When we feel we need a job, we negotiate from a position of weakness rather than strength. And this makes us more vulnerable. As a result, we make price concessions that, although they win the job, make us feel we are being paid too little.

There are two types of need that weaken us: financial and psychological. Financial need is the need for money. In tough times, many of us aren't making as much as we used to. Others aren't making it at all. So when your plate is empty and you've hit a dry spell, and a big fat project is dangled in front of you, you want to get it. You need the money. And you're willing to bargain.

The other type of need is psychological. Some of us cannot stand "slow" or "down" times. We need to be busy: either because it makes us feel secure or because we need the approval of others—and getting hired by clients is the ultimate form of approval. A minority of service providers even have a psychological need to be busy because they are workaholics: they're not happy unless they have more business than they can handle and are working from early morning to after dark.

The question is: Should you let either financial or psychological need affect your negotiating posture when it comes to fees? I cannot answer this for you. I can only present the two schools of thought and let you be the judge.

The first school of thought says, "Negotiate the job as if you don't need it, as if you don't care whether you get it or not. No matter how badly you want it, be willing to walk away. That's the only way you can negotiate from strength. Otherwise, the client will perceive you as weak and take advantage of you."

The second school of thought says, "While ideally the foregoing may be true, in reality you have to do what is best for you at the time. If you have a strong need to win a project, either for financial or ego reasons, there is nothing wrong with doing more or charging less to get it—as long as you realize that that's what you are doing and are comfortable making such a concession.

"After all, in today's tough economic times, clients are spending less than ever before. So why risk losing the job? If the job normally goes for $2,000 and the client wants to pay $1,000, and you have nothing else on the docket, isn't it better to make $1,000 this week than zero? Take it!"

I vascillate between these two positions; however, what I think is not important. What is important is that (1) you can choose to follow either path and (2) if you choose to negotiate more when you are in need, you should realize there is nothing wrong with it.

It is nothing to be ashamed of; everybody does it; and those who say they do not are either lucky or liars. Dr. Robert Gilbert says, "The ultimate skill is flexibility."

WHAT TO DO IF YOU OCCASIONALLY LOSE JOBS BECAUSE OF YOUR HIGH FEES

Nobody gets every job they bid on. If you do, you know that your fees are way too low and that many clients would probably pay more than you are now asking for.

If you are priced reasonably, in line with what others of your caliber and experience are charging, you will find that when existing clients ask you to bid on new work, your price will be acceptable to them as is, or with some minor adjustment, from 70 to 90 percent of the time.

That means 10 to 30 percent of the time, your price will be a little too high for that client for that particular job. Most of the time the reason is that the job does not warrant bringing in someone at your high level to handle it, but the client doesn't want to do it in-house or trust it to an inferior vendor. So they figure, "Why not ask Joe and see what the price is. Maybe we can sneak it into the budget somewhere." So the 10 to 30 percent of the time when the job never materializes, it's because asking you for a quotation was more of a "let's check and see if it's feasible" situation rather than a definite assignment.

The conclusion is this: if you occasionally lose jobs because of your pricing, but you win the majority of jobs you quote on, your prices are in the right range, and your fee negotiation techniques are working. So don't worry about trying to improve the win ratio by lowering fees or being more flexible than you already are. You can if you wish, but it isn't necessary. Your pricing is already right on target.

HAVE A NEGOTIATING HIERARCHY

Although "haggling" over fees has become a fact of life for service providers, there is no need to haggle with everybody. You should be flexible and accommodating only with those whose business you want to get and keep. On the other hand, for those whose business you don't need and are willing to do without, you can be less flexible and more insistent on sticking to your guns—although this too should be done in a polite, friendly, and helpful way rather than rudely or confrontationally.

Which clients do you accommodate and which are you tougher with? The choice is yours. I have established a "client hierarchy" for my business which I use to determine how flexible I will be with any particular person. This hierarchy, in order, is:

1. Existing clients, good
2. Potential clients, good
3. Existing clients, marginal
4. Potential clients, marginal

Good existing clients. My existing accounts—the good ones, anyway—are my number one business priority. I define a good account as one that is profitable, pays good rates, gives me a lot of assignments of the type I enjoy doing, pays bills on time, and is pleasant to work with. These are my most precious business assets, and I will do everything in my power to keep them happy. Interestingly, although I will be the most accommodating with these clients, they are the ones seeking the fewest concessions.

Good potential clients. Good prospects are second in importance. When I am negotiating fees with a prospect who has all the characteristics of a good client (except they are not yet *my* client), I will be creative in trying to package my services and fees to fit their needs. If I do, they will become a good client, and you can't have too many of those.

I always place the needs of my good clients before good prospects; serving existing accounts is even more important than selling. And you want your clients to know you feel that way.

Marginal existing clients. Third on the hierarchy is marginal accounts. Because they are clients, I will treat them well. But if the account is not enjoyable or profitable, I cannot make too many price concessions—otherwise we would reach a point where the work is simply not worth doing.

Marginal potential clients. At the bottom of the hierarchy are marginal prospects. If someone is not a client, and is not a person or company I particularly want to do business with, I am fairly firm and unyielding in my fees and terms.

Since you cannot please all of the people all of the time, I recommend you establish your own client hierarchy. With it, you'll quickly be able to determine who you negotiate fees with and who you do not, so at least you can please some of the people most of the time.

WHAT TO DO IF YOU CONSISTENTLY LOSE JOBS BECAUSE YOUR FEES ARE TOO HIGH

If you consistently lose jobs from existing clients and the reason is price, it is an indication that your fees are not realistic, are not in line with what others in your profession are charging, or at the very least are on the upper end of what is considered "reasonable."

You might object, "But I've been charging these fees, and *getting* them, for years." Yes, but we're not in the 1980s any more. The economic climate has changed. The client, not the service provider, is in control. The marketplace is more competitive.

In many industries and professions, fee increases have not kept pace with inflation. In others, fees have remained flat or actually *declined* in recent years. One well-known direct mail writer summed it up best in a letter he sent me which said, "There are twice as many vendors competing for half as many jobs as there were six years ago, and fees today are half of what they were then."

Your profession may not have suffered so greatly, but it is unreasonable to assume that you can charge today what you charged in the past and continue to win and keep clients. You have to be aware of what clients are paying in today's market, what your competition is charging, and whether your fees are high, low, or medium.

I recommend that you or someone you know call up your major competitors and either ask for their sales literature and rate sheets or ask them to quote a fee on a typical job. You should be aware at all times of what your competitors are doing to win and keep clients and how much they are charging. If you are shy about doing this research, ask or hire someone to do it for you.

HOW TO PRICE IN COMPETITIVE BID SITUATIONS

Most of us serving clients on an ongoing basis charge a fair price for value delivered. We don't overcharge or rip off clients. But we don't undercharge, either. With a good client who is a "regular," you figure they like your service, are comfortable with you, and will pay your fee as long as it's not unreasonable or outrageous.

We assume with our ongoing clients that, when they ask us for a price, it's because they want to know what the job will cost before we start, not to compare our price with bids from other vendors. We don't think of ourselves as "competing" for the job; we assume the job is ours as long as the price is not out of whack.

But more and more, clients are seeking second and third bids from your competitors on jobs that once would have been sole bids by the preferred vendor—you. Why? Not necessarily because they are eager to switch. They aren't. Most clients prefer to work with a "known quantity" and seek other sources only when given reason to. The reason for the multiple bids is to make a comparison check between your price and those of your competitors, to ensure that you have not gotten "too comfortable"—that is, to make sure your prices are still competitive.

Even if your prices are fair and competitive, this can be a problem. The reason? Your competitors are hungry for new clients and very, very eager to take the client away from you or at least get a "foot in the door" by doing a job for the client. And you would prefer for that not to happen. After all, once the client sees what your competitor can do, they might like it. And suddenly, you have half the business instead of all of it, and a second vendor has muscled in on you.

This means that if you know or feel fairly certain you are in a "competitive bid" situation—that is, the client is getting estimates from more than one vendor—you should probably price a bit more competitively on this project than when you know you are the sole bidder.

How much less? As a rule, make your price in a competitive bid situation 5 to 15 percent lower than the amount you would bid if you were the sole bidder and there was no competition. This increases the probability that your bid will in the same range as the others, yet keep it high enough so it's not obvious to the client that you are low-balling.

In such a situation, where you are the preferred vendor and where the client is seeking competitive bids as a "reality check" to ensure your prices are in line, you need not be the low bid to win. In fact, the client wants to hire you and is looking for justification to continue doing so. All they need is to be reassured that your prices are reasonable, not that they are the lowest. A 5 to 15 percent reduction in cost will usually accomplish this.

HOW TO OFFER THE CLIENT A LOW PRICE AND STILL RETAIN THEIR RESPECT

Why are you offering a lower price to the client, and why are you so willing to negotiate? Because you want the job, yes, but also because you want to serve the client and help them find a way to afford and benefit from the services you offer. Fee negotiation is a service function as well as a sales function. It's not done because you're a wimp or are scared of the client. It's done because you want to be the client's partner and help him achieve his goals (while you achieve yours as well).

Too many service providers feel lousy about haggling over fees, and this feeling comes through to the client. If you think it's undignified or a sign of weakness to negotiate fees, you will perform the task in an undignified and weak manner, and that is how you will come across to the client.

On the other hand, if you view fee negotiation as part of the process, as a positive rather than a negative, you will perform the task in a professional and helpful manner. You'll feel proud, and your dignity and self-esteem will be high. This too will come across to the client, enabling you openly to discuss fees in a manner that lets you retain your dignity—and makes the client see you as dignified and professional.

To continue this train of thought, what we are doing when we negotiate fees is help the client—specifically, we help him or her benefit from our service by finding a way to make our service affordable.

The desire to help clients is a key attitude of all successful service providers. By conducting fee negotiations in the framework of helping clients rather than begging for work, you do it in a way that makes clients grateful for your flexibility in money matters, yet does not make you seem desperate or unsuccessful in their eyes.

There's a difference between telling the client "I need the work; please give me the job; I'll do it for any price" and saying "Let's see if we can work out an arrangement that enables your company to use my services at a price that meets your budget." The former is indicative of someone who is desperate and needs the work; the latter is indicative of a successful professional who is supportive of his clients and cooperative with them.

MAKING IT UP ON VOLUME

"Being flexible to help meet the client's needs" is one justification for negotiating prices. Another is the volume argument, which goes something like this:

"My fee for recording a radio commercial is $400. I cannot lower that fee for a one-shot assignment. But, Mr. Client, you mentioned you need six commercials. If you give me all six to do at one time, I can give you a volume discount and do the entire job within your budget of $2,000."

This makes sense for you—and the client. From the client's point of view, many of the things he buys are cheaper if bought in volume, so why not your services? A volume discount is something he is used to getting, so when you present it as the rationale for lowering your fee to meet his budget, it makes perfect sense and does not seem arbitrary.

From the service provider's point of view, doing the six commercials all in one shot will probably take less time and cost less than doing six separate commercials at six different times for six different clients. The six spots can be done in sequence faster than the individual commercials; it means one trip to the studio and one day's rental of studio time instead of six; the similarities in spots probably mean the series can be done in less time. So you are making more profit on the series than when doing one-shot commercials, and it's perfectly reasonable to pasw part of the cost savings along to your client in the form of a volume discount.

MAKING "CONDITIONAL" LOW-PRICE OFFERS

Another was to lower your price without seeming to come out the loser is to request concessions, conditions, or special terms from the client in exchange for agreeing to reduce your fee. In essence, you say to the client, "Okay, I will perform the service within your budget, but in return, I want X, Y, and Z." What are some of the concessions, conditions, and terms that are possible?

- *Getting cash up front.* "We will reduce the fee 20 percent to meet your budget, but at this low price, we cannot bill you and would need payment up front."

- *Offering improved terms.* "We will reduce the fee 20 percent to meet your budget, but at this low price, we would want to be paid in full net 15 days, not the usual 30 or 60."

- *Limitating service.* "We will reduce the fee 20 percent to meet your budget, but at that low price, revisions and changes are not included, and if desired, would be billed at a rate of $75 an hour additional."

- *Sharing work load.* "We can do the job for $500 instead of our regular fee of $750, provided you handle the booth set-up, hire the personnel, and coordinate the service requirements and hospitality suite directly with the conference sponsor. If we can handle the rest without being involved in those details, we can give you the $250 fee reduction you said you needed to go ahead with the job."

- *Easing time frame and other work requirements.* "I will do the job for the reduced package price of $2,875 provided there is no rush and I can take as long as I want to do the work and I can do it from the office via phone or fax, with no on-site meetings or conferences."

- *Having client provide "extras."* "My normal fee for a speech is $2,000. But I'll tell you what. Do you have videotape capabilities? If you can professionally videotape my talk and give me a master of the tape, I will waive the fee and speak for just a copy of the tape and the $250 honorarium you offer your speakers."

HOW A VENDORS' NETWORK OR BUREAU MAKES YOU IMMUNE TO PRICE-BASED OBJECTIONS

Many service providers are "lone wolves." They do not network or associate with peers; view others in their trade as dangerous competitors; and avoid contact with those competitors for fear that these firms will steal business from them.

But a better strategy is to form alliances with your competitors in which you sell their services to your clients, through your company, and at a profit to both you and the other service provider.

Let me give you an example. For years, I have been writing technical documents for different clients nationwide. I have a company, The Center for Technical Communication (CTC), that provides writing-related services including technical writing, writing seminars, editing, and so on.

In the past, whenever a job came up that I could not handle—because I was too busy, the client didn't have the budget, or it was something I didn't do—I would just say, "No can do."

Then I thought, "If I can't do these jobs, why not offer the work to my competitors through my company?" I spoke to my competitors, got their rates and resumes, put them in a file.

Now, when a client calls with a job I cannot personally handle, I say, "I can't do it for that price, but we have a large number of associate writers who work for us at a variety of rates." I look in my resume file and match the client with a writer who charges what they can afford to pay for the job. My commission is 20 percent, which is taken out of the writer's fee; the client pays what they would pay if hiring the writer direct, so there is no penalty to the client for using CTC.

This is a win-win situation for all parties. Clients benefit because they get a solution to their problem for a price that is within their budget.

I benefit financially because, instead of wasting leads that come to me from my marketing efforts and other sources, I can now convert those inquiries to a sale. For instance, on a $5,000 writing project, I earn a commission of $1,000.

More important, however, I receive an additional benefit: I now get to say "yes" to clients and prospects instead of "no," and I *never* have to turn away a client because my fee is too high: if clients cannot afford to pay my hourly rate, I will get them a writer they *can* afford.

As a result, fees are never a point of disagreement, confrontation, or contention. If I quote my rate and the client says, "Too high!" I simply say, "Fine. Tell me what your budget is, and one of our CTC associates can do the job for you!"

The writers also benefit. I am not ripping them off taking a 20 percent commission, because CTC eliminates the need for the writer to market and sell himself or herself. There are no sales visits to make, no direct mail to send out, no showing the portfolio, and no follow-up. When we bring the writer a job, it's a done deal. So we save him or her an enormous amount of expense and time, well in excess of the 20 percent commission.

This has been so successful in CTC's technical writing business that I have also established such a network for the speaking and seminar side of the business. Our CTC Speakers Bureau allows me to provide any client with a speaker or seminar leader to fit their budget. If the client cannot afford to pay me $3,000 for a day of training, I ask, "What is your budget?" and then find them a speaker in our files who knows the topic and whose rates are in line with what the client wants to pay.

Can this strategy work for you? Build a network of people who perform your service or related services. When you cannot personally perform the job because your fees are simply too high, or for any other reason, instead of sending the client away empty-handed, match them with an individual or firm that *can* perform the service at their price. You do it through your company, and you take your commission as a percentage of the vendor's fee.

Afraid these vendors will go behind your back and try to steal your client? It does happen. Your best bet is to make the vendor sign an agreement saying they agree not to work for any client of yours, or at least any client you hire them to work for, for a period of one or two years. You may want to ask your attorney to help you draft this document.

Referrals—Fee or Free?

If you refer work to other vendors, do you do it out of kindness or for some financial reward? The answer is: you can do it either way.

Referring a client you cannot help to someone who *can* help them is an example of putting the client first and rendering superior client service. After all, we exist to help our clients find solutions to their problems.

If we turn them down and then don't provide an alternative solution, we are not being very helpful. The client walks away with his problem still unsolved. And he does not feel that we have helped him or been cooperative.

By telling the client "I can't do this assignment, but here is the name and number of someone who can," you are helping the client find a fast solution to the problem. And although someone else and not you will get the work, you will have made a favorable impression that paves the way for future business.

So overall, making referrals when you can't take on the job is good practice. It benefits you and the client. The question is: Should you do it for fee or free?

At the most basic level of referral, there is no compensation at all. You simply refer clients to someone you feel can help them, with no expectation of renumeration or reward of any kind. This is still good for you for the reasons discussed: you never lose by doing good for your clients.

Of course, you want to make referrals to vendors who (1) you know are qualified and will do a good job and (2) won't try to steal future business from you or promote themselves to your client.

At the next level, you refer clients only to vendors you know personally. The expectation, often unstated, is that in return for the referral business you give them, they will make every effort to give you an equal amount of referrals. If someone does not reciprocate, you simply stop referring business to them and start referring it to someone else. And by the way, I see nothing wrong in telling the person, "I am referring so and so to you. They are a good client, so please take care of them. And by the way, all I ask in return is that when you get a job you cannot handle and need to refer out, you think of me first."

The highest level is where direct financial compensation is involved, where you have a network of service providers or suppliers you refer work to in exchange for a percentage. You can either refer the work to them and have them send you a commission check after they are paid by the client, or you can arrange for them to do the work through your company, as discussed in the previous section and the example involving CTC.

Referrals usually build goodwill all around, and even if you are not immediately rewarded, the rewards eventually do come. For example, there was one writer to whom I referred several lucrative projects over the years and who never sent me a thank you note or referred any business back to me. I told my wife, "This disproves the theory that being kind pays off; being kind gets you nothing."

A year later, the writer retired. He referred two of his three clients to me (the third was one in a field I do not handle), and both became clients of mine. So I was wrong—goodwill does pay off.

OFFER SERVICES THAT PEOPLE WILL BUY IN ORDER TO AVOID PAYING MORE FOR OTHER SERVICES

There is one way to get your price, even if it is high, and even if the client is short on funds: offer services that *save* the client money or *eliminate* the need for them to buy an alternate, more costly service.

The best example is the home remodeling business during the recession. In a recession, people want to hold on to their money and not spend it. And home remodeling is one of the most expensive things you can buy. Yet during the recession of the early 1990s, the home improvement business was booming—at least in our neighborhood, where you saw more dormer additions, second story additions, porch conversions, and add-on family rooms than ever.

Why was this so? Although people didn't want to spend money, they were increasing their families, and they simply had to have more space. In a good economy, they would have simply traded up to a bigger house. But this is an even bigger investment than remodeling, and more of a financial commitment: it requires a large down payment that can consume the bulk of an average family's savings and also involves a long commitment to a large monthly mortgage payment.

For the family that had to have more space but could not afford or was afraid to commit to buying a bigger house, remodeling was the *only* alternative. A new addition might cost $10,000 to $50,000 or more, but it eliminated the expense of moving, closing, points, and a bigger mortgage.

I don't know what business you are in, so I don't know if this strategy can work for you. But here's how to analyze it. Look around at your market. Are clients reluctant to purchase your primary service because it's too expensive? This will hurt you as well as your competitors. You can gain the edge by coming up with an alternative service that enables clients to get some of the benefits they want, while spending less.

True, this service might sell for less, so profit margin is reduced. But because buying this service saves the client the cost of buying the more expensive service, they will buy. Hence, you will have plenty of business, while your competitors stand there gaping and scratching their heads.

Note: The alternative service you create need not be an alternative only to what *you* are currently offering. The only requirement is that it be an alternative to *any* costly service that the consumer wants to avoid buying and *can* avoid buying by hiring you instead for less money.

By using this strategy, you will eliminate most of the price resistance on the part of the client, so that fees become less of an issue and the negotiating process described in the rest of this chapter is eliminated or at least reduced to a minimum. That will make you happy, right?

WHAT TO DO WHEN CLIENTS FEEL THEY ARE PAYING TOO MUCH

What happens when the client agrees to your price, but later expresses to you that she feels you really "squeezed her" and took advantage of their neediness? Or what happens if the client gives in and agrees to your price, but reluctantly and sullenly, rather than happily and enthusiastically?

Another problem is when the client agrees to your high price seemingly without hesitation or concern, but, as you begin to perform the service, comments that they don't seem to be getting extraordinary service or results, considering the high fee you are charging.

These things are bad. The goal is not just to force the client's hand and win the negotiation and get your price; the goal is to have clients who are comfortable with what they are paying and feel they are getting their money's worth.

Here are some techniques for making clients feel they are not getting ripped off and are receiving a good value when they agree to pay the higher price you asked for.

Present The Price in the Lowest Possible Unit Terms

For example, for a training seminar, quote the price as "$100 per student for 25 attendees," not "$2,500 per day." The former is a bargain, the latter may cause resentment among some clients who feel that no one should be making $2,500 for a day's work.

Recap or Summarize All the Services Being Performed for the Fee

Instead of saying, "My fee to write the capabilities brochure is $3,200," say, "The fee for creating the corporate capabilities brochure is $3,200, which includes the following: research, review of all client materials, interviews with engineers and scientists, on-site visits to client facility, teleconferences, outline of brochure, first draft, rewrites, and all revisions until client is satisfied with manuscript. Text to be submitted as hard copy with an IBM-compatible floppy disk included at no extra charge. Writer will also review layouts and make design recommendations at no additional cost."

The former seems like a lot of money for a small thing; the latter like a lot of service and work for a modest fee.

Compare the Price to the Result

Copywriter Mike Pavlish charges high fees to write direct mail packages and ads for his clients. In his promotional mailings, he addresses the possible objection to his high fees before it is even voiced by pointing out, "My fee is a *drop in the bucket* compared to the tremendous increases in sales and profits my copy will generate for you." If your service makes or saves the client a large amount of money, point out that your fee, although seemingly hefty, is miniscule when measured as a percentage of the money the client will make or save using your service.

Compare the Cost Differential to the Result or the Importance of the Job

Sometimes the objection is not the fee itself but your fee in comparison to what a competitor is charging. This is even easier to handle, because you don't have to justify your fee; you just have to show that the *difference* between your fee and theirs is really insignificant compared to the extra quality you offer, your greater experience, your track record, or the results you achieve.

For instance, you are charging $5,000 to do a project. The client says, "Someone else will do it for $4,200." You say, "I understand. $800 is not insignificant, and no one wants to spend $800 if they don't have to. But even if our system is only a *little* better than the other, we will save you $3,000 in materials the first month of operation. Tell me, would you spend $800 one time to save $3,000 per month every month?"

Compare the Fee for Your Portion of the Job to the Fee for the Entire Job

Sometimes we forget that our service is not the entire job but just a small portion of a larger job.

Let's say you are a landscaper and a wealthy client wants you to do the landscaping for a new $800,000 home they are building. They choke on your quote of $15,000. "That's a lot of money for bushes!" the husband says stiffly. You reply, "I understand. $15,000 is not an insignificant sum. But, Mr. Client, the landscaping sets the tone for the entire house and determines, to a large degree, whether the outer appearance impresses friends and relatives and how the whole exterior of the property looks. Tell me: Do you want to skimp on the landscaping when it comes to making your $800,000 home look the best it can be?"

Emphasize the Quality and Value

The client may not appreciate the work, labor, skill, materials, quality, or value of what you do. So tell them. If your landscape design uses rare and valuable Ooka-ooka trees that only you can get and will be the envy of the neighborhood, say so. If you are saving the client time and expense on future upgrades of their manual because you store the page layout on computer disk permanently at no extra charge to the client, remind them. If you give a free wash and wax with detailing of every car interior and your competitors do not do this, or if you clean out every crevice with a perfumed cotton swab, say so.

Many clients do not realize the value of what they are getting. So tell them. When they realize the value, the work and skill that goes into it, they'll feel they are getting their money's worth, and won't have any regrets about the price.

Throw in a Few Freebies

If the client still isn't convinced they are getting their money's worth, throw in a few freebies. For example, a client wanted to hire me to give a seminar; his boss would not sign off on the approval. When we asked why, after hemming and hawing, he finally said, "I know your proposal says you include handouts and course materials, but for this kind of money, I'd think you could throw in a copy of your book for each of our trainees as well." I replied, "If I could give each trainee a copy of the book at no extra cost, would you be able to go ahead?" He said yes. I shipped the books, closing a $4,500 seminar for an extra $100 in out-of-pocket costs for the 20 free books.

LEARN TO SAY "NO" IN A WAY THAT LEAVES THE CLIENT'S DIGNITY AND THE RELATIONSHIP INTACT

Occasionally, despite your best negotiating efforts, you and the client will *not* be able to come to terms on a particular project. You cannot do the work at the low price they are willing to pay. And so you must turn down the assignment.

This can be unpleasant and awkward. Or it can be pleasant, dignified, and professional. It's not the situation that determines it; it's how you handle the situation. It's entirely up to you.

Learn to say no and turn down client requests gently and gracefully. For example, "Michelle, I am really sorry. I would like to take on this project for you, but no matter how we adjust the scope of work or the numbers, I can't even get close to your budget figure. If there's any way you can do some of the work in-house, we can handle a *portion* of it for that fee. Or, is there any way to get money from other budgets? As much as we'd like to do the whole job right now for the fee you have offered, we can't—much to my regret."

When you cushion the blow this way, the client can more easily absorb it and react in an equally agreeable, friendly manner. But when you turn them down in an abrupt, terse manner, they feel uneasy and a bit offended. Saying no to a client is never beneficial to the relationship, so if you have to do it, do it tactfully. And always make a few last-minute suggestions or offer some additional alternatives when you're giving your turn-down. This shows that you genuinely want the deal to work out and that your door is always open as far as this matter is concerned.

NEGOTIATING TIP FOR BEGINNERS

My only extra piece of advice is that, if you're a beginner, you should be even more flexible and accommodating about fees (and everything else) than I've already suggested.

Now is the best time to be in a service business, and the most challenging. It's the best because the entrepreneurial spirit is flourishing in America, with more and more people going into service businesses than at any time in recent memory. It's the most challenging because the flood of people entering the service sector creates stiff competition for jobs and clients, and because, in today's tight economy, there are fewer assignments to go around.

Every service provider must be competitive, but for the beginner with no client base, no experience, and no track record, it's even tougher. For the beginner, the winning attitude is to see what experienced service providers are doing to win and keep clients, and to *do even more*! Because you lack a reputation and list of satisfied clients, you need a competitive edge to beat out your more established competitors. That competitive edge is the willingness to do what others are not doing to get jobs and satisfiy clients.

If you extend yourself, do more for the client than your competition, you will soon be ahead of the competition and, in fact, not have any. Once again I quote motivational expert Dr. Rob Gilbert, who notes, "There's no traffic jam on the extra mile."

CHAPTER 8

Handling The Client Who is Dissatisfied With your Service

A wise client once told me, "Subjective judgment is the death of the service business." No matter how carefully worded our agreements, how tightly written our contracts, whether the client is ultimately satisfied is determined by their subjective judgment of us, our service, and our treatment of them.

Since you do not control any individual's subjective judgment, or the mood or external circumstances affecting that judgment, you cannot totally control the client's reaction to your services. Therefore, no matter how good you are, or how hard you try, you are invariably going to run into situations where the client is not satisfied with you or your service.

Some of your peers will tell you that this *never* happens and that their clients are *always* satisfied. Either they're lying, or they handle so few clients that a problem hasn't happened yet. It will.

Given that clients will become dissatisfied and that client dissatisfaction can hurt your business—it reduces your income, tarnishes your reputation, and can cause loss of accounts—you must learn strategies for coping with clients who become dissatisfied. That's what this chapter will help you do.

EARLY DETECTION OF DISSATISFACTION: THE BEST CURE

For many human illnesses, doctors tell us that early detection is the best cure. Caught early enough, the eye disease won't blind us, the cancer won't kill us. It's only when we ignore the symptoms and let the disease progress undiagnosed and untreated does it grow to a point where it can cripple us or do us in.

It's the same with the disease of client dissatisfaction. A client complaint, even one that seems serious at first, can be handled in such a way that it does no permanent harm to the client/vendor relationship—provided it is detected earlier and dealt with swiftly and effectively.

Client dissatisfaction can hurt us only if it goes undetected or ignored. Then the problem festers and grows to the point where it kills the healthy relationship and we lose the client and his or her business.

So the number one rule in coping with dissatisfied clients is: act fast. If you suspect there's a problem, bring it out in the open where it can be dealt with. When you have a problem, acknowledge it. Be up front with the client and discuss it with them. Don't think it will go away if you ignore it. It won't.

Find a solution that not only solves the problem but also restores the client's faith and confidence in you. Don't hold back; do what it takes. Even if the solution costs you more than you want to spend, do it. You must not let dissatisfied clients remain dissatisfied. When you do, you lose their business, and they tell others, and you quickly gain a reputation that will cause others to shun you.

DISSATISFIED CLIENTS TELL OTHER CLIENTS

As noted earlier in the book, investment consultant John Cali says a dissatisfied client will tell ten to twenty or more people about their bad experience with you. You can read that and it may not sink in; you have to experience it for the statistic to have meaning.

Here's an example. I recently gave a speech at a local advertising club. Before giving my talk, people at my table—all ad agency executives—were discussing different printers, photographers, copywriters, artists, and typesetters: which were good, which were bad, which were expensive, and so on.

The name of a copywriter friend of mine came up. To my amazement, one of the agency executives—also a friend—immediately told the others not to hire that copywriter. "He was difficult, rude, uncooperative, and his bill was much higher than his estimate," said the executive. "We agreed to pay it, but said we would have liked to make two payments over a two-month period. He screamed at us, demanded his money immediately; threatened to tell our client he would sue them unless we paid right away. We did pay him, but would never use him again; you should not, either."

I was stunned. Could you imagine how this copywriter would have felt at that moment, sitting at home, if he could somehow be transported to the table and see what was being said about him? There were people representing eight other New Jersey ad agencies sitting there; he will probably never be able to sell to any one of them.

The point is, the same has been (or will be) said about you, without you knowing it, at least once in your lifetime, by someone who for some reason doesn't like you or feels you did not treat them well.

Do dissatisfied clients deliberately *go out of their way* to slander you and besmirch your reputation? I don't think so. They don't sit at the telephone and call all their friends to get even with you or send out mailings saying you stink.

On the other hand, keep in mind that the dissatisfied client, while not "out to get you," is not hesitant to talk about you and give her opinion when asked or when the subject comes up, as it did at the ad club. If asked about their experience with you, dissatisfied clients will probably give the truth as they see it, which, since they are dissatisfied, means a negative report.

For this reason, you want to work hard to prevent client dissatisfaction from happening, and when it does happen, to minimize its negative effects. It's not client dissatisfaction that ultimately harms your business; it's what you do to find and fix client dissatisfaction when it occurs.

A wise man once said, "It's not what happens to you in life; it's how you handle it." Screwing up with a client is bad, but it won't kill your relationship with that client. It's how you respond to the problem and what you do about it that determines whether the client's satisfaction is restored or the client's dissatisfaction is made worse.

DON'T MAKE EXCUSES TO CLIENTS

Most books on customer service tell you, "No excuses. Do whatever it takes to serve the customer. People hate to hear excuses." I agree, but not totally. What I agree with is that (1) you should keep your promises and (2) you shouldn't get in the habit of making excuses.

Just as "my dog ate my homework" doesn't cut it with teachers, clients don't want to hear what so many difficult, unresponsive, unpunctual vendors tell them:

"The materials haven't arrived yet."

"It's not me—it's my supplier."

"We'll come *next* Friday, I *promise*."

"I'm sorry, but we got really busy this summer."

"My assistant is sick."

"My daughter wasn't feeling well."

"I had to take my wife to the doctor."

"Our photocopier broke down."

"Our computer broke down."

"We tried to call you but your line was busy."

"I thought you said *Thursday* morning, not Tuesday morning."

"We said *maybe* it would be ready Friday."

"I thought my secretary sent that to you. Didn't you get it?"

"Someone else does that; it's not my fault."

"It's in the mail . . . ."

Get in the habit of meeting commitments, not making excuses. Think of a commitment as a promise you cannot break. Clients want to deal with vendors who are reliable and get the job done no matter what, no excuses.

On the other hand, I do not agree with those who say you should never give an excuse or a reason for the problem. We live in the real world, not the ivy-covered tower of some theoretician imaging business the way it *should* be.

And in the real world, things *do* happen. Computer systems crash. Delivery trucks go off the road. Flights get canceled. People become seriously ill.

If the client's dissatisfaction is the result of a problem with your service caused by something that was unavoidable, catastrophic, or could not have reasonably been predicted or anticipated, my advice is to be honest with the client and tell them precisely what happened and why the problem occurred rather than try to hide it.

Clients are human beings, with feelings. If you had to miss a deadline because your son was hit by a car, only the most unfeeling of clients would expect you to stay at your desk to complete their report, proposal, drawing, or design.

So do not be afraid to tell the truth. Rather than annoy the client, the truth will make them sympathetic, even helpful. When they know and understand the reason for the incident or action that caused their dissatisfaction, their anger will lessen, and it will not be a permanent blot on your record with them.

Those of us who are sole practitioners or the principal service providers of small businesses are particularly vulnerable to the threat of interruptions in client service caused by personal illness or other catastrophe. At a big company, for example, a technical writer whose computer stops working can simply go to the store-room and sign out another machine. But the freelance technical writer, unable to afford a second PC, loses the ability to get work done while his machine is in the shop being repaired.

In the same way, if an employee is absent from her job due to illness or personal reasons, the corporation will still function, the department will continue to be productive. If I have a cold and stay home in bed, however, "Bob Bly Inc." gets no work done that day.

While in some businesses it's difficult for a substitute to step in and take over when you're unable to perform, in many other fields it may be a good idea to make such an arrangement with a friendly competitor: when you get laid up or put out of commission, your backup takes over and handles the work load until you can return. Every doctor makes such an arrangement with another "covering doctor"; why not you too? It makes sense and can prevent service interruptions that are the cause of lost deadlines and much client dissatisfaction and frustration.

TEN REASONS CLIENTS MAY BECOME UNHAPPY WITH YOUR SERVICE

Although there are many things that can cause clients to become unhappy or frustrated with you, here are ten of the most common:

1. The client is not happy with the quality of your work.
2. Your service has failed to achieve the desired or expected result.
3. You have performed poorly or have made a mistake.
4. You behave unprofessionally or have a conflict with the client.

5. You miss your deadline.
6. Your bill exceeds your estimate.
7. The client wants more service than what you can provide.
8. The client wants a different service than you are providing.
9. The client wants more freebies and extras.
10. There is a misunderstanding, miscommunication, or poor communication between you and the client.

Let's take a brief look at each cause of client dissatisfaction, along with ideas on how to handle them and how to prevent them from occurring in the first place.

Reason 1: The Client Is Not Pleased with You or the Quality of Your Work.

The first step is to find out *why* the client is unhappy with you or your work.

Here I am assuming that you did not do something bad, inept, or incompetent, but the client's displeasure is based on some subjective negative assessment of you and your service. For example, the client feels you turned in a sloppy report (even though you think it's good) or the client thinks you did not provide good service and were not attentive to her needs (even though you got the job done on time and from your point of view communicated with her in an efficient and service-oriented manner).

If the client does not come straight out and tell you she is dissatisfied, you can usually detect it in their manner of dealing with you. Instead of being friendly and relaxed, as usual, the client becomes distant, curt, and uptight. Whenever you call or visit, you get the sense that they are angry. This is not by accident: although the client is afraid or unwilling to tell you she is angry, she is subconsciously doing so through body language and tone of voice.

If you suspect there is a problem, say, "Rita, you seem angry and upset. Did I do something wrong?" or "I must have really done something bad to get you this angry and upset. Can you tell me what it is?" This "opens the dam" so to speak, and the client will give forth with a torrent of words, emotions, and information telling you what you did to get them ticked off at you.

So far, so good. But here's where most of us fall: when we get the client to tell us what's wrong, and we hear it, our immediate response is to *argue* with the client's feelings or viewpoint, that is, tell them why they are wrong or why they shouldn't be angry.

We tell them that (1) it's not our fault, (2) their account of what happened is not accurate, or (3) their perception is wrong. This doesn't work. You can't tell someone who is angry, "Don't be angry," and expect them to say, "Okay." They'll only get angrier that you are arguing with them or are treating their opinion and feeling as invalid.

There are two things you must do to set things right: (1) acknowledge the client's feelings and point of view and (2) begin the process of taking corrective action. Note that it is almost irrelevant at this point whether you were wrong or right. The goal is to make the client happy again, get her in a calmer and more receptive state. Later, when she likes you again, a discussion at the right time may get her to acknowledge that it really wasn't your fault or at least correct some inaccurate perceptions. But for now, that doesn't matter. So when the client tells you the problem, you say, "You're right, and I'm sorry. Tell me, Rita, what can I do to set things right for you?"

Notice the two-step process. First, you acknowledge that her opinion, feelings, and perceptions are correct. After all, as the saying goes, the customer is right, even when she's wrong. Second, instead of *telling* her or recommending to her what should be done to solve the problem, *you* ask *her* how she would like you to handle it: "What can I do to set things right?"

All you need to do to correct the situation is take the corrective action she asks for and feels is appropriate. And surprisingly, what the client says is needed after you ask is usually *much, much less* than you would have imagined or offered had you not inquired.

By the way, unless her request is absolutely impossible or unreasonable, promise to do it immediately—and then do it immediately. Do not start negotiating, hemming or hawing, or modifying what she asked for because it's more convenient for you. At this point, you want to suspend your self-interest and do whatever the client wants you to do, regardless of how difficult or time consuming it is.

Reason 2: Your Service Has Failed to Achieve the Desired or Expected Result

Many of us selling services sell them based upon a result that is implied, predicted, or promised but not guaranteed. A direct mail consultant, for example, will not guarantee or promise a particular response rate (doing so violates the code of ethics of the Direct Marketing Association), but will strongly imply that, by hiring him, the client is getting a pro who almost always increases direct mail response rates for other clients and will do so for this client, too. The problem, of course, is that when you overpromise to sell the job, your results are often not what you led the client to expect. What to do?

My strategy is to prevent this problem from happening by not overpromising in the first place. Instead, give the client a realistic assessment of what you can do and what results to expect.

If you have a track record of achieving record results for other clients, by all means let clients know it when selling your services to them. But at the same time, make sure they know that you cannot guarantee the same result from them; all you can guarantee is that you'll give it your best effort. You are like a mutual fund in that "past performance is no guarantee of future yield."

"I can't do that!" you protest. "My competitors are all making big claims when they sell, and if I'm a milktoast about it, I won't get any projects." Actually, while this fear sounds logical, I've found the opposite is true: by being honest with potential clients and *not* overpromising, you stand out from the crowd because what you say sounds more honest and believable. Says stockbroker Andrew Lanyi, "The more you tell the client you are not a witch doctor, a rainmaker, the more credibility you get."

Example: A large industrial manufacturer in my area was looking for a new copywriter to write their product literature. When interviewing me, the marketing director said, "Our complaint with other writers is that what they produce is not right the first time and we have to spend a lot of time rewriting it. If we give you a trial product sheet to write, can you promise that it will be right the first time?"

My answer shocked him. "That would be impossible," I replied. "Until I learn your preferences, style, and method of working, the drafts are going to have to be rewritten two or three times before they are perfect. However, I can promise that I will do all rewrites at no charge until you are satisfied, with a minimum of work on your part, although you *will* be required to review carefully and comment on each draft. Also, after the first three or four projects, the first drafts will be much closer to finished, as we gain more experience working with each other. But guarantee the first draft on the first project will be acceptable without changes to you?

Impossible. I can't do it, and anyone who makes such a promise doesn't know this business or is a liar."

The advertising manager later told me, "They were impressed with your honesty." Also, by setting up a realistic expectation at the start, satisfaction was far easier to achieve, because I did not have to live up to an expectation that would have been nearly impossible to satisfy. I got the trial project and soon became the firm's regular copywriter for all product literature. Now let's consider the other scenario, where you did overpromise and the client is complaining that the result was not achieved. What to do? You have several options:

Deliver on your promise.   If you promised a specific result and did not achieve it by performing the work contracted for, you might want to consider doing additional work on the project, at no charge to the client (or at a reduced charge), until the result the client expected is achieved.

Give them a credit.   If you generated some results but fell short of the goal, you might refund part of your fee. Rather than give the money back, you might give the refund as a credit the client can apply toward purchase of more services. This has the advantage of costing you nothing out of pocket, and the credit compels the client to try your service again.

Refund their money.   If you promised to generate the result, and that promise was based on a money-back guarantee, or if your fee was contingent on getting that result, the client at this point gets a refund or doesn't pay. Of course, to avoid this, you can always offer to try again, at your expense, to get the result you promised.

Give them freebies.   Another option is to give them more service at no cost to make up for not achieving the initial result promised.

Reason 3: You Have Performed Poorly or Have Made A Mistake

This is different than the first problem of dissatisfying the client in that here the dissatisfaction is caused by apparent and obvious error or poor performance.

First, analyze what caused the poor performance. Did you accept an assignment that was too big or complex for you? Was it something you'd never done before? Was the deadline too tight?

Second, take steps to ensure that the problem doesn't happen again to this client or any others in the future. Exhibit 8-1 lists a few of the typical causes of poor service—and their cures.

Third, in dealing with the current situation, the best strategy is to be up front with the client. If the job was bigger than you anticipated, say, "I made a mistake. I hadn't managed an entire project like this before, and it was much more work than I anticipated. The mistake was mine."

Always take full blame; do not attempt to "share blame" with clients. If they really feel that it is partially their fault, they will tell you so to make you feel better and let you off the hook. If not, you only make a bad situation worse by inferring that they are partially to blame.

Fourth, apologize and ask clients how they would like you to rectify the situation, letting them know that you will do whatever it takes to correct things and get back in their good graces: "I'm really sorry, Rita. Tell me: What can we do to set things right?"

Always expect work to take more time than you think it will, not less.

Reason 4: You Behave Unprofessionally or Have A Conflict with the Client

Whether you can fix this depends upon the severity of your transgression. If this happens frequently, you need to examine the source of your conflicts and poor treatment of clients. Perhaps you really don't like your clients or enjoy what you do. That can cause depression and lack of self-esteem which in turn affects your work.

You may have to resign some accounts because of your inability to deal with that particular client in a cordial and decent way.

You might also consider a sabbatical or slowdown to reexamine your career and make sure you are in a business that brings you pleasure and satisfaction as well as financial rewards. Don't do something just for the money. You should enjoy your work, too. If you don't, this will reveal itself in your dealings with your clients.

By being happier in your work, and working with clients you like and enjoy, you are less likely to act in a rude, abrupt, or discourteous manner, and there will rarely be an incident that causes problems.

Table 8-1.   Reasons for poor performance.

CAUSE	CURE
Deadline is too tight.	• Negotiate for longer deadlines. • Do not take on projects if deadline is too short. • Do not take on more assignments than you can handle. • Add staff. • Subcontract work to other vendors.
Project is too complex to manage (has too many tasks and activities for you keep track of).	• Do not take on projects too complex for you to manage. • Take seminar in project management to improve your project management skills. • Hire an employee to be project coordinator/manager. • Acquire and learn to use project management system or software.
You lack the expertise needed to perform project adequately.	• Do not take on projects that you do not have the expertise to handle. • Subcontract to other vendors with the expertise you lack. • Hire employee with skills to handle this type of work.
You lack the time needed to perform work adequately.	• Do not take on more work and projects than you can handle. • Hire more employees. • Cut back on workload. • Make sure deadlines are sufficient and realistic.
Constant client contact and communication interfere with your successful performance of the work.	• Hire an account representative to handle client contact. • Work with clients who do not demand intensive "hand-holding." • Educate clients on level of contact appropriate and necessary for successful completion of the work. • Set a regular schedule of client contact to reduce unscheduled interruptions. • Use voice mail or assistant to screen phone calls. • Take calls only during certain hours.

CAUSE	CURE
Project is more work than originally anticipated.	• Make more realistic estimates of time and labor required to do job when making bid or quoting fee. • Always expect work to take more time than you think it will, not less.
Client changes interfere with timely completion of the work as scheduled.	• Have a policy or contract that calls for deadline extensions and fee increases when client changes job requirements in midstream.
Your dislike of project interferes with quality of work.	• Be selective and take only take on projects that interest you. • Assign boring and routine tasks to freelancers, subcontractors, or staff.
Your dislike of client interferes with quality of work.	• Be selective and deal only with clients you like and can work well with. • Have staff account coordinator be primary contact with "nonfavorite" clients.
Tiredness or lack of energy interferes with your ability to do a good job.	• Take a vacation to "recharge your batteries." • Take on less work. • Get more sleep. • Get more relaxation. • Take up a hobby. • Spend more time with family. • Achieve better work/personal life balance. • Exercise. • Improve diet.
Boredom or lack of interest causes poor performance.	• Take a vacation to "recharge your batteries." • Take on less work; take on more interesting projects. • Consider career change or change in business activities.
Job involves doing tasks you do not enjoy or have the skills for.	• Consider cutting back on scope of work and sticking to tasks you do well and enjoy. • Do not try to expand too quickly into peripheral areas.

CAUSE	CURE
Paperwork and administrative details bog you down and prevent you from attending to essential work.	• Hire secretary or clerical support staff. • Farm out secretarial work to outside word processing or office support service. • Hire temps as needed for each job.
Employee, vendor, or subcontractor performed poorly on their portion of the project.	• Discuss problem with employee or vendor. • Look for alternative sources of services.

Should an incident arise, the best course of action is an immediate, direct apology: "I was curt just now, Wayne. I'm sorry. We were up all night with a sick child, I didn't get any sleep, and I'm on edge. Please accept my apology." Most clients will react in a human fashion ("I understand; I have a two-year-old myself"), and the incident will be forgiven and forgotten.

Occasional rudeness, abruptness, or less than perfect behavior, while not desirable, is only human and rarely causes permanent damage in the client/service provider relationship. What you want to avoid is major or frequent conflict or problems with clients.

If you have a short temper, you must learn to control it. A good technique is to pause and mentally count to 5 when you feel yourself about to explode or let loose with a client.

The pause will give you time to gain control, calm your emotions, and formulate a rationale, nonoffensive response to whatever the client said or did to set you off. Use some body language (e.g., eyes looking off to the distance, as if in concentration) or some tone of voice ("hmmmm . . .") to make the client think you are carefully thinking about your answer rather than controlling your temper. Force yourself to smile to convert negative to positive mood.

Reason 5: You Miss Your Deadline

As we discussed earlier, here are the rules regarding deadlines:

1. Never miss a deadline.
2. Try to complete work slightly ahead of the deadline, if possible.
3. If you are going to miss a deadline, notify the client as soon as you are sure that missing the deadline is unavoidable.

If the deadline is for an intermediate step or task, assure the client that it will not affect the final due date. Mail or fax a revised schedule to show how you will still complete the work on time, despite having missed the intermediate deadline. Then do whatever it takes to make up the lost time, with any additional expense or extra effort to be expended by you, not the client.

If the deadline you missed is the final deadline, see if you can do something so that the client does not suffer loss or hardship as a result of your having missed it.

For instance, if you were supposed to deliver printed brochures to the client's office on October 1 so they would be ready for a trade show exhibit in Texas on October 6, and the brochures will not be printed until October 5, arrange for express overnight shipment of the appropriate number of brochures from your printing plant to the client's booth at the convention center, at your expense. Be sure to let the client know what you are doing, and in your invoicing, show what you paid to have the brochures shipped via overnight express, so the client realizes the expense you incurred in taking care of the problem.

If missing the deadline cannot be avoided, and there is nothing you can do to mitigate the damage, ask the client, "What can I do to set things right?" Let them tell you, rather than you tell them.

The client will be unhappy about the missed deadline and may be seriously considering ending his relationship with you. What you should do is acknowledge the breakdown, apologize, give any legitimate reasons why the breadown occurred (letting the client know that you consider these factors as reasons but not excuses, and that there is no excuse), and end with this promise: "If you can trust us again, I promise that every job will be delivered by the deadline date or sooner—or you don't pay us." Promising to sacrifice your payment if deadlines are not met should show the client you are sincere and serious about not repeating your mistake.

Reason 6: Your Bill Exceeds Your Estimate

Clients do not like it when your bill exceeds your estimate, and giving them such a bill risks nonpayment. Many fixed-price contracts today even call for cost overruns to be paid out of the vendor's pocket.

There are three important things you can do to prevent billing problems.

Make sure your clients understand your billing procedures and charging policies before you begin work.   You, the service provider, not the client, are responsible for making these policies clear.

For example, I often hire graphic artists to work for me, as many businesses do. I will give a description of a job, and the graphic artist will come back with a quotation that says, "For design, layout, type, illustration, and camera-ready mechanicals of a four-page product brochure—$1,250."

The written estimate almost never addresses contingencies, such as "What happens if the client does not like the design?" "Is there a charge to redo it?" And "What is the cost if the client changes the text after the type is set?"

The artist doesn't put these things in because he's afraid mention of these extras will make the client feel his service is too expensive and will lose him the job.

But not every client is experienced in graphic arts or educated in what the typical procedures are. Let's say the artist submits three designs and the client rejects them and asks for another. The artist says, "Okay, but of course, that will be extra."

The client says, "For what? Your quote says $1,250 including design. To me, that means a design I like—and I didn't like what you did." The answer is phrased in a more disagreeable tone than the client had intended, because he is taken aback by this sudden issue of paying more money for work that was, to him, no good in the first place.

The artist, feeling he is being insulted, answers stiffly, "The three designs were excellent by any standard. It was your decision not to use them, not mine. By your logic, we could do five hundred layouts and you could still say you were not satisfied; obviously I cannot do that for $1,250." From this point the conversation degenerates quickly from discussion to argument.

What the artist should have done is explain, in writing or verbally, the policies and procedures for making changes. For example, the contract should specify that $1,250 entitles the client to *up to three* layouts but no more, and if the client does not select one, additional designs are X dollars apiece. It should also say that the charge for changing the mechanical after copy has been approved for $50 an hour or whatever the fee is. That way, when the client gets the final bill showing extra charges for "changing his mind," he may not be *happy* about it, but at least he will not find it objectionable or inappropriate.

Give the client an estimated price before you begin work. The second strategy for eliminating confrontations and problems concerning billing is to give the client a specific dollar quotation for any extras, changes, revisions, or add-ons to jobs at the time they are requested.

To give you an example, when our contractor was at our home putting on various room additions, we would ask him to do small jobs around the house from time to time. I never bothered to ask him what these would cost since they were all small jobs. He never bothered to tell me, and the amounts were nominal.

One day, I asked him to put an additional electrical outlet in what was then a home office (I no longer work at home). He did, and when the bill came, it was $450!

When I complained, he explained that, because of the location of the room in relation to wiring, he had to spend over a day drilling and running wires, had to put in a special kind of outlet, and so on.

I was still unhappy, and said, "Mike, you should have told me that it would be that much *before you started*; if you had, there's no way I would spend nearly half a thousand dollars on a *socket*." He apologized, but did not directly offer to reduce the charge (I sensed he would have done so if I requested it, expected me to request it, and was hoping and praying I would not—and I didn't). I paid the bill, extremely unhappy about what had happened. In time I forgave the incident, and we hired him to do more work, but it nearly cost him all future business with me. And to be honest, for a long time I stopped referring business to him, so miffed was I about the incident.

Keep the client informed of the charges for your work.
A third strategy for preventing billing problems and misunderstandings is to bill in a timely manner and send regular monthly
statements that show clients what they have spent with you and
what they owe you. Some clients who do a lot of business with you
call you for a lot of different tasks, and they lose track of how much
they're spending with you.

When they get a huge, unexpected bill, they become upset and
unhappy. Their complaint: "Yes, I ordered all these services, but I
didn't know we were spending so *much* with you this month; you
should have *told* us."

For frequent users of your service, a monthly statement lets
them know where they are at so they can control spending and
keep the bills at reasonable size.

Reason 7: The Client Wants More Service than You Can Provide

At times the client may want:

- A higher level of customer service and "hand-holding" than
  you have time to provide
- Services that you do not currently offer and prefer not to offer
- More services than originally contracted for (e.g., additional
  assignments, increasing the scope of the current project) in
  the same or an even more compressed period of time

Because clients like it when you say "yes" and dislike it when
you say "no," you should comply unless:

- You are unable or unequipped to offer the services they want
- You are not experienced in offering the services they want,
  would probably do an inferior job, and know where they can
  get it better elsewhere.

Even in such cases, you want to avoid simply saying "no" and
leaving the client high and dry, with no explanation why you are
refusing them and no other options for them to pursue with you.
The best strategy is to tell the client the truth about your limitations or preferences, but still offer to handle the work if he or she
desires. For example, "We have never done this before, and are not

experts in it. We would be happy to try it and do our best for you, if that's what you need. As an alternative, we will find a firm that does have this service for you, review their work, and make a recommendation. We can also supervise their work and manage it for you, so you don't have to spend your time worrying about it."

The idea is, if you cannot give an unconditional "yes," at least you do not want to give an unconditional "no." Rather, you want to offer the client a range of options, so you they can choose how they want you to proceed.

The client will be pleased that you are willing to help in any way you can. He or she will also appreciate your honesty when you admit your shortcomings and lack of ability in a specific area; it adds to your credibility and does not create an unrealistic expectation for superb performance in a discipline you've just said you know little about.

Reason 8: The Client Wants a Different Service From What You Are Providing

If the client wants you to provide a service other than what you currently provide, you have to make a decision about how important that account is to you and what business you are really in.

For instance, let's say you are in the business of booking entertainment at corporate meetings and events. An important client comes to you and says, "We want a big celebrity and a band at our next event, but our corporate meeting department has been downsized, and we have too much work. In addition to booking the entertainment, we want you to plan and coordinate the entire meeting from start to finish, from creation of a theme, to the catering and site selection, through on-site management. Can you have a proposal to me by Friday?"

Since flexibility is the ultimate skill, one positive way to approach this request is to say to yourself, "The client is very perceptive; we've always been more than just talent agents; we have always helped plan and create successful events for our clients. So yes, we'll bid on this. In fact, the client has given me an idea: Why not start a division of our firm specializing in meeting planning and management? Could be very profitable and will help us provide more and better service to those accounts who have wanted us to do more for them."

At the same time, however, you cannot do everything everyone asks, and there may be requests that you cannot accommodate.

There are some services you are not comfortable rendering, some you are not competent to render, and some that you just don't want to be involved in because they're not "your thing."

The strategy is to *always help clients find the solution to their problem* in cases where you yourself are not going to solve the problem directly via application of your services. This is done by forming a large network or "database" of service providers and other vendors in allied fields who can provide your clients with those services they need but you do not provide.

For example, a meeting planner would have a network of service providers and vendors who could provide their clients with every conceivable service related to putting on meetings and special events. These would include photographers, printers, caterers, travel agents, independent meeting planners, florists, electricians, carpenters, set designers, audiovisual production houses, speakers bureaus, hotels, resorts, convention centers, furniture rental outlets, uniform suppliers, and a host of others.

When the client calls and requests a service other than what you provide, you do not want to say "No, we don't do that." Instead you want to say, "No problem. We don't do that, but I know three of the best [set designers/caterers/videotaping services/etc.] in town; here are their names and phone numbers. Mention my name when you call and you will get good service. If they don't work out, call me back and I will provide additional names for you to contact."

If the client has a request for a service that no firm you know of can provide, say, "I don't know the answer to that. But let me research it and I will get back to you with some names and recommendations; no charge of course."

Then you call others within your network to see if they know of a company that can handle the request. Within two or three phone calls you'll get someone who says, "We don't do that, of course. But I know a guy . . .". Then you call that service provider, check him out, and relay the information to your client.

It is extremely important to maintain a large network of quality, reputable service providers to which you can refer your clients. Many clients today want a turnkey, "single-source" solution, and if you cannot provide it through referrals to qualified vendors, they may call your competitor instead.

In fact, for those clients who want "single-source" service, you may want to hire the appropriate vendors as subcontractors, add a management fee or markup, and offer the entire meeting (or whatever it is you're providing) as a complete start-to-finish service.

Do all clients want it that way? No. The answer is, some clients want one vendor to handle all the details, don't want to hire and coordinate multiple vendors, and want to buy the service as a "package."

On the other hand, many clients prefer to manage the project themselves, hire the most qualified vendor in each field on an individual basis, and pay the lower price of using independents versus a larger single-source service provider who adds a markup or charges more for management of the project or overhead.

You can choose to be just a specialist, offering your one service. Or you can present yourself as a full-service firm, "doing it all." In each case, there are plenty of clients wanting both types of service. But you can please a wider number of clients by being flexible and going either way.

For example, if you're an independent, and the client wants a full-service firm, you can provide the full-service by hiring and managing other vendors to do the whole project.

On the other hand, if you're a full-service firm, and the client only wants you to provide service X, you can satisfy that client by offering service X on an à la carte basis, instead of saying, "No, we either do the whole thing or nothing."

The more flexible you are, the greater the number of clients you can please.

Reason 9: The Client Wants More Freebies and Extras

Some clients want to squeeze every last penny of value from every vendor. It's not malicious; it's just they way they are. They feel they are paying a lot and therefore should get everything they can. This often results in clients trying to get lots of extras and freebies out of you: free copies of your books and tapes, free advice, free services.

How far should you go to accommodate such clients? My feeling is it's better to err on the side of being too generous and accommodating rather than being too limiting and restrictive.

Clients like to feel that they can go to you freely for advice, help, and assistance on small matters on an informal basis and that you are available, willing, able, and glad to help them out.

If clients get a bill every time they spend ten minutes on the phone with you or have you do some small favor for them, they will resent it and feel you are just out to extract as much money as you can from them. Obviously there are limits, and these limits differ with the client: you give more extras and freebies to a $14,000-a-year client than a $400 one-shot project client.

It's a good investment, for example, to spend an hour of your billable time (worth anywhere from $25 to $200 or more, depending on your business) to do a favor that will retain a $14,000 account. It's not a sensible investment to spend a lot of time talking to a client that spent $200 and may, if you're lucky, spend another $100 with you this year.

Interestingly, it is often the big accounts who require the least hand-holding and make the fewest requests of you, while the smallest accounts expect and demand the most extras and attention from you.

When you do extra favors and give freebies to clients, let them know, in a polite, indirect way, the value of what they are getting from you. For example, if you give a half hour of your time to a client at no charge, send him a bill for a half hour of your time, in which you charge zero dollars ("NO CHARGE") but show the dollar value of the time (see sample "Courtesy Discount Invoice" in Chapter 5).

When you communicate to clients the fact that what you are giving away for free has a dollar value attached to it, they appreciate the value of what they are getting and the magnitude of your favor.

When you do not educate and inform the client of the real dollar value of the freebies and extras, they do not appreciate the value of what they are getting, nor are they especially appreciative of what you are giving them for free. They take it for granted, and feel it is something they are automatically entitled to, rather than a valuable bonus you are giving them as a favor.

When a small or marginal account becomes too demanding, you may decide not to give away a freebie or extend further favors. Do not directly refuse them with a "no" or "I can't do that for you," or tell them that you are tired of their taking advantage of you. Instead, simply agree to do the service and, almost as an after-thought, quote the cost of it. For example, "I'd be happy to make those calls and collect that information for you, Diane. We'll just bill you our hourly rate, and I estimate it will take one or two hours to complete. Shall I proceed?"

The client will appreciate that you are telling them the service is not free in a polite, nonconfrontational way. After you quote the estimate, they are highly unlikely to argue and try to get the service for free, as they originally had hoped. Instead, they will either say "go ahead" if they want to pay you for it, or if not, "I'll think about it" or "let's hold on that."

Reason 10: There Is a Misunderstanding or Miscommunication Between You and the Client.

For the busy service provider juggling lots of clients and projects, there is a great opportunity for miscommunication and misunderstandings with clients.

While we should take the time to clarify every point and be totally clear with clients, because of time pressures, we often don't do this. We rush phone calls, run from meeting to meeting or job to job, fax hastily written memos rather than mail carefully considered letters, and in general are always in a hurry and therefore don't spend as much time as we should on careful communication.

How can you help reduce and prevent client miscommunication and misunderstanding? And how can you get back on track when such misunderstandings and miscommunications do occur? Here are a few suggestions:

Call reports.   After every in-person meeting write a short report or memo summarizing who said what, what was agreed to, and the actions to be taken by you and the client. Send the report to the client and keep a copy in the client's file. The purpose is not so much to inform your client of what happened in the meeting (after all, he was there), but to (1) make sure everyone is in agreement about what was said, (2) eliminate any potential misunderstandings, and (3) provide a record proving what was said and done if later a dispute arises and people have different recollections of who was supposed to do what, and when.

Phone call memos.   A short memo summing up and confirming key decisions made or actions taken after phone calls is also a helpful tool in preventing miscommunication and misunderstandings. For example, if the client asks you to do something during a phone call, and no purchase order or contract is to be issued, you should write and fax a memo summing up the request, confirming your go-ahead, and giving the price you quoted.

Repeat back.   A useful habit for ensuring understanding is to repeat, in your own words, what the client told you, then ask if you have expressed it correctly. For example, "So, Mr. Client, what you're saying is that the system should have an automatic sensor that opens the back-flow valve if the pressure exceeds the safety limit set by the process engineer. Correct?"

"You're right."   Since the responsibility for making sure communication is clear and that understanding is mutual is yours, we operate on the principle that 99 percent of misunderstandings and miscommunications must primarily be the responsibility of the service provider, not the client.

Therefore, when a misunderstanding does arise, the first necessary step is to acknowledge that the client is right and you are wrong. When the client tells you, "No, we distinctly said *purple*, not green," you reply, "You're right. I had written 'green' in my notes, but I must have made a mistake."

The exception is when written records confirm that you, not the client, are correct. Even in such cases, the goal is not to prove to the client that you are right and they are wrong, but to point this out in a tactful way that doesn't insult or belittle the client. For example, "Well, I had thought so too, but if you look at the original call report we both signed off on, it does in fact call for a butterfly valve instead of a ball valve."

"What can we do to set things right?"   After acknowledging that the client is right (or gently pointing out that they are in error), you immediately move to the more important issue of taking corrective action. If the action is not directly specified by the client, dictated by the situation, or obvious to you, ask the client how he wishes you to correct the situation, for example, "What can we do to set things right?"

IF EVERYTHING FAILS

If everything fails and the client is still dissatisfied, don't spend any more time thinking about it. You've apologized and done everything humanly possible to set things right. What else can you do? Nothing. Therefore, if there's nothing else you can do, it's now up to the client whether he or she will forgive and forget, or whether he or she will refuse to reconcile with you.

Since it's up to the client, and out of your hands, do not spend further time pursuing the matter. Your efforts will be futile. Do not spend any more time thinking about it or feeling bad about it. What's the point?

Feeling bad or guilty or unhappy, or punishing yourself, isn't going to change the client's mind about you or alter the situation in any way. Since "beating yourself up" achieves no desirable result, why do it? It can only waste your time and hurt you more than you've already been hurt.

Here's a saying that seems sensible and helpful: "You can't be responsible *for* the client; you can only be responsible *to* the client." If you've done everything in your power to correct a problem situation, and the client is still unhappy, he or she is *choosing* to remain unhappy and mad at you. You can't be responsible for or help other people's behavior, thoughts, or emotions. You can only act in a responsible manner as a professional service provider, which you have done.

So do what you can do to set things right. Most clients will appreciate the effort and give you a second chance. That's wonderful. As for the others, you've done all you can do. Let it go.

As honor high school student Aazim Hussain observes, "If you have a goal, you have to work hard and stay focused. Have courage and faith in God. That's all that motivates me to do well."[1]

---

[1] Par, Pearl, "Teen Seeks More From Life Than a Routine 9-to-5 Job," *The Record*, December 11, 1991. p. NV-8.

CHAPTER 9

Coping with Difficult Clients

$\mathbf{A}$s mentioned earlier in the book, many service providers have the attitude, "This would be a great business—if it weren't for the clients!" Especially in today's marketplace, where the clients are in control, and the supply of service providers outweighs the demand, you are going to encounter the occasional "difficult" client.

A difficult client is a person who gives you a hard time, seems to do it deliberately, and is interested in exerting power and control over you rather than working *with* you to achieve a mutually beneficial result. Although the majority of clients are not in this category, there are enough difficult people out there to warrant a chapter on how to deal with them.

WARNING SIGNS OF A DIFFICULT CLIENT

You don't need me to tell you whether any of your clients are giving you a hard time; if they are, you already know. On the other hand, some client relationships seem promising enough, and so you go ahead with the work, only to discover that the client is going to be difficult to work with, impossible to please, and hard to get along with.

Here are some warning signs to watch out for that indicate the client is a difficult person:

1. Every time you show up for a meeting, the client keeps you waiting in the lobby for 10 to 15 minutes or longer and never seems sorry for it.
2. The client seats you in a "low-power position" in his office. That is, he is seated on a comfortable straight-back chair

behind a desk, while you sit in an uncomfortable, soft chair into which you are sinking, which forces you to literally look upward at them when you speak.

3. The client never offers a cup of coffee, soft drink, or lunch.

4. The client's manner is curt, clipped, terse, and humorless.

5. When you ask questions, the client responds in monosyllables.

6. The client never smiles.

7. The client never asks you anything personal and does not engage in small talk.

8. You sense no humanity or warmth radiating from the client.

9. The client seems pressured, unhappy, and put-upon.

10. The client complains in a disgruntled manner about her job, boss, assistant, coworkers, colleagues, assignment, and so on.

11. When you volunteer additional ideas or suggest new ways of looking at the client's project, the client tunes you out; the client wants you to stick exactly to the recipe or formula.

12. The client rarely compliments your work, and when he does, it's for being punctual or neat, not the quality or originality.

13. The client is in a dead-end job or is in a position that is usually held by someone many years younger than he or she.

14. The client has a difficult, troubled, or unhappy personal life.

15. The client's tone of voice always seems angry, annoyed, rushed, or disinterested.

16. Nothing makes the client joyful or happy.

17. The client radiates zero enthusiasm.

18. The client is very dictatorial in his dealings with you and not open to suggestions, collaboration, or new ideas or concepts.

19. The client gives you orders instead of making requests.

20. The client doesn't return phone calls and, when there, usually tells you he is too busy to talk, without suggesting that the call take place later.

21. The client thinks nothing of making unreasonable demands in terms of deadlines and deliverables and is quick to anger when you attempt to discuss setting a new or revised work schedule.

22. The client is almost always annoyed if things are not 100 percent perfect, and does not seem happy or appreciative when you render extraordinary or excellent service.

23. The client complains about your fees on every cost estimate, every job, and every invoice.
24. If the client's question is not answered instantly, he immediately becomes angry, short-tempered, and sullen.
25. When the client calls, you get a queasy feeling in your stomach.
26. You are beginning to dislike the client intensely.
27. You go out of your way to avoid contact with the client.
28. You do not enjoy working on the client's projects and tend to procrastinate on his jobs.

If you found yourself agreeing with six or more of the items listed, you are probably dealing with a difficult client and it is taking its toll on you.

REASONS WHY YOU SHOULD AVOID DEALING WITH DIFFICULT CLIENTS

Here are the negatives that result from putting up with a difficult client:

1. It causes stress.
2. It raises your blood pressure.
3. It makes you angry.
4. It makes you unhappy.
5. It makes you want to act in an unprofessional manner (telling the client off, etc.).
6. It affects your ability to do good work for this difficult client.
7. It affects your work for other clients.
8. It keeps you up at night.
9. It makes you want to stay in bed and not go to work.
10. It affects your appetite.
11. It darkens your mood and makes you less pleasant to be around.
12. It gives you gray hair.
13. It affects your physical health.
14. It affects your mental health.
15. It does not bring you satisfaction.

16. It makes you depressed.
17. It makes you tired.
18. It drains your energy.
19. It gives you ulcers.
20. It gives you migraines.

Life's too short. So, what to do? The solution is simple, and there are only three options: (1) live with it, (2) get rid of the client, (3) learn to deal with the client so the relationship is less unpleasant for you and so, it is hoped, you can help the client improve his or her disposition and behavior.

TAKING ACTION

There are so many variables that I cannot cover all situations here, just the main ones. Here are the most common situations that make client/vendor relationships difficult:

- Clients who demand perfection
- Unreasonable requests for changes and revisions
- Unreasonable demands for rush service
- Clients who take unfair advantage of your guarantee
- Uncommunicative or close-mouthed clients
- Clients who are overly controlling
- Rude, abusive clients
- Arrogant clients
- Clients who think they "know it all"
- Personality conflicts between you and the client

Let's take a brief look at each situation and one or two strategies for handling them effectively.

How to Handle the Client Who Demands Perfection

"I won't have any problem with a client who is a perfectionist," you say to me. "After all, I'm a perfectionist myself."

But watch out. What is perfect to one individual may seem severely flawed, inadequate, or inferior to another. Perfection in most things is the perception of an individual based on their subjective judgment. It's why one Olympic judge gives a diver an 8.4, while another scores the very same dive 9.2.

A good example of a perfectionist is a client who fusses over the shape, appearance, and style of every single letter in the typeset proof of his new brochure, who endlessly agonizes over color schemes and choice of paper stock and the placement of photos and drawings—to the point where he's far fussier than the graphic artist doing the job.

Strategies for dealing with the perfectionist? First, don't ridicule his Felix Unger–like behavior. You don't have to agree with it, but you should at least show empathy and understanding for his preferences, habits, and way of looking at things. The wrong thing to do is to say in an impatient, condescending, or annoyed tone, "Oh, that doesn't make any difference!" To the client, it does, and if you say otherwise, that's an indication to the client you don't share his attention to detail and commitment to quality.

Second, if the perfectionist's nitpicking is interfering with timely, cost-effective completion of projects, let him know that in a kind, gentle way. Say that you share his appreciation and concern for quality, but point out the extra expense and delay that result from being *too* perfect.

If the client's fussing does not visibly improve the end result to the majority of those who will evaluate your work, or does not deliver a measurable increase in benefits (e.g., sales will not increase as a result of all this agonizing), educate the client that this is so. Most perfectionists will retreat from their inflexible stand if they feel their superiors or colleagues will view them as wasting time and resources.

If the perfectionist doesn't budge, insists on an endless quest for improvement, and is not happy with a job you know is more than excellent, consider a third-party opinion. Having a neutral third party review the work will most likely reinforce your opinion that it is fine as is, and the credibility of the neutral opinion gives greater force to your argument and increases the odds of persuading your client.

Also, if *you* are critical of the client or in strong disagreement with them, they might get angry with you. But if the criticisms and dissenting opinions come from a neutral third party, the client will not fault you for bringing them to his attention.

Once I ghosted an article for a client who is a perfectionist when it comes to writing. I thought my draft was excellent and said so; he spent six hours rewriting, agonizing over every word change.

I said, "If the editor of one of the country's top business magazines read our drafts and said both serve the same purpose and are equal in quality, will you agree that the rewriting was not necessary?" We then paid a professional business editor for a neutral third-party critique; as expected, it supported my argument.

How to Handle Unreasonable Requests For Changes and Revisions

What do you do with the client who changes his or her mind a dozen times? The most effective strategy for dealing with this problem is to address it up front when you are negotiating the terms and conditions of your work agreement.

You should spell out how many revisions or changes the client is entitled to make for the fee being paid, whether there are any restrictions on the scope or range of changes that can be requested, and what the charge is for making additional revisions not covered by the original fee.

Once that is done, revisions cease to be a problem area; if the client makes an extraordinary amount of changes, and your contract calls for an extra payment at your usual hourly rate, what do you care how many revisions are made? In fact, each puts money in your pocket! It is only *unpaid* revisions and changes that cost a service provider time and money and that we don't enjoy making.

Some service providers have come to me and said, "That's all well and good, but right now I am working for a client who is being totally unreasonable about changes and revisions. We did not discuss charging for revisions in advance, but what they are now asking for is unreasonable by any rational standard. What do I do?"

To a large degree, you are stuck; while *you* may not think doing a zillion versions is reasonable, the client's attitude may be, "I'm paying for a satisfactory job and, so far, I'm not satisfied. What's the beef?"

Since you didn't discuss the revisions and changes issue up front, the blame is really yours, and you should probably grin and bear it, make the necessary changes, have an unprofitable experience on this job, and not make the same mistake in the future.

If things really get bad, you can always try to explain things to the client and negotiate either a higher fee for the extra work, or ask for a "kill fee"—a reduced payment to you for services rendered so far in exchange for ending the contract. This may be the best choice if you simply cannot abide doing more revisions on this project but the client is insistent on doing it over and over again.

How to Handle Unreasonable Frequent Demands for Rush Service

For many of us, tight deadlines are a fact of life, and for the most part, we have to get used to it. Especially in today's competitive, client-driven service marketplace, clients want and demand fast turnaround and immediate action. In business, the modem, computer, and fax machine have also served to "spoil" the client when it comes to expecting everything to be done right away.

For example, if a client wanted some changes to a design in the old days, they would mail you the drawing with their changes. It would take two or three days for it to arrive in the mail. You'd review it, make the changes, and mail it back. The whole thing would take about a week, and that's the turnaround time the client was accustomed to.

Now, with the fax machine, the client faxes you the changes at 9 AM; you invariably get a call at 10 AM saying, "Have you looked at it yet? Can I have it by lunch?" The "mail float" has been eliminated and the turnaround time reduced from one week to twenty-four to forty-eight hours. This puts enormous pressure on service providers handling multiple projects for multiple clients, because for every component of almost every project, instant turnaround is fast becoming the norm instead of the exception.

What to do? The *wrong* solution, practiced by only a few hold-outs, is not to get a fax machine. Clients expect you to have one, and most will not deal with a vendor who cannot receive or return fax transmissions.

The answer is that the cause of the problem is not only client demand, but service provider reluctance to set reasonable limits. Because we are so eager to please our clients, we sometimes are too quick to comply with demands—including demands for rush service—even though it isn't good for us or, ultimately, them.

My advice? Start asking (not demanding) more time, longer deadlines, slightly more relaxed schedules. Explain that this is not to make your life easier or for your benefit, but that when everything is rushed beyond normal limits, it can increase the probability for lower quality, cause more frequent and more serious errors, and incur rush charges.

Start small. Don't tell clients, "Now I need one month instead of three days." But when a client asks for it by next Tuesday, say, "How about Thursday or Friday." Most times, the client will pick Thursday, and you've just gained a precious two extra days to make the job that much better.

When a client sets an unreasonably tight deadline, I always ask, "Is there an event or particular milestone driving this deadline, or is it that you just need it as quickly as possible?" Some deadlines—completing the construction of a trade show exhibit in time for the show, for example—are event-driven and cannot be compromised or negotiated.

Most other deadlines, however, are usually tight simply because (1) the client wants it "as soon as possible" (versus having a real deadline) or (2) the client was late getting the work to you and now wants you to make up for their tardiness with fast turnaround.

In a way, these reasons are still legitimate reasons for wanting the service done quickly. The client has a right to want something as soon as possible without there being an event or other reason for it. And as far as the service provider getting squeezed by a rush job because the client was slow on their end, well, that's part of what they pay us for.

However, nonevent-driven deadlines do have some inherent flexibility that event-driven deadlines do not. Therefore, when a client presents a tight deadline, you should ask, "Is this driven by a specific event?" For a room addition on a home, for example, that event might be the arrival of a new child; the client wants the room completed and furnished weeks before the baby's due date.

If the deadline is not event-driven, then say, "Rich, let me ask: What would happen if we delivered the [report/drawing/water softener] to you a week from Friday instead of Friday?" The trick is not to come out and ask the client to move the date, but to ask "What would happen if" the deadline were a week or two weeks or longer.

When clients consider your question, it helps them see that their deadline is indeed "artificial" and that *nothing bad* will happen if the project is done two or three weeks later. In many cases, they will either agree to push the deadline ahead to the time frame you suggest or else pick a deadline that's halfway between yours and their original. So my suggestion is if you want a one-week extension, ask for two weeks or one and a half weeks, and aim to negotiate an extension of one week or more.

In some instances, however, the client will inform you the deadline is indeed not flexible. A strategy that works here, if you are one of several vendors contributing to a project, is to request that the deadline pressure be shared equally by all the vendors involved.

For example, many times when writing copy for a client, they will tell me, "We need to get it in five days, because it is due on August 26th and the graphics studio says they need eight weeks to design, set mechanicals, print, and bind."

I reply, "I want to work to help you make this happen, but you have agreed that copy is a key element, and five days will not enable us to do the quality work you seek. I don't like anyone to work faster than they feel comfortable, but to meet your emergency need, both the studio and I will have to share in the burden. Ask them to do the job in seven weeks instead of eight, and I will do the copy in thirteen days instead of my usual three-week turnaround. Fair enough?"

One final tip: If a client's deadline date falls on a Thursday or Friday, I ask for an extension to Tuesday, explaining that this gives me an extra weekend to polish and perfect their work. Very few clients will object to a vendor who offers to work weekends on their behalf.

How to Handle the Client Who Takes Unfair Advantage Of Your Guarantee

Let's face it: Most of us offering strong service guarantees don't expect clients to abuse or take unfair advantage of their guarantee privileges. When they do, it's a pain in the neck, and we resent it.

I'm not talking about someone who asks for reasonable extra service according to the terms and conditions of the guarantee. I'm talking about the rare (but it does happen) client who is going to hold you to the letter rather than the spirit of your guarantee and wring you for all the free service he or she can get out of you.

How to handle it? First, be pleasant. Even if making the service call is a pain in the neck to you, act friendly and happy to help the client.

Second, err on the side of being too generous with your guarantee and providing extra service at no charge rather than being too strict with your guarantee and arguing with prospects who think they should be covered but you claim are not according to your contract with them.

For example, if you offer a thirty-day guarantee on a service and the prospect asks for some changes to the job on the thirty-second day, don't say the time limit has run out and too bad for them. Instead, make the changes or fix the problem, but do let the prospect know you are doing it because you care about their welfare, even though their guarantee has technically expired.

Third, make your guarantees as generous, lengthy, and unconditional as practical. You might think this increases the chances of clients taking unfair advantage of you. But, actually, the opposite is true. The more generous your guarantee terms, the more people trust you and trust in the quality of your work. A guarantee with a short time limit and numerous restrictions and conditions is like giving people a piece of paper to sign with lots of fine print and tiny type—it creates instant distrust, suspicion, and hesitation.

For example, mail order booksellers have found that a fifteen- or thirty-day guarantee helps increase sales versus a ten-day guarantee or no money-back guarantee. The reason? If the buyer has only ten days to examine the book and make a decision about whether to keep it, he will feel rushed and pressured. If he is busy and doesn't have time to review the book immediately, he may return it unexamined simply to avoid having the guarantee period run out. With a longer guarantee period, the buyer keeps the book for later review, and the longer he keeps it, the more he forgets about returning it.

The best guarantee for service is one of buyer satisfaction. My wife and I recently called a toll-free service, 800-MATTRES, to order a mattress and have it delivered to our home. The advantage of this service is you can get the same brand-name mattress you'd buy in a store just by dialing a toll-free number; no shopping or store visit is required.

The disadvantage is that you don't get to test out the mattress for comfort, firmness, and so on before buying. The 800-MATTRES company, realizing this, offers this guarantee: "We will unpack the mattress, install it on your bed, and let you try it out right then and there. If you do not like it, tell our driver; he will pack it up, take it back, and you won't owe us a cent."

A *conditional* guarantee would have said the mattress is guaranteed to be the right brand and model, or guaranteed to be in undamaged condition. We would not have bought sight unseen; what if we didn't like it? The *unconditional* guarantee of satisfaction — telling the buyer, "We guarantee your satisfaction no matter what" — is what clients want today. And, increasingly, that's what service providers must offer.

How to Handle the Uncommunicative or Close-mouthed Client

Uncommunicative or close-mouthed clients are difficult to deal with for two reasons. First, their lack of communication makes it difficult for you to extract the information needed to do a good job for them. Second, their unresponsiveness may be symptomatic of worse problems, such as dissatisfaction with your service, hidden anger, or resentment at something you did.

It's stressful to deal with clients that only answer your questions or respond to your comments in monosyllables. It makes you feel as if you're doing something to offend them, only you don't know what. As a result, you become apologetic in your behavior without quite knowing why, and find yourself doing everything possible to carry the conversation.

How to handle it? I have found that difficult, uncommunicative, tight-lipped people generally act that way for two reasons: first, because they are not naturally outgoing, and this is their basic personality; second, because *they think they can get away with it.*

Being deliberately uncooperative and uncommunicative is a way of showing disdain for people or exercising power or control over them. It's also a way of announcing to the world "I'm antisocial," "I'm an introvert," or "I'm not a people person."

The person doing it *knows his or her behavior is not normal* and that the behavior is unpleasant. But as long as they think they can get away with it, the behavior continues.

The trick, then, is *not to let them get away with it.* My experience is this: when you let the deliberately difficult, deliberately uncommunicative person know that they *are* being uncommunicative, and that it's not appreciated, they realize they've been "found out," that we're onto their game. Caught in the act, they stop this behavior — or at least open up a bit more, let their guard down, and become a little more human.

For example, if someone is answering me in monosyllables, I will pause, then say, "Betty, is there a problem? Have I done something to offend you?" This, or a variation of it, is your subtle way of telling Betty (1) you know what she's doing, (2) you want her to *know* that you know she's doing it, (3) it's not appropriate or productive behavior, and (4) you would like it to stop and want her to treat you in a normal manner.

Another tactic for handling uncommunicative clients is to allow silent stretches in conversation. When you ask a question to which an appropriate response would be some conversation, and instead you get a monosyllable answer ("yes," "no," "not sure"), your natural tendency is to blab on some more to draw the person out. The result is the unpleasant pressure of trying to conduct a two-way conversation in which one participant isn't playing.

Don't do this. Instead, if a longer answer is natural, but the other person answers abruptly, *do not respond*. If you're on the phone, be silent. If you're there in person, smile, look pleasant, and don't say anything. *Eventually, the other person will break the silence* because he or she can't stand it — it's awkward and uncomfortable. And the only way he or she can break the silence is to *start talking*, which forces the client to *continue the conversation*.

By waiting it out and making the client the one to break the silence, you again communicate that (a) this tight-lipped, one-grunt-per-answer treatment isn't cutting it with you and (b) two can play that game. The trick is to wait without talking first — in a conversation, a 5-second pause seems like an eternity. Believe me, the other person cannot handle the silence, and if you wait long enough, he or she will be forced to respond.

Eventually, the client will get the picture and the conversation will become less forced, more natural. In time, you'll have trained this person to conduct normal conversation, which he or she will learn to enjoy and which will make you much more comfortable in dealing with them.

How to Handle Controlling Clients

All clients are in control of the client/vendor relationship, because the client is the customer, the customer is always right, and the client pays the bill. But the difference is in how that control is used and to what degree. A good client realizes that the most productive client/service provider relationship is more a partnership than a master/slave relationship. True, in this partnership, the client is the senior partner; the service provider is the junior partner. But it's still a partnership. The spirit is one of mutual respect, trust, and cooperation, with both parties working toward an agreed upon set of mutually beneficial goals.

At the other end, the worst, least productive client/vendor relationships are those in which the clients elect to exercise their power of control over their vendor to the maximum degree possible.

In this type of relationship, the client consistently pushes the service provider around, taking maximum advantage of the service provider's natural desire to be of service, please clients, and satisfy client requests.

Some clients who exhibit this behavior do it because they are pressured by circumstances (e.g., financial situation, boss, spouse) to get the maximum productivity out of the vendors they hire, and they truly believe the best way to achieve this maximum performance is by being a consistently tough, stern, and demanding taskmaster.

Other clients, admittedly a minority, exert this power and control simply for the sake of doing so, and because they enjoy it. Lord Acton said it: "Power tends to corrupt, and absolute power corrupts absolutely."

The solution? Start by assuming the client's controlling, demanding behavior is driven by external factors, not by a controlling personality. This approach allows you to be empathetic rather than angry and to try to help identify the source of this external pressure.

Instead of the client becoming your enemy, you identify what's really bugging him and then make that thing your common enemy — an enemy that the two of you work together to destroy or overcome. Once that's done, not only does the relieving of pressure on the client relieve the client's pressure on you, but his gratitude will make you a saviour in his eyes, and saviours usually get better treatment than servants.

An example? A client was continually pressuring me into accepting tight deadlines, and then, once I agreed to them, would call halfway through the job and ask for the work to be done even sooner. Finally, I asked why every job needed to be done in two days—was there any problem the client had that forced them to make every job a rush and was there anything I could do to alleviate it?

The client admitted that his boss always gave him projects to do at the last minute and then demanded immediate turnaround, and in turn that forced him to push me for faster delivery. We talked about the entire process of producing marketing materials, and I learned that his art design studio typically took three weeks for design and mechanicals of product sheets.

I introduced him to an excellent desktop publishing service that could give equivalent quality, at half the cost, with only *four days* turnaround! This not only solved a production problem for the client, but bought me more time on the writing end, and eliminated the constant pressure to do every job sooner than I could.

On the other hand, you may find that there is no external reason why the client is so demanding and controlling and that he or she just *enjoys* being that way. What to do?

You might try having a heart-to-heart talk, and it might work, but frankly, I doubt it. You are the client's service provider, not his therapist, and therefore you are unlikely to achieve significant changes in his personality or behavior. The only choice is to live with it or walk away from the account.

Which option you choose depends largely on the severity of the client's behavior, how you handle it, and how much it affects you. I find I am not bothered by clients others have told me they could not work with. I am able to say to myself, "I'm not doing anything wrong; it's just the way they are" and move on from there.

The clients want to be controlling? My attitude is—fine. I'm here to serve them, and if they want to be demanding, it's their right. As long as they're not abusive and my bills are paid, it's a matter of indifference to me how they behave. Would I like it better if they were friendly and pleasant? Of course. Who wouldn't? But I simply do not allow the behavior of others to affect my attitude or my work for them in a negative way.

Remember, it's not what happens to you; it's how you handle it that counts. I agree with Dr. David Burns, director of the Institute for Cognitive and Behavioral Therapies, who says, "Your moods are created by your thoughts and, to a great extent, are caused by forces within your control—the way you are thinking about things.[1]

How to Handle Rule, Abusive Clients

Even the best people are occasionally rude, and an outburst every now and then can be forgiven. But you should not put up with clients who

---

[1] David Burns, *Superachievers: Portraits of Success*, pp. 79–80, published by PERSONAL SELLING POWER INC.

- Are constantly rude and abrasive
- Insult or demean you
- Sexually harass you
- Use objectionable language
- Act in a manner deliberately calculated to make you uncomfortable or attack your self-esteem
- Threaten you physically or slap or hit
- Abuse you in any other way

We are all in the business of service, but service is not a synonym for subservience or submission. Every human being has the right to expect decent, civil treatment from his or her fellow human beings. You can politely but firmly let the other person know that what they are doing is unacceptable behavior and must stop for the professional relationship to continue.

For example, "I'd like us to continue our association, but there is one problem that I would like to discuss with you and see if we can resolve." Many people who have been exhibiting abusive behavior will stop when the victim explains why the behavior is wrong and how damaging and inappropriate it is.

Unfortunately, many others will continue despite your plea. Some view you as a "hired peon" and do not care how they treat you. Others have different values and simply cannot understand that what seems good-humored and "all in fun" to them is not to you.

Once again, the choice is to stay or walk. If you find the behavior truly abusive and offensive, and damaging to your happiness and self-esteem, you really have no choice other than to end the relationship and walk away.

When you do it, by the way, do it politely, in a calm, rational, dignified manner. If you want to avoid an unpleasant telephone confrontation, or think the person would react badly or violently if this were done face to face, a letter is fine.

Don't stoop to their level. Thank them for their business, express your regrets that it didn't work out, and wish them well. You may have the overwhelming urge to get emotions off your chest and really let the client "have it." Resist the temptation. While it might provide temporarily satisfying, there is no long-term benefit to making enemies.

How to Handle Arrogant Clients

The way to handle clients who have a big ego is: let them. Right now, you're letting their bragging and boasting bother you. Don't. If the client wants to make himself feel big and important, even at your expense, so what? He is the client; we are the service provider. He's *supposed* to get all the glory, that's what he's paying us for.

The real reason we find arrogant clients with big egos difficult to deal with is that many of us have pretty big egos ourselves. We're specialists in our trade or skill and are proud of our ability. So when a client lords over us that he or she is more successful, or makes more money, or is more important, we find it hard to take.

Service providers have an especially tough time dealing with the client who implies that he could do the job and do it better than the service provider he is hiring "if only he had the time." Arrogant people frequently build themselves up by dismissing your ability or talent and indicating it is just one of many things they can do.

Samm Sinclair Baker, best-selling self-help author, tells this story[2]

> At a large party, a boor interrupted a conversation among several writers, "Big deal—it's a cinch to write, anybody can do it!"

> "Sure," I agreed. "You just put your hands on the type-writer keys and let your fingers go."

The tendency in dealing with the egomaniac or arrogant client is to "Call his or her bluff"—that is, to go out of your way to show them that what they said isn't true, and they're not as superior as they claim.

Don't do it. The only possible result from pointing out that the client is lying or exaggerating is to embarrass him, make him feel bad about himself, and possibly humiliate him in front of his peers. If you do that, how much do you think he will want to associate with you and work with you in the future? That's right—he won't.

---

[2] Samm Sinclair Baker, *Writing Nonfiction That Sells* (Cincinnati, Ohio: Writer's Digest Books, 1986) p. 65.

Instead, when a client tells a whopper, *let it pass*. Don't make snide little comments or ask seemingly "innocent" questions designed to reveal the client as a phony or braggart. At the same time, you don't need to gush over a boast or claim of superiority, either. Just listen, acknowledge it politely, and move on. Let the client think you are impressed. Let the client retain his dignity and inflated ego. That will make him a happy client. And clients who are happy when they are around you are clients who will hire you.

How to Handle Self-Proclaimed Experts

A variation of the arrogant client is the self-proclaimed expert. For example, the client who hires your interior decorating firm because she loves your work and wants the best, and then rejects every suggestion, every color scheme, and totally redesigns every room layout and plan herself.

I don't mind working with clients with strong opinions and ideas stemming from a claim of expertise in my field, because many in fact do have good ideas. Where my copywriting, consulting, and training are concerned, I encourage client input and feedback, and I value their suggestions and ideas.

Don't assume the client is an ignoramus in your field before you know the facts; otherwise, you may embarrass yourself. Recently I met with the vice president of engineering at a large manufacturing firm; he was interested in having me train his employees in writing skills.

During our talk, he began to suggest improvements to my presentation technique and ways to make the training better and more interesting. I was thinking, *Hey, I'm the training pro, you're the engineer; why don't you leave it to me?* Then he casually mentioned that he had been a professional trainer and teacher for eighteen years before becoming an engineer. Actually, his suggestions were excellent, and this explains why. I am glad I listened and did not dismiss his ideas or try to prove my superior knowledge of training to him (he had been in training longer than I had!).

Although you are the expert, many clients do have some knowledge. And nobody knows everything: you and I always have something more to learn. If you are open to client input instead of hostile toward it, you'll be amazed at what your clients can teach you.

Also, while you are the expert in your field or skill, the *client* is the expert in their own needs, wants, situation, business, life, and requirements. They know more about their company, their goals, their employees, their product, their competition, and their technology than you ever will.

So rather than have the attitude that you are the guru and the client should sit still and keep quiet, be glad that the client wants to take an active role in helping you do the best job possible.

Naturally, when the client suggests something that is not practical, feasible, technically correct, or desirable, you must speak up and say so. But don't simply dismiss the client's suggestion; show him or her why it doesn't work and how you propose to do it in a more effective way. Many clients like to learn, and part of our role is teaching them to do more and more on their own so, over time, they don't have to totally rely on outside suppliers for assistance.

What if the client *thinks* she knows it all but actually is not knowledgeable? Again, no need to dismiss her, diminish her role or value, or act as if what you're doing is beyond her comprehension. Instead, show the client what you are doing and why as you go along and suggest other resources—seminars, adult education classes, books, tapes—that can increase her knowledge of the subject.

What you should never do is tell the client that she is stupid or ignorant, that you are the expert, and that she should butt out. That's sheer arrogance on your part, and guess what? The client is paying the bill and need not put up with it—or you.

What to Do When There Are Personality Conflicts Between You and the Client

There are some difficulties in client/service provider relationships for which the precise cause or contributing factor cannot be clearly identified. Sometimes no one thing the client does is making him difficult to deal with our annoying to you; sometimes it's simply a matter of personal chemistry: you and the client do not get along.

As we discussed in Chapter 2, this situation can be avoided by opting to do business only with clients you like and feel you can get along with. Personal chemistry is a key factor in determining whether a client/vendor relationship can work and should be initiated.

But what if you entered the relationship without much prior exposure to the client, and now you find the client difficult to get along with? Your action depends on how great the differences in

personality are and the degree to which you and the client are
having trouble.

You can't change the client's personality, and she cannot
change yours. But you can change the way you *react* to and deal
with each other. For example, if the client has a habit or mannerism that is annoying to you, you cannot get her to stop it. And you
probably can't get yourself not to be annoyed by it. But you *can*
control your reaction to the habit or mannerism; you can *choose*
not to let the annoying habit interfere with your ability to serve
the client or to treat her warmly and kindly.

The key, as sports psychologist Dr. Rob Gilbert says, is simply
to change *buts* to *ands*. For example, instead of saying, "I want to
be nice to Anita, but her pompous accent annoys the heck out of
me," you substitute "and" for "but" and say: "I want to be nice to
Anita, *and* her pompous accent annoys the heck out of me." That
is, Anita's accent will remain pompous and annoying to you, but
you will refuse to let that annoyance color your dealings with her,
and you will be nice to her and treat her as if the accent did not
exist.

The same technique can work for any client habit or personality quirk that makes you impatient, angry, or annoyed with
them. For example, instead of saying, "I want to do a good job for
Joe, but he is always changing his mind," you say, "I want to do a
good job for Joe, *and* he is always changing his mind." In the first
statement, the fact that Joe changes his mind is what prevents you
from doing a good job for client Joe.

In the second statement, you take control of your emotions,
actions, and reaction to Joe's behavior. Yes, Joe is always changing
his mind. But you choose not to let this interfere with your service
to him. As Dr. Burns contends, moods—and therefore actions
dictated by mood—are within our control rather than controlled
by external forces, such as what Joe or Anita do or do not do.

THE ONE CLIENT YOU CANNOT SUCCEED WITH

Jim Alexander, founder of Alexander Marketing Services in Grand
Rapids, Michigan, once made a comment that stuck in my mind.
We were talking about working with clients who are dictatorial,
ignore the service provider's advice, and redo everything the service provider turns in because the client believes he or she can do
it better.

"I can handle a client who is arrogant but knowledgeable," said Jim. "And I can handle a client who is ignorant but admits he doesn't know what he's doing. The one client that no service provider can succeed with is the one who is arrogant *and* ignorant—doesn't know anything, but thinks he knows it all."

Realize there are some situations in which you cannot win or salvage a good relationship because the client is simply too difficult. In those situations, the strategies suggested in this chapter may fail. If that's the case, you have two choices remaining: keep the account, or resign it.

HOW TO RESIGN A DIFFICULT ACCOUNT WITHOUT MONETARY LOSS

Let's say none of my techniques worked, the difficult account is still difficult, and you're thinking, "Who needs this?"

You want to resign the account, because you know it will make life easier and more pleasant. On the other hand, you don't want to lose the billings. What to do? Simple. *Go out and get more accounts.* Do a direct mail campaign. Run some ads. Send out a press release. Make sales calls. Pick up the telephone and call some prospects. Go on some meetings. Make presentations.[3]

Do these things until the revenue from the new clients equals or exceeds the revenue from the difficult accounts you are resigning. That way, the emotional upset that comes with severing relationships won't be compounded by an accompanying loss of income. And you will feel more secure about your action.

---

[3] For recommendations on how to market and sell your services more effectively using direct mail, postcard decks, print advertising, public relations, sales brochures, telemarketing, and personal selling techniques, request a free copy of my "Sales and Marketing Resource Guide." You can get it by contacting Bob Bly, 174 Holland Avenue, Dept. CSRG, New Milford, NJ 07646, phone (201) 385-1220.

CHAPTER 10

How to Prevent a Dissatisfied Client From Leaving You

In Chapters 8, and 9 we covered the subject of how to deal with a dissatisfied client. In this chapter we expand on those principles and discuss new strategies for dealing with what I called the "critically dissatisfied client"—which I define as a client whose level of dissatisfaction is so great that there is a high probability he will fire you or take his business elsewhere.

THE EARLY WARNING SIGNS OF CRITICAL CLIENT DISSATISFACTION— AND HOW TO SPOT THEM

How do you know when client dissatisfaction has reached the critical level—the level where he is so unhappy that you are in danger of losing the account? Here are a few of the warning signs:

1. The client's manner of dealing with you suddenly shifts from warm and friendly to cold and distant.
2. When you visit the job site or client's office, the client avoids you, doesn't make eye contact when talking with you, and seems in a hurry to leave you.
3. The client does not return phone calls.
4. When the client does answer the phone and you get through to him, his tone of voice is stiff, clipped, terse, and icy.
5. The client frequently complains about various aspects of your service.

6. The client repeatedly complains about a single flaw or aspect of your service which you have been unable to rectify to their satisfaction.

7. The client delays or defers assigning routine work to you that would normally be yours without question.

8. The client cuts back on the quantity of business given to you.

9. You discover that the client is using your competitors, trying them out on various projects—and is not telling you about it.

10. The client gives what you perceive to be false reasons why his level of usage of your service has dropped or stopped altogether.

A FIVE-STEP PROCESS FOR HANDLING THE CRITICALLY DISSATISFIED CLIENT

Okay. Let's say you spot these warning signs, but the client has not directly *told* you she is dissatisfied. What do you do? The goal, of course, is to eliminate or reduce the client's level of dissatisfaction so that you are no longer in danger of being fired and can retain the account. There are five steps to achieving this:

1. Bring the client's dissatisfaction out in the open.

2. Separate the issue of "blame" (who's fault it is) from the issue of what the problem is and what can be done about it.

3. Address the blame issue in a manner that puts the responsibility on your shoulders, not the client's.

4. Get the client to agree that the important issue is solving the problem, not criticizing or blaming, and get her to commit to solving the problem with you.

5. Solve the problem for the client in a heroic manner.

Let's look at each step in more detail.

Step 1. Bring the Client's Dissatisfaction Out into the Open

Client dissatisfaction is like a pile of uranium getting hotter and hotter: when it reaches critical mass, there will be a tremendous and devastating explosion. Your job is to get the client to "cool down" and get her dissatisfaction level *below* "critical mass."

The first essential step is to get the client to admit she is dissatisfied, tell you so, and tell you why—to get her to "vent" her frustration and unhappiness with you and your service.

Now, if the client has already said, "I'm fed up!" this first step is accomplished and you can move on to step 2. But how do you bring up the subject of critical dissatisfaction with the client who has *not* openly voiced it?

The wrong strategy is to pretend the dissatisfaction doesn't exist and hope that you are "safe" as long as the client isn't openly irate or complaining. This fails because, left untreated, the problem only grows worse, the chasm wider.

The right strategy is to quickly, directly, and professionally—without hesitation or awkwardness—bring the problem out into the open. For example, "Betty, you seem angry or annoyed with me. Have we done something to offend you or make you unhappy with our service?"

Given this direct query, most clients will open up and vent their frustration. While it's not always pleasant to hear, and while no one enjoys being "scolded," this is, as I've said, a necessary step in solving the problem.

Step 2. Separate the Issue of "Blame" (Who's Fault It Is) From the Issue of What the Problem Is and What Can Be Done About It

Okay. You've gotten the client to admit they are peeved. Now what?

The tendency is to become defensive and "argue" with the client. For example, if you are a seminar leader, and the client says, "I feel your presentation isn't very lively," your immediate impulse is to do what? To say, "You're totally, 100% WRONG!!! I'm a GREAT seminar leader and ALL MY CLIENTS SAY SO! You are just WRONG!"

This is the wrong strategy. Arguing with the client only makes her dissatisfaction grow worse. Obviously, from her point of view, you *have* done something wrong or offensive, and she is not going to argue with her own perception of reality.

Instead, defer the issue of blame, or who's right or wrong, to the next step. Now you simply want to identify the problem—the cause of the client's dissatisfaction—and also to communicate to the client that you understand exactly why she is dissatisfied with you and that you are treating it as a valid complaint. The easiest way to do this is to repeat to the client, in your own words, your understanding of the problem as she's expressed it.

For example, instead of saying, "You're WRONG! My seminars are NOT dull—they're GREAT!" say, in a friendly, cordial manner, "So, Norman, if I understand you correctly, you're dissatisfied with the seminars because you feel the presentation isn't lively enough or entertaining enough. Is that right?"

"That's right!" Norman replies. "I mean, the information you present is good and all, but I just think a seminar should be more, you know, entertaining. It's not that you're *bad*, but for the money we are paying you, I expected a more dynamic presenter."

"So what you're saying, Norman," you reply, "is that you feel the seminar and the material are basically strong, but for the fee I am charging, you wanted someone who was more dynamic, more motivational, or entertaining. Is that right?"

By having this kind of very open, honest conversation with the client, you are achieving several things.

First, you are already alleviating the client's dissatisfaction with you. Part of the reason Norman was so unhappy is that you were not performing up to his expectation and *you didn't seem to even know it!* But now, as a result of this discussion, he sees that you understand his complaint—and even better, seem genuinely interested in hearing how he feels versus getting defensive and arguing, as he expected.

Second, before he had voiced this complaint, Norman had an all-encompassing, severe dissatisfaction with having engaged you to do the seminars, because he didn't like what he was getting. After the discussion, he sees that the scope of his dissatisfaction is smaller than he originally thought. "The program isn't really that bad," he thinks. "In fact, it's pretty good. As he says, my complaint is really only with style of presentation, not with the whole program." So the level of dissatisfaction is further lowered below the critical point.

Third, Norman realizes that you are isolating and pinpointing the problem for the purposes of discussing and formulating a *solution*. That is, rather than fight with him, you are working with him to address his issues. This increases his comfort level with you, makes him hopeful, and further cools down the nuclear chain reaction of critical client dissatisfaction.

The key is not to react to the client's criticism personally, or to argue with the client, tell him he is wrong, or say "You're right—but it's not my fault." Instead, you want to acknowledge the problem, identify and isolate its cause, let the client know you understand what the real problem is, and let him know your goal is to help solve it, not get defensive.

Here are some things *not* to say to the client who has a complaint about your service:

- "You're wrong, the quality is very good."
- "You're wrong, you don't understand enough about the subject to make an informed judgment. I am an expert, have been doing this twenty years, and am telling you the work is excellent by any standard."
- "You're wrong, I am not [whatever the client said you are]; I did not do [whatever the client says you did]; it isn't true that [whatever the client said was true]."
- "I am the best in my field and my ability to do this work is beyond question."
- "It's not my fault, you are responsible on your end because [reason why it is the client's fault, not yours]."
- "I have been in business doing it just this way for X number of years, and you are the only client to ever complain."

Step 3. Address the Blame Issue with the Attitude That the Primary Responsibility for a Smooth Working Relationship Is Yours, Not The Client's

Once you identify and isolate the problem, should you get into the tricky area of assessing who's fault it is, laying blame, and especially defending yourself if you truly believe that it is not your fault?

Here are my rules of thumb:

- It is generally futile to argue with clients; since they are the ones buying and you are the one selling, they can easily win any argument just by putting away their checkbook.
- If the problem is clearly your fault, you should accept the blame. Say it is your fault, and tell why it happened if there is a logical reason. Remember that you are giving the reason just so they can understand and perhaps be a little more forgiving; you are *not* presenting it as an excuse which automatically gets you off the hook.

- If there is a real question as to whether the problem was caused on your end or the client's end, step in and take the blame. The logic is this: since you are the service provider, and they are the one being served, you have greater responsibility than the client to make sure things come out right. So even if they did wrong, it was your fault for not being diligent enough to check up on them and make sure they did right.

The "gray" area is: What if the problem is clearly and solely the fault of the client, not the service provider? This is the most difficult situation to handle. If you lay back and take the blame, you may in fact lose the account or at least incur wrath for something that you did not do.

On the other hand, if you deliberately point out to the client that the problem is clearly his fault, it may only serve to annoy him further rather than pacify him. Many clients believe the old saying "Even when I'm wrong I'm right," applies to all client/vendor relationships.

Let me give you an example. A client called last Tuesday morning and said, "Bob, I am looking for the copy for our ad. Did you fax it? Where is it? It was due yesterday."

I was stunned: I had written in my calendar that the ad was due Thursday, not Monday. "I had it as due Thursday," I replied, "and I'm sure that was what was written in the letter of agreement I sent you on this job." I opened her file, frantically searched for the written confirmation of the assignment, found it, and saw my date was correct. "Look on page 2 of the confirmation," I told her. "It says August 8, not August 5. That's Thursday, not Monday."

"Well, I didn't read it," she snapped back irritably. "And in our meeting, I distinctly remember discussing August 5, and that's when it was due as far as I am concerned."

At this point, I should have backed off, because as I have told you repeatedly, arguing with a client is a losing proposition—and you, the service provider, are the loser in it.

"But, Judy," I continued. "I have to assume that when I give you a contract with a deadline date in it, and you sign it and send it back to me, that you have read it, including the due date. In fact, when I first faxed it, you told me you had read it and that everything was fine except you wanted to reduce the fee by $100, which I did in the revised contract."

"Listen, it's a waste of time to go on and on about who's fault it is," she snapped even more irritably. "I have an ad due at the publishers in two weeks and no copy—I'm really screwed. What can you do for me?"

Based on this experience, I recommend the following steps for handling client dissatisfaction in which the client, not you, clearly made the error that resulted in the problem:

- Put your agreements—fees, due dates, job specs—in writing. Give the client a copy. Keep a second copy for your files.

- If a dispute arises, and you did nothing wrong, but the problem was caused on the client's end, point this out once, citing your signed agreement or confirmation letter as evidence. But do it gently, not in an arrogant manner (no "Ha-ha, I'm right and you're wrong"). If the client agrees with you and says, "Okay, it's my fault," don't say "I told you so" or go on and on about it. Instead move on to the next step, which is helping the client solve the problem.

- If, rather than forgive you, the client is irrational, remains angry, and blames you despite the proof, find a way to agree (at least partially) with his assertion that he is correct, and then move on to solving that problem.

In my case, when Judy told me she hadn't read the schedule she signed off on, I *should* have said, "You know, I think we did discuss Monday as the deadline in the meeting, and when I worked out the schedule with a different due date, I should have called you to bring your attention to it and make sure it was okay with you. I know you don't have time to read the fine print in everything you sign—I certainly don't—so I'm sorry. It's really my fault."

See how much better this is? After the shock of not getting the material by the deadline date wears off, and the crisis is averted, Judy will realize that the error was hers, not mine. At that point, she'll be especially appreciative of the way I handled it and deflected the blame off her shoulders onto mine.

Step 4. Get the Client to Agree That the Important Issue Is Solving the Problem, and Get Them to Commit To Solving It With You

It should be you, not the client, who makes blame the peripheral or minor issue and taking corrective action to solve the problem the major issue. You should say something like, "I agree with you that we messed up here, and we can address that later; obviously, we will do whatever we can to make it up to you. But tell me, Norman, regarding the current situation, should we spend a few minutes now discussing exactly what is wrong and what we can do to set it right?"

The client cares more about getting the problem fixed, meeting his deadline, getting his driveway blacktopped, or whatever than in giving you grief. So he'll welcome your suggestion and almost always accept whatever help you can give in resolving what he perceives to be the problem situation.

In many cases, you and the client become so focused on the problem and how to fix it that you get caught up in the teamwork, and the original dispute or dissatisfaction, while not forgotten, takes on much less importance in the client's mind. Once the problem is fixed, the client, who at one point was so miffed about the whole thing that he wanted to fire you, might now say, "Well, that's water under the bridge. Let's move on, and I'm sure there'll be many other projects coming up for you to work on shortly."

Step 5. Solve the Problem for the Client in a Heroic Manner

When you are working to resolve a situation or solve a problem that is causing a critical level of dissatisfaction in your client, you want to pull out all the stops and do whatever it takes to handle it correctly, in the fastest, most efficient, most service-oriented manner possible.

In the case of my deadline misunderstanding with Judy, I said, "What's the problem you are up against?"

She replied, "I needed to get the copy Monday so I could review it Tuesday, give you any changes, and send it to the art studio by Wednesday. Thursday is too late; I'm leaving on vacation Wednesday night."

"I have a suggestion," I replied. "Today is Tuesday. I will call some other clients and rearrange and reschedule some work and meetings. It will be tough, but I can do it. I will then work on the ad all of today and tonight if necessary, and fax it late tonight so it is on your desk first thing Wednesday morning."

I continued, "I know you get in early, so if you can, review it first thing and get back to me. I will stay at my desk all day waiting for your call, so you won't miss me or have to play 'phone tag.' I will make the revisions immediately. Then I can fax the final copy to you, and directly to your art studio for you, so you don't have to stay late and can leave for vacation. Judy, how does that sound?"

She liked it, of course. I stayed late into the night to do the job, and faxed it to her early next morning. When she called me to give me her changes, I was bleary-eyed. After we went over them, I again apologized for the misunderstanding about the deadline, saying I was sorry.

"Oh, don't be," she said brightly and warmly. "Misunderstandings happen. And now, thanks to your extra effort, we're back on track and we won't miss our publication deadline. Thank you."

I wished her an enjoyable vacation and she ended by saying, "Let's talk when I get back; we have more work for you."

So, when correcting a critical problem situation, don't hold back. Don't give it a second-class effort because you're busy or because it's costing you extra money or time. Rather, give it all you've got—a 110 percent, heroic effort to do whatever it takes to meet the client's need, no matter how difficult or rushed the job is.

And, when you put forth this heroic, almost superhuman effort on the client's behalf, *let him or her know it*, in a gentle, good-natured, almost fun way. For example, when Judy called Wednesday to go over the changes, she asked, "How are you?" I replied, "Oh, a little bleary-eyed and tired, but no worse for the wear."

"It looks from what you've sent me that you were up late," she commented. Yes, I said, and in early that morning as well.

"I appreciate it," she said quietly and sincerely. And that made it all worthwhile for me.

HOW TO HELP THE CLIENT FIND A WAY NOT TO FIRE YOU

Here's another little secret: the client who is ticked off at you, no matter how disgruntled, unhappy, or angry, is actually not looking to fire you. In fact, what he'd like, aside from an apology and an effort to correct the defect in your service, is an excuse or reason to *continue using you.*

Clients don't switch vendors as quickly and easily as you might think. After all, if your service has been good until now, your delivery on time, and your prices reasonable, and you are pleasant and easy to deal with, you're a real asset to that client—an asset they'd rather not lose. So when a critically dissatisfied client is giving you indications that the account is in jeopardy, ask *him* what it would take for you to keep the business. He'll tell you. And if you do it, he'll be happy and will keep using you.

For example, "We've discussed the problem, and you've seen what we have done to correct it. Norman, your business is extremely important to us, and we value our relationship with you. Can you do me a favor? Tell me—*what would we have to do to keep your business and not lose your account?* We would hate to have a great five-year relationship end because of this one glitch which we seemed to have solve. So tell me—what would it take to get us back on track with you?"

The client will react in one of three ways.

1. About half will become friendly and cordial, reassuring you that the problem was not so bad as they thought and that you shouldn't worry about losing their business—they like you and want to continue with you.

2. About a quarter will name a specific improvement they would like to see in your service before they can make a decision about continuing the long-term relationship for you. And this is easy to handle. You correct the flaw that made them unhappy. They try you on a new job. They see that the flaw is eliminated and the service is now to their liking, and—comfortable with this knowledge—continue retaining your services as they did before the crisis arose.

3. A quarter will be unfriendly and unreceptive to your offer of putting things right and continuing the relationship. Some of these will tell you flat out that, because of what happened, they are not going to continue with your services. Others will answer in a neutral or noncommital manner, then simply not call you any more or use your services any longer. You don't hear from them and find out that they've switched vendors only when you see a job that someone else has produced for them.

Making The Secretary or Assistant Your Ally

One effective strategy for getting back in the good graces of a dissatisfied client is to enlist the secretary or assistant as an ally.

If you are having a problem with a client, you might call the assistant, and when she picks up the line, say something like, "Betty, this is Bob Bly calling."

"Hi, Bob," she will say. "Do you want to talk to Mr. Boss?"

"No, Betty," you say, surprising her. "Actually, I wanted to talk to you. Got a minute?"

From this point you must be up front and totally honest about why you are calling. For example, "Betty, last time we spoke with Mr. Boss, I could tell he was pretty upset over the cost overruns on the Johnson Project. Tell me, Betty, you know him better than anyone. How serious is this, really? We value our relationship with him; are we in danger of losing him as a client?"

Betty will probably give you a fair, accurate assessment of her boss's feelings and outlook on the situation and is likely to answer you in a sympathetic, even empathetic manner rather than bruskly as Mr. Boss himself might.

When you get Betty's assessment of the situation, you then say, "Betty, let me ask you a favor. Could you give me your advice and tell me how you think I should handle the situation? Should I stop by for a visit and talk it out with him face to face? Should we waive the fee for the XYZ service he bought but didn't like? What do you think we should do?"

Betty will give you an answer that is probably the best guide to what action you should take. After all, she knows him best. She'll even suggest other options for handling the situation that you may not have thought of.

Do what Betty says and then *let her know you are doing it*. This shows Betty that you value her opinion and that you consider her an important person.

In addition, to prove to you and to herself that the advice she gave you was indeed accurate, she will put forth her own effort to make Mr. Boss respond positively to what you are doing and will become an advocate for you, helping you win back the account and beat off competition. The combination of knowing what to do and having the client's closest advisor or assistant tell the client he should respond positively to your efforts makes it likely that you will retain the account.

Using the No-Risk Offer to Overcome the Objection

Let's say that, despite your best efforts, the client says, "I'm sorry but I think we're going to try going with someone else."

What you want to do in such a situation is *not* resell yourself to recapture the entire account—that's too big a step, and too unrealistic—but to get the chance to do *one more job* for that client so (1) the relationship continues, albeit on a greatly reduced scale, and (2) you can demonstrate in your performance of this task that the defects which caused the client to become dissatisfied in the first place have now been eliminated.

Once the client sees that the problems you had on previous jobs are no longer present on the one small job you are now doing, he will likely either trust you with more and more of his business again as time passes or reinstate you as his primary vendor for the service.

The easiest way to get one more chance to prove yourself to the client is simply to ask for it. For example, "I know you feel there has been a problem with print quality on the last two jobs, but that was a problem with a press operator, and he has been replaced by someone who is a skilled, experienced printer. Let us do your next small-quantity flier, so you can see the improvement and feel comfortable about continuing with our service for whatever printing needs you have."

If the client is still not open to your offer, you can motivate him to accept by making the offer risk-free to him. Say, "I understand. You're not certain. I'll tell you what. We will do the job for you and guarantee delivery on the deadline date or earlier. You look at it and tell *us* whether we have met your high standard of quality. If for any reason you don't like it, we will rerun it entirely at our expense and guarantee your satisfaction. How does that sound?"

Using the Free Offer to Encourage Continuation of Service

Even more powerful than the no-risk offer is an up-front offer to perform services free just to "prove" to the client that you have eliminated the undesirable defects from your service. This will motivate many buyers. After all, if it's free, there's absolutely no risk to them. This is your "secret weapon"—the big gun you can pull out when all the other strategies fail to get the client to give you another chance.

You say, "Jim, I understand why you're reluctant. So let me do this. We'll cater the next board meeting—absolutely FREE—so you can see how we've changed the menu and improved the food to make it even better. No charge whatever. If the meeting is perfect and you are delighted with our service and the food gets rave reviews, all we ask is that we be considered for the next catering job you have. Fair enough?"

Using the Fax and In-person Visits When the Client Won't Return Phone Calls

When you can't get through to a client and are always blocked by an assistant or voice mail, put what you want to say to them over in a memo and fax it. Say somewhere in your fax, "No need to dictate a reply or make a call. Just jot your response at the bottom of this note and fax it back to us."

Many clients who are avoiding you and don't want to take your phone call will read the fax, because it's nonconfrontational, allows them time to formulate a response, and is a quick and easy way of communicating.

Some situations are so severe, some accounts so important, that a face-to-face meeting may be necessary to resolve the crisis and retain the business. If you're in the neighborhood, a spontaneous visit give you the opportunity you need to have a personal talk with the client face to face.

Or you might schedule a meeting. Since you know the client may not want to see you, act as if you're not making a special trip and therefore don't expect to take up a lot of the client's time. Say, "Well, I'll be in your area next week, and I would like to spend just five minutes of your time discussing the problems we've had on Project X, as well as present some ideas that may help accelerate the schedule and get us back on track to meet the deadline. Would tomorrow afternoon be good?"

Most clients with whom you've had some relationship with have enough invested in you that they will grant this five-minute audience. This should give you enough time to work through the conversation of the five-step process. Once you reach step 5, and the client becomes receptive and interested, he'll forget about the five-minute limit and give you as much time as you need.

Soon you'll be working together again, as a team, as if nothing ever happened. You keep the business, he keeps you, and everybody is happy, as long as you resolve to do everything in your power to *keep your clients satisfied* from that day on.

Index

A

Abusive clients, 131-133,
    245-246
Accessibility of service
  and client satisfaction,
    91-92
  importance of, 91-92
Agenda, for client
    communication,
    111-113
Appreciation, communication
    of, 136, 138-139
  with gifts, 169-171
  with personal favors,
    171-172
  with thank yous, 168-169
Arrogant clients, 247-248
Associated Air Freight, 54, 61
Availability
  as customer criteria for
    using service, 60-61
  determining availability
    needs of client, 59-60
  instant access, readiness
    for, 145-147
  meaning of, 60

B

Beepers, popularity of, 60-61
Bidding, pricing in
    competitive bid
  situations, 195-196
Bonding with client, 121-122
Bullying by client, 131-133,
    245-246
Business atmosphere
  buying characteristics of
  changes in buying
    authority, 15-16
  demand for give-aways,
    22-23
  growth of in-house
    systems, 18-20
  incremental buying, 17-18
  lack of customer loyalty,
    20-22
  price sensitivity of
    market, 9-12
  shrinking of purchase
    price, 12-15
  and competition, 5-6
  downward mobility, effects
    of, 8-9
  surviving the recession, 3-5

professionalism, 141
prompt response to
clients, 147-148
scheduling calls/meetings,
110
sequential problem
solving, 114-116
taboo topics, avoiding,
143-144
taking responsibility for
contact, 107-108
use of fax, 128-129
Compensating client, for
problems, 94-95
Competition, 5-6
Controlling clients, 243-245
Convenience
as customer criteria for
using service, 58-60
determining convenience
level of client, 59-60
importance of, 58-59
Cooperation, communicating
cooperation, 162-163
Cost of living, 8-9
effects of, 9
Courtesy discount invoice,
142-143, 228
Customer Needs Assessment
form, 73-74
Customer satisfaction survey
advantages/disadvantages
of, 149
use of, 136-138

D

Deadlines
beating the deadline,
101-102
event-driven deadlines, 239

missing deadlines, 221-222
rules related to, 221
setting realistic deadlines,
54-55, 238-239
See also Time pressures
Demand
and changing service, 74-75
See also Supply and
demand
Dependence of client,
reducing dependency,
154-155
Diagnostic tools, to assess
client needs, 70-72
Difficult clients
abusive clients, 245-246
arrogant clients, 247-248
controlling clients, 243-245
demands for rush service,
238-240
giving up without financial
loss, 251
perfectionistic client,
handling of, 235-237
personality conflicts,
249-250
reasons for avoiding,
234-235
reasons for difficulties, 235
requests for
revisions/changes,
237-238
self-proclaimed experts,
248-249
taking advantage of
vendors, 240-242
uncommunicative clients,
242-243
warning signs about,
232-234
Disagreements with clients,
124-133